THE CIVIL WAR IN KERRY

THE
CIVIL WAR
IN KERRY

Tom Doyle

MERCIER PRESS

WHAT YOU NEED TO READ

MERCIER PRESS
Cork
www.mercierpress.ie

Trade enquiries to:

Columba Mercier Distribution,
55a Spruce Avenue, Stillorgan Industrial Park, Blackrock,
County Dublin

© Tom Doyle, 2008

ISBN: 978 1 85635 590 2

10 9 8 7 6 5 4 3 2

 Mercier Press receives financial assistance from
the Arts Council/An Chomhairle Ealaíon

This book is sold subject to the condition that it shall not, by way of trade
or otherwise, be lent, resold, hired out or otherwise circulated without the
publisher's prior consent in any form of binding or cover other than that
in which it is published and without a similar condition being imposed
on the subsequent purchaser.

Printed and bound in the EU.

CONTENTS

Acknowledgements

This book would not have been written without the assistance, encouragement and help of many people. I am particularly grateful to Michael Houlihan, whose knowledge of computers proved invaluable at every level in the compiling of this work. Special thanks are also due to Mary Foley-Taylor and Seán Ó Suilleabhain – both from Killorglin, and James Fitzpatrick, Cork, for their help and advice.

I would also like to thank all the staff at the Local Studies Unit, Cork City Library, Grand Parade, Cork and the staff of the Local History Department, Kerry County Library, Tralee, who enabled me to consult contemporary newspaper accounts of the conflict both from a local and a national perspective.

INTRODUCTION

When people are asked about the Civil War in Kerry those with an insight into the conflict in the county usually mention Ballyseedy, or the series of landmine explosions that occurred in early March 1923. In fact, the explosions – one perpetrated by republicans, three carried out by government troops as reprisals on republican prisoners – are not typical of the war. They represent an extreme response to a continuous conflict that stretched back to early August 1922, ironically a point at which the war was already over in most other parts of Ireland.

Why did the Civil War go on for so long in Kerry, and what factors contributed to the bitterness which both sides brought to the conflict? The answers to these questions are complex, involving both local factors – such as the fact that Kerry possessed suitable terrain for waging a guerrilla campaign, the type of campaign carried out by republicans – and national features, namely the fragmented nature of the independence movement itself, where its political and military wings (Sinn Féin and the IRA) operated in tandem, but with a good deal of autonomy. Added to this, local rivalries and personality clashes that sometimes transcended both local and national spheres and issues affected the way the centre (Dublin) and the periphery (Kerry) viewed each other. The national organisation and its local structure in Kerry had a shared – but also a distinct – experience of the independence struggle. While united by the common purpose of undermining British rule in Ireland, these differences were brushed aside. Once difficult choices had to be made between July and December 1921, from the truce and Treaty negotiations, latent fault lines deepened between the moderate and the more extreme view points within the movement.

The movement in Kerry was a manifestation of both the GAA's club structure and IRB influence within that organisation – Austin Stack and Paddy Cahill emerged as leading figures in the separatist (Irish Volunteers) wing that supported Eoin McNeill's line when John Redmond, leader of the Irish Parliamentary Party, pledged in September 1914 that the National Volunteers would support the British war effort in the First World War.

Initially, Michael Collins viewed both Austin Stack and Thomas Ashe as embodying the best of the Kerry Fenian tradition. Following the failure of the Kerry Volunteers to land arms and ammunition in advance of the Easter Rising, and Stack's subsequent failure to rescue Roger Casement following his arrest, Stack's reputation was tarnished, with some figures questioning his abilities as a leader and an organiser. As the Volunteers metamorphosed into the IRA during the War of Independence, Collins – assisted by Richard Mulcahy – took a leading role in organising armed opposition to the British. Cathal Brugha, technically Minister for Defence, resented the way Collins stole his thunder. Collins also tended to belittle Austin Stack's running of the Dáil courts system, his responsibility as Minister for Justice. Brugha and Stack's friendship deepened as their hatred of Collins grew, so that by the time Collins returned from London with the terms of the Treaty in December 1921, they wholeheartedly supported de Valera's opposition to the agreement. General Headquarters Staff, IRA

(GHQ) in Dublin regarded the Kerry IRA's performance during the War of Independence as inadequate, to the extent that they sent a national organiser to overhaul both Kerry No. 1 and Kerry No. 2 brigade IRA in the summer of 1921. The move generated a good deal of anger across the board in the county. If Dublin saw the Kerry IRA as mediocre, the willingness of the negotiating team led by Collins to accept less than a republic was viewed as a betrayal of the sacrifices endured and the gains won in Kerry during the 1919–21 campaign.

As local IRA (predominantly anti-Treaty) units took over RIC and military barracks over the spring of 1922, they saw their acceptance of these facilities as their reward for the successful military campaign they had waged in Kerry since 1919, and not the political dividends won by what they perceived as a 'weak' negotiating team led by Collins in London. Nationally, the pro-Treaty faction accepted the Treaty as a partial achievement of the struggle for national independence. They still saw themselves as republicans, but viewed opposition to the agreement as jeopardising the real gains achieved in London. For the republicans the settlement the Provisional Government accepted from the British was an inadequate result and the republic was still there for the taking, a prize to be won if the war continued. The elections held on 16 June 1922 showed that an overwhelming majority of the population in Ireland wanted peace, not war. As in the 1918 and 1921 general elections Kerry voters were not able to voice their opinions, as the 1922 election was not contested in the county. On 28 June, less than two weeks after the election result, government troops began shelling the Four Courts, which had been the republicans' military headquarters for almost two months.

There had been a Provisional Government force (250 men, recruited locally) based in Listowel since March/April 1922. In May 150 republicans billeted themselves in the town and for the next two months there was a military stand-off in Listowel. The outbreak of hostilities in Dublin forced the republicans in Listowel to challenge the garrison militarily on 30 June. Neither side wanted to fight, and one soldier was killed and another wounded on the Free State side before a ceasefire, brokered by a local seminarian, brought hostilities to an end later that afternoon. The two opposing commanders – Thomas Kennelly on the government side and Humphrey Murphy on the republican – issued a joint statement that as Kerrymen they didn't want to fight a civil war. It is possible that the battle for the Four Courts was seen as a 'Dublin quarrel' at this point that might not necessarily have long-term repercussions for Kerry. The fact that its sole military outpost in Kerry not only collapsed in the face of hostile fire, but fifty troops – about one in five – of the Free State garrison joined the republicans confirmed to the military authorities in Dublin that if there was further fighting in Kerry it would involve sending troops from outside the county to quell the uprising, with no great sympathy for the locals – be they either civilians or republicans.

In the five weeks or so from the fall of the Four Courts garrison to the beginning of August 'Free State' forces gained control of large areas of the country as the republicans surrendered their principal assets without offering much more than token resistance. In early August 1922 the republican front line in Munster theoretically ran from Limerick to Waterford. During the first fortnight in August sea-borne landings along the Cork and Kerry coasts took the republicans totally by surprise.

In separate but co-ordinated landings at Tralee and Tarbert (2 and 3 August) and Kenmare (10 August) almost a thousand troops were successfully deployed in Kerry while the flowers of the Kerry IRA brigades were still based in Limerick. The bulk of the troops – the Dublin Guard and the 1st Westerns, predominantly from the national capital and the Clare/Galway area – had no local knowledge of either their surroundings or their enemy in Kerry and expected to be in the county for a relatively short tour of duty. Michael Collins optimistically predicted the war could be over by early September, and his visit to Tralee on 12 August 1922 was intended to open discussions to bring the conflict in Kerry to an end.

Collins did not live to see the end of August, much less the end of the conflict he so much wanted to avoid. Without his guiding hand, the Dublin Guard, whose officer corps was drawn from the remnants of the Squad, the assassination unit he had set up during the War of Independence to counter British intelligence agents, was the driving force in Free State campaign in Kerry. They viewed the IRA in Kerry with disdain considering what they perceived as their low profile during the war against the British. On 2 August, the first day of the landing, republicans opened fire on army medics operating under a Red Cross flag as they tended to the wounded in Tralee. The double killing of two off-duty medics (unarmed) boating on Killarney lakes later that month and the shooting of the two O'Connor brothers during the republican assault on Kenmare in September convinced Free State troops that they were facing a ruthless and unprincipled enemy in Kerry. During the first two months of the conflict Free State dead (thirty-five soldiers) equalled the total police fatalities in the county during the War of Independence. By this time the

Squad cohorts in the Dublin Guard had re-activated their assassination skills and were carrying out both summary executions of prisoners and reprisal killings.

The introduction of the Emergency Powers Act in early October gave the government draconian powers to execute republicans for possession of arms and ammunition. While the intensity of the conflict and the corresponding death toll (on both sides) in Kerry diminished considerably in the last three months of 1922, this was due as much to the limitations winter imposed on the republican campaign as it was to Free State army successes in capturing men and materials. The Irish Free State Government's formally succeeding the Provisional Government on 6 December 1922 should have been proof that republican attempts to overturn the Treaty-based administration had failed. The symbolic taking of Kenmare on the same day by troops led by both Brigadier Paddy O'Daly, O/C Dublin Guard, and Colonel Michael Hogan, O/C 1st Westerns, was probably done in expectation of the war being over by Christmas. A Free State officer visiting republican prisoners in Kerry in May 1923 remarked that the reason the conflict went on for so long in the county was because the rank and file IRA man believed their brigade commanders' assertion that the Civil War was basically a continuation of the War of Independence, with the Provisional Government doing Britain's bidding to destroy the republic. This deference to authority seems to have extended right up the republican chain of command. The deference shown to Liam Lynch, the IRA chief of staff, who more than any other individual on the republican side refused to countenance defeat, was a significant – if not the principal – factor for the campaign extending into the first four months of 1923.

1

IRELAND 1912–1918: A REVOLUTION?

Herbert Asquith's Liberal administration's Home Rule Bill (Ireland) was passed by the House of Commons in April 1912. A year earlier the House of Lords veto was abolished, to be replaced by a two-year delaying mechanism on legislation. Thus, failing a major catastrophe, home rule would be on the statute books by September 1914. The 1912 bill granted an Irish assembly fairly modest powers and limited autonomy. While not euphoric, the public response among the majority of nationalists was positive. And in election terms the majority of voters stood squarely behind the Irish Parliamentary Party. In the 1910 general election, for example, two of Kerry's four Nationalist Party MPs were returned unopposed. In the remaining constituencies, South and East Kerry, both the home rule candidates, John Pius Boland and Tim O'Sullivan, comfortably defeated both (William O'Brien's) Independent Nationalists.[1]

The Irish Parliamentary – 'Home Rule' – Party had evolved as the political wing of the Land League in the 1880s, with the twin objectives of 'peasant proprietorship' and a home rule parliament for Ireland. By 1912 both objectives were virtually achieved. The Wyndham (Land) Act of 1903 made money available (through the Congested Districts Board) for land purchase. Over the summer of 1911–12 most Kerry farmers secured title deed to their holdings, thanks to government loans to be repaid over thirty years. And while the issue of land annuities rankled, the majority of the rural population were content to be land owners.

In 1908 old age pensions were introduced, the first step towards social legislation, while ten years earlier (1898) the grand jury system (local government – presided over by landed gentry) had been abolished, to be replaced by a network of local councils chosen by elections. The county councils, through their dispensaries and public health nurses, provided a rudimentary form of health care. All in all a substantial section – if not an absolute majority – of Kerry's population (and nationalist Ireland in general) were content with their lot in the summer of 1912. Household suffrage had been the norm since 1885 and people accepted that constitutional politics – as reflected in elections – was the best way to bring about gradual change in their everyday lives.

Poverty was widespread in Kerry at this time (by twenty-first-century standards) but not as acute as it had been in the late 1870s, much less the Famine years of the 1840s. In the ten years between 1901 and 1911 a total of 22,881 people emigrated from Kerry, the lowest net outflow from the county in any of the six- to ten-year cohorts since 1851. Rather than being a flaw in an otherwise 'balanced-contented' society, emigration was the pivot that kept the mechanism in equilibrium. It served as both an escape route and a safety valve for people whose life chances/employment prospects were slim (to non-existent) in an Ireland that offered little more than subsistence farming, if they were lucky enough to inherit the holding. For those who left there was the hope of better opportunities in

America, the preferred country of 'choice' for the bulk of the 234,184 emigrants who left Kerry between 1851 and 1911.[2]

From the point of view of those who remained in Ireland, competition for scarce resources and limited opportunities was radically reduced. In many cases emigrants who fared reasonably well in their country of adoption underwrote the viability of the home country in both the short and longer term. In the former case they sent home the 'passage' (fare) to allow their younger brothers and sisters to emigrate, and in a more structural way remittances acted as a cushion in harder times. It is probable that the American 'letter' was as important in late nineteenth- and early twentieth-century rural economy as their EEC/EU transfers would be for modern Ireland from 1973 onwards.

Following the 1885 Reform (Electoral) Act the Home Rule Party held the balance of power at Westminster. Though a Tory by temperament, Charles Stewart Parnell saw Gladstone's Liberal Party as the best option from the point of view of delivering a home rule assembly for Ireland. In Ulster the prospect of a 'national' – or more precisely, a nationalist dominated – assembly in Dublin was an anathema. When the Liberals introduced a Home Rule Bill in 1886 the Tories wooed the unionists, where Sir Randolph Churchill urged that the Orange card was the one to play.

Both the 1886 and 1893 Home Rule Bills failed as the (Tory dominated) House of Lords had the power of veto over the (lower) House of Commons. This changed in 1911 when Herbert Asquith abolished the Lords veto to enable a budgetary measure to be introduced in the Commons. Instead of the veto, the Lords could impose a two-year delay on legislation. Thus, when the 1912 Home Rule Act was passed it was only a matter of time before it would be the law of the land. In September 1912 in Belfast a substantial majority of Ulster's adult male Protestants signed the Solemn League and Covenant, a quasi-religious oath pledging their lives to defy and resist the imposition of home rule on Ulster. In January 1913 Edward Carson and James Craig set up the Ulster Volunteer Force to channel loyalist physical force elements into a politically constrained organisation, under their leadership. The UVF grew rapidly and soon had over 100,000 members in its ranks.

Taking his inspiration from the Ulster Volunteers, Professor Eoin McNeill, co-founder of the Gaelic League (along with Douglas Hyde) in 1893, penned an article, 'The North Began', in September 1913. McNeill's argument was that southern nationalists should set up a parallel volunteer force to bring pressure to bear on the British to implement the Home Rule Bill. The Irish Volunteers in Kerry seems to have grown out of the GAA clubs structure. And this is perhaps why Austin Stack emerged as the leading figure in the movement in Kerry.[3]

Secretary of John Mitchel's GAA club, Stack played on the side that won eight successive county finals. Captain of the Kerry team that won the All-Ireland football final in 1904, he served as secretary of the Kerry County Board from 1904 to 1908. In addition to his sporting achievements, Austin Stack came from a staunch republican family; his father, Moore Stack, was involved in the Fenian movement in the 1860s. Nominally, Kerry was one of a few locations where the Fenians 'came out' in the 1867 Rising. According to Anthony Gaughan, Moore Stack was so determined to convince the police of his seniority within the movement that he went above and beyond the call of duty to help the constabulary with their enquiries.[4] Of course Austin Stack – or most of his contemporaries – would not have been aware of this. In 1908 his standing as a republican was acknowledged when no less a person than Cathal Brugha swore him into the IRB. Stack and Brugha would remain both close personal friends and political allies within nationalist and republican groupings for the rest of their lives. In Kerry a corresponding bond existed between Austin Stack and Paddy Cahill, both within the GAA and the Volunteers.

Over the spring of 1914 events took their own momentum within both the Ulster and Irish Volunteers. On 24 March 1914 Brigadier Gough, a senior army commander with unionist sympathies, declared that he would not move against the UVF if they took up arms against the imposition of home rule. The 'Curragh mutiny' indicated that the British army would be passive supporters of the UVF. The shock this caused to the body politic was to see thousands of nationalists join the Irish Volunteers, which had 150,000 members by June 1914. It was an army without weapons. The same cannot be said of the UVF who – with the assistance of senior Tories – over the night of 24–5 April landed 24,600 rifles and 3,000,000 rounds of ammunition at Larne and Donaghadee. In July 1914 Erskine Childers landed 900 Mauser rifles and 25,000 rounds of ammunition at Howth. Comparatively the Irish Volunteers could arm little more than a battalion; the UVF could equip two divisions, with the logistics, transport, etc., that one could expect from a largely urban/industrialised society like Belfast.

When Britain declared war on Germany in August 1914, the UVF joined *en masse*, forming the 36th (Ulster) division of the British army. In order to convince the British that a home rule Ireland would not abandon Britain in her hour of need, and that nationalist Ireland could be as loyal as unionist Ulster, John Redmond urged his followers to volunteer for the British army in September 1914. The Home Rule Bill was on the statute book by this time, but its introduction was postponed until the war ended, which most people anticipated would only be in a couple of months.

Even so, Eoin McNeill repudiated Redmond's call to the flag and urged his followers to leave the movement. Nationally about 12,000 members heeded his advice and formed the Irish Volunteers. The vast majority, perhaps in excess of 180,000, remained with the Redmondite group who became the National Volunteers. Of course only a fraction of Redmond's supporters joined the British army.

While the responsibility for bringing the gun back into Irish politics rests firmly with the Ulster unionists – through the creation of the UVF – neither they nor their rivals in the Irish Volunteers proposed to use their weapons to bring about a radical, much less a revolutionary, transformation of either Ulster or Irish society. On the contrary, loyalist militancy was essentially a reactionary movement responding to their centuries-old fear of being swamped by Catholics. While governed from London alongside England (Anglican), Scotland (Presbyterian) and Wales (Methodist), reformed (Christian) churches would always be in the majority. If, however, the island of Ireland was treated as a separate unit, then Roman Catholics would be the dominant denominational group. As God's elect among 'heathen papists', and thus superior to a mere majority, the UVF harked back to the seventeenth century – 1641 and 1690 – for its physical force tradition.

The National Volunteers, on the other hand, were essentially more loyal to the British parliamentary tradition than the (self-proclaimed) loyalists. In essence they wanted a very mild form of regional autonomy (that a genuine federal system such as the German Länder, or the Swiss cantons, would regard as risible) to be introduced, as had been agreed by parliament in 1912. That the aspiration of nationalist Ireland for a generation (since the 1880s) was to be kicked to touch to placate Ulster's threat to use force struck many home rulers as an act of betrayal and – more seriously – undermined their faith in constitutional politics. If force of arms carried more weight than force of argument, it was a negotiating tactic both sides could use.

In June 1914 the House of Lords proposed an amendment to the Home Rule Bill allowing the nine Ulster counties to opt out. At the Buckingham Palace conference in July, John Redmond secured a compromise from Edward Carson whereby just six of the north-eastern counties would be outside the jurisdiction of the home rule assembly in Dublin. This gentleman's agreement became academic on 3 August 1914 when Britain declared war on Germany and the implementation of the Home Rule Bill was postponed until the end of hostilities.

Britain would later claim to have entered the conflict that became the First World War to defend the rights of small nations, an irony that did not go unnoticed in Ireland. The Irish Volunteers, in spite of McNeill's titular leadership, had already been infiltrated by the IRB who intended to strike a blow against British rule in Ireland. An armed uprising would validate Ireland's moral claim to self-determination and secure national independence for a small nation. It is unlikely that there would have been a military uprising in 1916 without the wider precedents set by the First World War. This is not just the cliché, 'England's difficulty is Ireland's opportunity', although this was central to the IRB's plan of action, which was based on the expectation of assistance (arms and ammunition) from imperial Germany on the basis that 'the enemy of my enemy is my friend'.

What the First World War provided was both a rationale and a rhetoric for military action, and a language that was universal across European territorial and cultural boundaries in the summer of 1914. It would have been surprising if Ireland had not been infected by the virus. The small nation Britain had in mind in 1914 was Belgium. The Treaty of Brussels (1830) gave Britain a right to intervene to protect Belgium's territorial integrity if the country was invaded. Basically this was a legacy of the Battle of Waterloo (1815), the last salvo of the Napoleonic wars. It also recalled the Spanish Armada of the 1580s, when a land army based in the Netherlands was to invade England following Spanish realisation of naval supremacy in the English Channel. By the spring of 1915 it was becoming apparent that the war was going to last a number of years rather than a number of months. In May 1915 a National Coalition government was formed in Britain, with the unionist leader Edward Carson (the leading legal mind of his day) serving as attorney general. John Redmond was offered a place at the cabinet table but he rejected the offer. As the war progressed political unionism grew closer to the mainstream of British politics, while nationalist Ireland gradually drifted away. If the 1914–18 war is addressed at all in an Irish context it is treated as little more than a footnote to the 1916 Rebellion. Ironically, far more Irishmen served in the British army and were either killed or wounded in the conflict than participated in the series of conflicts that took place in Ireland from 1916 to 1921 and the Civil War in 1922/3. This would be equally true in Kerry where far more families were bereaved as a result of the First World War than lost their relatives in the county during the War of Independence and the Civil War. Yet this aspect of history has been airbrushed out of national (and nationalist) consciousness and has virtually no place in collective memory:

'Twas on Good Friday morning all in the month of May,
A German ship lay signalling way out upon the bay.
We've twenty thousand rifles all ready for to land,
But no answering signal did come from the lonely Banna Strand.

So begins the ballad 'Banna Strand', a song that ranks alongside 'The Valley of Knockanure' as one of the most plaintive and evocative songs to emerge out of Kerry's experience of the 1916–21 struggle for national independence.

In 1916 Good Friday fell on 21 April, not in May as recorded in the ballad. Apart from Casement's capture, the plot to land the arms suffered a further setback later that night when a car carrying four volunteers *en route* to the cable station at Valentia (to make radio contact with the *Aud*) drove off the pier at Ballykissane – about a mile from Killorglin – resulting in the deaths of three of the passengers (Con Keating of Caherciveen, Charles Monaghan from Belfast and Donal Sheehan from Newcastle West), the first casualties of the 1916 Rising.[5] Ironically, had the men reached their destination, their mission would have failed. There was no radio transmitter on the *Aud*.

The sub-text of 'Banna Strand' is an 'if only'. If only the arms consignment had been landed successfully, a full mobilisation of the Volunteers (both nationally and in Dublin) would have occurred. The Irish would have overwhelmed the British militarily and everyone would have lived happily ever after. This presupposed that the Kerry Volunteers could have successfully landed and distributed the weapons. Implicit in this operation was neutralising the garrison at Ballymullen barracks, commandeering the railhead at Fenit and severing telephone and telegraph contacts between Tralee and the outside world. In reality Austin Stack wasn't able to rescue Roger Casement from a lightly guarded RIC barracks in Ardfert and (later) Tralee, where Head Constable Kearney (who admired Casement) would not have hindered the escape bid. Assuming the Rising had taken place as originally planned by the IRB – with the fully armed and fully mobilised Irish Volunteer Force in the field and on the street on Easter Monday – would an Irish victory (militarily) have been the most likely outcome of the conflict? Probably not. The alternative history (a rebel victory) overlooks one small historical detail – the First World War. Over the spring of 1916 the French army was being bled dry at Verdun (90,000 casualties in six weeks). Joffre pleaded with the British to launch an offensive to take the pressure off the French, who, at that point, seemed on the verge of collapse. Had this occurred Britain would have had to fight Germany on her own, with the outcome far from certain.

In the war rooms of Berlin and Whitehall planners on both sides expected the 'big push' of 1916 would be the decisive campaign on the western front and ultimately determine the outcome of the war. In this context the British response to a full-scale rebellion in Ireland would have been to crush the uprising as quickly as possible. The outcome would have been brutal,

bloody and short, with thousands of deaths among both combatants and civilians. In less than a week in Dublin over 400
lives were lost, the civilian death toll (over 250) far exceeding
the combined rebel and crown forces losses. It may be heretical
to say so – about one of the totems of Irish Nationalism – but
the failure of the *Aud* to deliver its cargo was probably a blessing in disguise, considering the alternatives.

It is worth noting that the supreme council of the IRB anticipated a German victory in 1916, or at the very least a negotiated end to the war. In this context it was hoped that Germany
would sponsor an Irish delegation (with negotiating rights) at
the 1916 version of the Versailles conference. Given the severe
terms Germany imposed on Russia at Brest-Litovsk (Germany
won the war on the eastern front, after all) IRB expectations
were probably a little naive.

The Rising took the British military authorities by surprise
and was generally greeted by the Dublin civil population with a
mixture of indifference and open hostility. That the outbreak of
the Rebellion coincided with the first anniversary of Gallipoli,
where so many Dublin Fusiliers lost their lives, angered many
servicemen's families. The outbreak of hostilities was accompanied by widespread looting by some of the inhabitants of Dublin's tenements. In fact the high number of civilian casualties
was the principal reason Patrick Pearse and the other leaders
decided to surrender on Saturday, 29 April. By this time the
Rebellion was already being referred to as the 'Sinn Féin' Rising, though it had nothing in common with the political party
founded by Arthur Griffith in 1904. Separatist in outlook, Sinn
Féin was non-violent and non-republican – Griffith advocated
a party of MPs abstaining from Westminster, but accepting a

dual monarchy in a similar fashion to the constitutional device in use in the Austro-Hungarian empire since the 1860s.

Between 3 and 12 May, acting under the orders of General Sir John Maxwell, the British executed fifteen of the leaders of the Rising, including the signatories of the Proclamation and all the battalion commanders except Éamon de Valera (who had US citizenship). As military governor, Maxwell did not have to take political considerations into account. In strict military terms the executions weren't excessive, if seen against the background of disciplinary measures implemented during the First World War. For instance, 346 British servicemen were shot for cowardice – or desertion – in the face of enemy onslaught between 1914 and 1918.[6] In France following the May 1917 'mutinies' the authorities courtmartialled over 2,300 troops, sentenced 432 to death and shot fifty-five.[7]

During the course of the fighting in Dublin no fewer than four Kerry Volunteers lost their lives, when the total Volunteer death toll was sixty-two. Outside of Dublin the only other (successful) operation mounted by the Volunteers was the attack at Ashbourne, County Meath on an RIC convoy, led by Thomas Ashe of Lispole and Richard Mulcahy, which left ten policemen dead and sixteen wounded.

In tandem with the executions, over 1,860 Volunteers were interned in Frongoch prison camp in north Wales under the Defence of the Realm Act (DORA) in June 1916. Almost a thousand were veterans of the Dublin Rebellion, but a cross-section of activists were arrested on a nationwide basis. Thirty-seven were arrested in Kerry, almost half in Tralee, among them Tom McEllistrim, Paddy Cahill, Thomas Slattery and Billy Mullins.[8] During their six months' incarceration in Frongoch the prisoners developed individually and collectively in an almost hothouse environment that accelerated the development of a cohesive purpose and a core of future organisers for a national movement. Following a general amnesty prior to Christmas 1916, the internees returned home to a heroes' welcome.

In February 1917 an embryonic Volunteer/Sinn Féin organisation made its first foray into electoral politics when it supported Count Plunkett, father of the executed 1916 signatory, Joseph Mary Plunkett, in the North Roscommon by-election, which Plunkett duly won. It was Joe McGuinness, however, then serving a prison sentence at Lewes jail, who received the Sinn Féin nomination in the South Longford by-election in May 1917 – where Michael Collins coined the phrase 'Put him in, to get him out' – and was the first Sinn Féin candidate to be elected on the party ticket. On the subject of prisoners, when the bulk of those interned in Frongoch were released in late 1916, the British still held a number of high ranking, politically sensitive prisoners – among them Eoin McNeill, Éamon de Valera, Austin Stack and Thomas Ashe – in custody until June 1917. Their release then was part of an amnesty which the British hoped would encourage Sinn Féin to participate in the Irish Convention, due to start its discussions in July 1917. Sinn Féin boycotted the assembly on an abstentionist basis – in the same way its MPs (or TDs) refused to take their seats at Westminster.

Around Ireland the Volunteers staged demonstrations – in uniform (in itself an illegal act), to provoke a response from the RIC. During one such demonstration at Ballybunion on 11 July 1917, the 'Riot Act' was read. In the ensuing gunfire, Daniel Scanlon, a local Volunteer, was shot dead by the police.

On Sunday, 11 August 1917, the Sunday nearest the first anniversary of Sir Roger Casement's death, a massive open-air meeting was held in and around McKenna's Fort (the site of Casement's arrest) where an estimated attendance of 12,000 heard speeches from Austin Stack, Fionán Lynch and Thomas Ashe.

Later in August, Ashe, then head of the IRB, was arrested for making a 'seditious' speech and incarcerated in Mountjoy prison. By mid-September there were thirty-nine Sinn Féin prisoners in the jail, including Austin Stack and Fionán Lynch. As leader of the group Ashe demanded political (POW) status, and went on hunger strike when the prison authorities refused to grant his demands. He died while undergoing forced feeding. His funeral at Glasnevin cemetery on 30 September was the equivalent of a 'state' funeral. Michael Collins' short oration following a volley of shots echoed the spirit – if not the words – of Patrick Pearse's tribute at the funeral of O'Donovan Rossa in 1915. The parallel wasn't just symbolic; Collins succeeded Ashe as the leader of the IRB.

In the spring of 1918 the Bolsheviks, under Lenin, signed the Treaty of Brest-Litovsk, bringing the war in the east to an end. The transfer of hundreds of thousands of German troops to the western front suggested the possibility of a 'big push' and a subsequent German victory in the west.

In January 1916 conscription had been introduced in Britain, but not in Ireland. Public opinion in England, spurred on by the popular press, regarded nationalist Ireland as shirkers. In April 1918 the introduction of a proposal to extend conscription to Ireland galvanised nationalist opinion, not just Sinn

Féin; both the Home Rule Party and the Catholic hierarchy also opposed the move.

It was Sinn Féin, however, that gained the most (politically) from the conscription crisis. In a tense and charged atmosphere many people were radicalised and were prepared to resist – under arms – being forced into the British army, where they faced a high risk of being killed or wounded on the western front.

Kerry people were shocked at the killing of Thomas Russell, a native of Dingle, and a Gaelic League activist, who was bayoneted to death by a British soldier in Carrigaholt, County Clare on 30 March 1918, while giving a language class in the local national school.

Indicative of the way some of the more perceptive of the Volunteers in Kerry were thinking, Tom McEllistrim led a raid on Gortatlea RIC barracks to obtain arms and ammunition for his column on 13 April 1918. Half the police garrison had gone out on patrol, and the Ballymacelligott party successfully overwhelmed the remaining officers and were removing the contents of the armoury when some of the RIC patrol returned unexpectedly. In the ensuing struggle, two Volunteers – John Browne and Robert Laide – were killed, and could be reasonably claimed to be the first casualties of the War of Independence.[9]

The conscription issue was defused by the arrival of US troops in France in April 1918, but the political damage – a self-inflicted wound – the British had done to the legitimacy of their continued rule over 'nationalist' Ireland was immense.

The First World War ended in November 1918 and was followed by a general election in December. In Ireland Sinn Féin increased its representation from six to seventy-three MPs, becoming the sole representative in twenty-four of Ireland's thirty-two counties. The Home Rule Party was reduced to six seats, four won in Ulster as part of an electoral pact to avoid splitting the nationalist vote, and thereby returning a Unionist Party MP by default.

Sinn Féin candidates were returned unopposed in twenty-five constituencies, including all four in Kerry, where Austin Stack, Fionán Lynch, James Crowley and Piaras Beaslaí (all then in jail) were the only nominees. In the remaining (contested) electoral battlegrounds, where the average turnout was 69 per cent, the Sinn Féin candidates secured 47 per cent of the vote in a 'first past the post' electoral system. Sinn Féin's victory was a landslide, but like most landslides it was built on a shaky foundation. Fr Michael Flanagan, president of Sinn Féin, noted, somewhat cynically: 'The people have voted for Sinn Féin. What we have to do now is explain to them what Sinn Féin is.'

2

THE WAR OF INDEPENDENCE
1919–1921

THE FIRST DÁIL

The Sinn Féin members elected in 1918 convened for the first time at the Mansion House, Dublin on 21 January 1919. While the party won seventy-three seats, a number of candidates winning dual/multiple mandates, sixty-nine representatives was the total returned. Only twenty-seven members attended the inaugural sitting of the Sinn Féin abstentionist parliament. Among the absentees, two were excused due to illness, a further five were on official business overseas, while thirty-four were in prison, including Éamon de Valera. In fact de Valera had doubts about the policy of mass abstention, observing, 'Westminster gave us a platform, which we now do not have.'[1]

The Dáil proceedings opened with a prayer in Irish, and a toned down version of the Democratic Programme (a draft written by Thomas Johnson, leader of the Labour Party) was read into the official record. It was a token gesture, 'rewarding' the Labour Party for not contesting the 1918 general election. For the majority of Sinn Féiners, if they thought about James Connolly at all, it was as a nationalist martyr rather than a socialist mentor. In the preamble to the Declaration of Independence, the Dáil stressed that the language, race, customs and traditions of Ireland are radically distinct from those of England. By implication a total separation from the government at Westminster was the natural outcome of this statement.

At its inaugural sitting, the Dáil – though physically severing the umbilical chord with London – was firmly imbued in the British parliamentary tradition. Rather than marking a radical departure from the British model (other than being a separate assembly) the Dáil retained the parliamentary language and procedures, as well as the functionaries and cabinet government format in use at Westminster. On its first day, business was conducted through the medium of English. The cabinet portfolios were allocated as follows: Internal (Home) Affairs (Griffith); External Affairs (Plunkett); Finance (Collins); Defence (Brugha); Local Government (Cosgrave); Labour (Countess Markievicz); and Industry (Eoin McNeill).

While the Dáil was establishing a precedent for *de facto* and *de jure* control over Irish governance in Dublin, a unit of eight Volunteers under the command of Dan Breen and Seán Treacy held up a cartload of dynamite on its way to a quarry in Soloheadbeg, County Tipperary. The ambush of the explosives convoy had been planned for a number of days, and it was purely coincidental that it occurred on 21 January 1919, the same day as the inaugural sitting of Dáil Éireann. If seizure of explosives was the sole reason for the Soloheadbeg raid, the Volunteer unit would have easily overwhelmed – and disarmed – the two RIC men guarding the convoy and seized their arms and ammunition. But the Volunteers wanted to set a precedent. So Constable James McDonnell (aged fifty-seven), a native of Belmullet, County Mayo and Patrick O'Connell (aged thirty-seven) from Coachford, County Cork were shot dead.[2] The assassination of the two policemen shocked most people in Tipperary as both men were popular members of their community. The Dáil also had mixed feelings about the action.

The Tipperary Volunteers had acted on their own initiative, without seeking political approval. As Minster for Defence, Cathal Brugha felt they had usurped his authority. On a wider level many of the newly elected Sinn Féin TDs were angry that the double killings in Tipperary overshadowed the attention given to the Dáil's inaugural meeting in local and national newspapers.

The events of 21 January 1919 showed that there were two nationalist organisations in operation – Sinn Féin operating in a political sphere, and the Irish Republican Army (IRA), as the Volunteers units now chose to call themselves, intent on pursuing a physical force campaign. Both organisations were interlinked and operated in parallel, yet maintained distinct values. During the course of the War of Independence it was never really established which strand in the movement – the political or the militarist – held supremacy over and/or dominated the republican agenda. failure to resolve these issues was a major contributory factor to the onset of Civil War.

During 1919 IRA assassinations of policemen were sporadic, intensely local attacks. The unit that carried out the Soloheadbeg ambush claimed the lives of five RIC men in Tipperary and Limerick, many killed in shootouts aimed at rescuing IRA prisoners. Elsewhere four policemen were killed; two in Clare in August; one in Meath in October and one in Cork in December, bringing the RIC death toll for 1919 to eleven.

Attacks on the RIC were the mainstay of the IRA campaign (1919–21) for several mutually supportive reasons. Firstly, the force was the most visible manifestation of the British presence in Ireland. Its intelligence-gathering role on both Sinn Féin and

IRA activities meant it would have to be confronted sooner or later. An armed police force, but with no real military training, RIC barracks – and officers – were a potential source of arms and ammunition, which the IRA needed to initiate and advance further attacks. Due to the small size of police patrols and the dispersed locations of their barracks it was much easier (comparatively speaking) to overwhelm and disarm them than it would be to mount an attack on the British army.

In April 1919 Dáil Éireann elected Éamon De Valera as president and agreed to send an emissary to the Peace Conference in Paris (Versailles), and to Washington, DC to gain American recognition for Ireland's claim for independence. Both diplomatic initiatives delivered few positive results. De Valera went to the US in June 1919 to solicit financial and political support. In his role as 'president of the Irish Republic' he was well received by Irish Americans, who subscribed over five million dollars in Dáil bond certificates. Initially intending just a short tour, de Valera would remain in the USA until December 1920. In his absence Michael Collins assumed a pivotal role in the struggle for independence.

In June 1919 Collins assumed responsibility as director of intelligence within the IRA general headquarters (GHQ) staff. Established in March 1918 to reorganise the Irish Volunteers to cope with the influx of new members during the conscription crisis, GHQ found its 'mass' membership evaporated as soon as the fear of a British 'press gang' receded in the summer of 1918. Within a year GHQ had revitalised itself to guide, coordinate and direct IRA activities. Apart from Collins, Richard Mulcahy and Dick McKee were the main players in the organisation.

Detectives in the RIC, Dublin Castle and the Dublin Metropolitan Police (DMP) such as Éamon Broy, Joe Kavanagh, David Neligan and James McNamara offered to assist the Volunteers. Their offers were not acted on as (understandably) it was assumed their motive was to infiltrate the new movement with a view to destroying it. Michael Collins thought differently and sought out their inside knowledge of how the political 'G' division operated, in collecting and collating information.

As well as police contacts Collins also built up a network of state employees; these included telephone operators and stenographers in the post office, railway telegraph operators in local government and, amazingly, secretaries/typists within Dublin Castle and military command structures at national and regional levels. Each IRA brigade also had its own intelligence officer at local level who provided Collins with summaries of the activities, strengths and weaknesses of both the police and army in their districts. Railway workers acted as a 'fast track' communications network between Dublin and provincial centres if Collins (or the local unit) needed a twenty-four-hour turnaround of information. It was a communications failure – after all – that had scuttled the *Aud*.

On the night of 7 April 1919 Éamon Broy smuggled Collins into the detective headquarters in Brunswick Street and allowed him to spend the night examining the 'G' division records. Within two days Volunteers accosted individual detectives and warned them that their lives were in danger if they chose to continue working in political/surveillance duties. Some took the warnings seriously and sought transfers to other departments. Others did not.

If the threat to kill non-compliant 'G' detectives was to have any deterrent value the IRA had to be willing and able to carry out assassinations at close quarters. Headed by Mick McDonnell, the 'Squad' consisted of nine men initially, and in January 1920 added three further members, earning it the title in popular imagination of the 'twelve apostles'. The Squad's first execution was that of detective Patrick Smith. He had arrested Piaras Beaslaí, editor of *An tÓglach* (*The Volunteer*) and Sinn Féin TD for East Kerry, in possession of inflammatory articles for his newspaper. Unwilling to abandon his prosecution, Sergeant Smith was challenged by the Squad near his home in Drumcondra on the night of 30 July 1919. Though he received multiple bullet wounds, Smith managed to return fire on his attackers as he succeeded in running and entering his own house to the amazement of Squad members. He later died from his wounds.[3]

IRA ACTIVITIES IN KERRY

Kerry was divided into three brigade areas following Mulcahy's GHQ organisation of the Volunteers in March 1918. To all intents and purposes this structure was to remain the template for the IRA during the War of Independence and the Civil War.

Kerry No. 1 brigade, under the command of Paddy J. Cahill, covered the western part of the county from Tarbert to Glenbeigh, including the Dingle peninsula. It consisted of seven battalions: 1st – Tralee, O/C Dan Healy; 2nd – Dingle, O/C 'An Seabhac'; 3rd – Castlegregory, O/C Tadgh Brosnan; 4th – Listowel, O/C P. Landers; 5th – Ardfert, O/C Tom Clifford; 6th – Killorglin, O/C Flor Doherty; 7th – Lixnaw, O/C B. O'Grady.

Kerry No. 2 brigade was presided over by Dan O'Mahony and covered the eastern part of the county. Its five battalions were: 1st – Castleisland, O/C Tom O'Connor; 2nd – Firies, O/C P. O'Riordan; 3rd – Killarney, O/C M. Spillane; 4th – Rathmore, O/C H. Sullivan; 5th – Kenmare, O/C John Joe Rice.[4]

The 3rd brigade was based in south Kerry, centred on the Iveragh peninsula, and consisted of about a dozen companies organised on a parish basis. J. O'Riordan and Denis Daly of Caherciveen were the principal commanders.

The first IRA operation in Kerry took place near Camp on 24 June 1919 when Sergeant Bernard Oates and Constable J. J. O'Connell were successfully disarmed. Embarrassed and humiliated by the experience, Oates identified five of the men involved in the attack and succeeded in getting convictions on four, who received prison terms ranging from three years to a year and nine months.

The initial success at Camp, followed by the jail terms, together with the failure of the attack on Gortatlea RIC barracks acted as a brake on IRA activities in Kerry throughout 1919. In fact the only Kerry fatality of that year occurred in Dublin on 29 November when Detective Sergeant John Barton, DMP (aged thirty-six), a native of Ballymacelligott, was shot and wounded on College Street, Dublin. He died of his wounds and was buried at Kells, County Kerry on 3 December 1919, becoming the Squads' fourth victim.

On 11 September 1919 the Dáil was proscribed by the British and towards the end of November, Sinn Féin, the Volunteers, Cumann na mBan and the Gaelic League were also banned. Rather than calm the situation the British moves undermined moderate opinion – and strengthened the hand of the militarists, such as Collins, Mulcahy and Stack, to ratchet up IRA operations.

The municipal elections held on 15 January 1920 (under proportional representation) delivered spectacular results for Sinn Féin, when it secured control of 172 of the country's 206 local councils. Especially gratifying were the Sinn Féin majorities in Tyrone and Fermanagh; and a Sinn Féin/Nationalist electoral pact securing twenty-one seats on Derry city council (and the mayoralty) against the Unionist tally of nineteen councillors. Not surprisingly, the results in the six-county 'exclusion zone' the Unionists proposed as their 'Lebensraum' did nothing to undermine the Sinn Féin view that partition was a non-starter, and an Orange 'mini state' was unfeasible.

As none of the general elections of 1918, 1921 or 1922 were contested in Kerry it is worth noting the seat distribution in Tralee, Killarney and Listowel urban district councils:

UDC	SINN FÉIN	LABOUR	IND.	UNIONIST	TOWN TENANTS
TRALEE	9	9	3	1	1
KILLARNEY	9	–	3	–	–
LISTOWEL	5	6	1	–	–

Table 1: Municipal election results, January 1920, Kerry UDCs.[5]

While crushing a plethora of nationalist organisations in the autumn of 1919, the British chose to down-play the significance of the IRA campaign. A comparatively low intensity conflict comprising ambushes and no-warning attacks that claimed the lives of fifteen policemen and one British soldier (killed in Fermoy, County Cork in September 1919) meant that the IRA were regarded as cowardly, unscrupulous killers fudging the boundaries between banditry and criminality. The task of suppressing the IRA, argued Sir Henry Wilson, the British military advisor on Ireland, was one best suited to police methods and not to the military.

Ironically, placing the RIC in the front line against the IRA undermined police morale, most of whom joined the force for mundane reasons: a sense of serving the community, the security of a government job with reasonable pay and promotion prospects and a pension on retirement.

As attacks on police patrols and RIC barracks intensified in the first six months of 1920 many RIC members left the force; some because they did not want to risk their lives in a role they felt should have been carried out by soldiers rather that policemen, while others only had a couple of years left to retirement and could afford to trade a reduced pension for a longer life. Finally many police were nationalist (if not republican) in sympathy, and quite a few assisted Sinn Féin (as neighbours) in both passive and active ways.

Over forty RIC men and four British soldiers were killed between January and June 1920 in a conflict centred on Dublin city and Munster – Cork and Tipperary in particular. Of RIC/DMP deaths, Cork accounted for thirteen, Tipperary seven, Dublin six, Limerick six and Kerry three. In other words, over 80 per cent of police fatalities occurred in five counties. And this trend was to continue for the final year (July 1920–July 1921) of the war.

At the summer assizes in June 1920 the presiding magistrate summarised the level of 'rebel' activity in Kerry since the turn of the year. In all a total of twenty-three police barracks, three court houses and four coastguard stations had been destroyed. There had been six attacks on police patrols at Camp, Ballyheige, Ballybunion, Castlegregory, Gortatlea and Scartaglen.[6]

The Gortatlea attack, led by Tom McEllistrim, took place on 25 March 1920, almost two years after the Ballymacelligott company's action of April 1918. On this occasion the unit captured six rifles, five pistols, two shotguns and substantial quantities of ammunition. In the attack three of the seven-member garrison were wounded before surrendering the post to McEllistrim, who phoned a doctor to tend to the wounded RIC men, even though some of his company urged the execution of all seven to avenge the deaths of Laide and Brown two years earlier.[7]

Individual commanders and their willingness to engage the police (either on patrol or in a smaller barracks – a hut essentially) determined the success of the 'national' campaign at local level. Basically an IRA unit was left to fend for itself – the Gortatlea arms seizure was to prove the core of the Ballymacelligott unit's weaponry for the duration of the conflict.

Some of the IRA killings were far from heroic. On 16 March 1920, Cornelius Kelly (aged forty), the caretaker at Caherdaniel courthouse, was shot dead in front of his wife and nine-year-old daughter. His slowness in handing over the keys to the shed where six bicycles belonging to the RIC were stored cost him his life.

By June 1920 the first of the new police cadets recruited from among British ex-servicemen began to arrive in Ireland both to augment the RIC (depleted by resignations) and provide both a core and a corps that had military training and were 'battle' hardened. Hastily assembled, the new force were not even issued proper uniforms and improvised a kit that included the bottle green (not actually black) of the RIC and the khaki of the military. They were nicknamed the 'Black and

Tans'. The 'uniform' might suggest a fusion of police and army, but the 'Black and Tans' had neither the local knowledge (and empathy) of a police force nor the discipline of an army. And their presence and actions in Ireland did more than the IRA could ever have done to undermine the legitimacy of British rule in Ireland in the minds of moderate public opinion in both Ireland and England. General Hubert Gough, perpetrator of the Curragh mutiny (1914), and no friend of nationalist Ireland, would write: 'Law and order have given way to a bloody and brutal anarchy ... England has departed further from her own standards and further from the standards ... of any nation in the world ... than has ever been known in history.'

The Black and Tans accompanied the RIC on their patrols and the mutual animosity was palpable. The Listowel police 'mutiny' of June 1920, well documented in J. Anthony Gaughan's *Memoir of Constable Jeremiah Mee,* is indicative of the moral dilemma many rank and file RIC men faced when told by their military overseers that soon they would be given *carte blanche* to shoot their own countrymen with impunity.

From July 1920 onwards conflict and confrontations between the IRA and the RIC and the Black and Tans became more frequent and bloodier, with civilians being killed and wounded in greater numbers and the property, homes and businesses of non-combatants being burned in reprisals for IRA attacks on policemen and soldiers.

In the six months between July and December 1920 122 policemen were killed and 184 wounded in Ireland; thirteen lost their lives in Kerry during 1920 while eight Kerrymen died elsewhere in Ireland in the course of their police duties. The British army, in contrast, suffered forty-nine dead and over eighty wounded in the same time frame.[8] Nationally, IRA volunteers took heavy casualties in 1920; thirty-two died in the first six months of the year, while 228 were killed between July and December.[9]

In Kerry the first two weeks of November 1920 were the most unsettled of the entire conflict in the county, with heavy loss of life to both police and IRA activists and a reign of terror in which civilians were attacked and their homes and property damaged. IRA GHQ issued orders that a series of attacks on RIC stations should coincide with the funeral of Terence Mac-Swiney on 31 October. The order was rescinded, but countermanding instructions did not reach Kerry in time. In separate attacks at Abbeydorney, Ballyduff, Dingle, Tralee and Killorglin six police officers were killed and eight wounded in IRA operations. It was no coincidence that seven of the fourteen IRA volunteers who died at the hands of crown forces in Kerry during 1920 were killed between 31 October and 22 November. In a surreal twist during the 'siege of Tralee' the British army garrison at Ballymullen barracks intervened to protect townspeople and their property from the Black and Tans, who went on a rampage around Tralee.

Nationally, the single most audacious act of the 'intelligence' war occurred in Dublin on the morning of 21 November 1920 when the Squad, assisted by the Dublin active service unit (ASU), targeted twenty British agents, killing fourteen and wounding six. The action was a pre-emptive strike on Collins' part as the British were poised to eliminate his organisation in Dublin. Later that afternoon (it was the day of the All-Ireland football final) the Black and Tans converged on Croke Park. Shots were fired, and in the ensuing panic eleven were killed and dozens injured; possibly more died in the stampede than from gunshot wounds. Either way the Croke Park incident became known as 'Bloody Sunday'.

A week later, Sunday, 28 November, at Kilmichael, near Macroom, County Cork, Tom Barry's west Cork brigade attacked an auxiliary column, killing seventeen men in circumstances that are still considered controversial.

Introduced into Ireland in September 1920 – on Churchill's recommendation – the auxiliaries were recruited from ex-officers and were regarded as an elite force. It was a huge body blow that an entire patrol was wiped out. In a reprisal action the commercial heart of Cork city was burned down. The combined impact of the events in Ireland's two principal cities during November precipitated the partial introduction of martial law focused on Cork, Tipperary, Limerick and Kerry.

During December 1920 serious efforts were made to open peace negotiations when Archbishop Joseph Clune of Perth, Western Australia engaged in shuttle diplomacy between more moderate factions within both the Irish and British administrations on a range of measures that would be the basis of the truce adopted six months later. It was the chief secretary, Sir Hamar Greenwood's belief, supported by his military advisers, that Britain was winning both the military and public opinion campaigns against the IRA. Had the opportunity been grasped hundreds of lives – both British and Irish – would have been saved.

Éamon de Valera returned to Ireland in December 1920 after an absence of eighteen months in America. While out of Ireland he was critical of the IRA's ambush/hit-and-run strategy and urged instead one good battle, about once a month, involving about 500 men in each. Such a policy was beyond the IRA's capacity – at every level; they had developed the flying column in the summer of 1920 to create a small (20–30 members), full time, effective, highly manoeuvrable force to avoid such engagements. In 1921 the conflict escalated in intensity and column activity nationally was spread across a much wider area, geographically, than had been the case during 1920.

In Kerry the level and extent of the campaign waged by the IRA was patchy and was complicated by personality clashes.

Paddy Cahill, brigadier of Kerry No. 1, was older than the average volunteer in his command, and owed his appointment to a close personal friendship with Austin Stack, rather than innate military ability. Conservative by nature, he avoided both military confrontation with the enemy and joint operations with neighbouring commands, and made little contact with GHQ.

Within the cabinet Austin Stack was given responsibility for setting up the Sinn Féin courts. His ineffective command of his portfolio soured his relations with Collins. Cathal Brugha, Minister for Defence, resented the inroads Collins and Mulcahy had made in their intelligence and GHQ roles, into 'his' department. It was a feeling of anger he and Austin Stack shared, and as time went on their common hostility towards Michael Collins deepened to the level of hatred.

On 21 March 1921 an IRA column led an attack on a troop train at Headford junction on the Kenmare–Killarney railway line. The two IRA officers leading the assault, Dan Allman and James Bailey, were killed in the attack; several civilians were killed and wounded in crossfire, while the IRA claimed British losses to be at least twenty. It is probable that more ambitious actions were countenanced in east Kerry due to high levels of cooperation between IRA units in that area and their Cork counterparts.

Liam Lynch was scathing of IRA intelligence in Tralee town and regarded the IRA in Lixnaw and Dingle as ineffectual. A GHQ report in June 1921 on Kerry No. 1 brigade noted that battalions acted independently of each other and had no basic military training, to such an extent that hardly 10 per cent of the men could shoot effectively. To put these criticisms in context, the IRA in Kerry was chronically short of ammunition and could not afford to waste what little they had improving marksmanship. Besides, from 1921 onwards, joint police–army 'sweeps' made it difficult to organise firing ranges because of the danger of the column being surrounded, captured and killed. In the final analysis it was the ability to pinpoint the location and timing of an ambush, and fire first (at close quarters) that gave the IRA its main advantage.

During the first six months of 1921 IRA attacks claimed the lives of twenty-three policemen, the high casualty levels resulting in the main from ambushes in May and June in the vicinity of Rathmore and Castlemaine which claimed the lives of eight and five officers respectively. Some twenty-seven IRA volunteers lost their lives in Kerry in the same time frame. In the country at large 324 members of the crown forces were killed and almost 500 wounded between 1 January and 11 July. IRA casualties numbered 182 dead, but as many as 4, 500 were interned and in jail, leaving about 2,000 active volunteers confronting a combined British army, RIC, Black and Tan and auxiliary of some 60,000 men. The population at large was war-weary and longed for an end to hostilities. In Dublin for example, between January and June 1921, forty-six civilians were killed and 143 wounded in crossfire during street ambushes.

May 1921 was the worst month for the British in terms

of casualties, with a total of seventy-two (fifty-six policemen and sixteen soldiers) killed. De Valera's advocacy of a large-scale action was finally agreed to with the seizure of the Custom House in Dublin on 20 May. The propaganda value of destroying the nucleus of local government, and one of Dublin's finest buildings, vindicated de Valera's strategy. The action cost the IRA five dead and many wounded and led to the capture of eighty of Collins' best men, rendering the outcome something of a pyrrhic victory.

It was the general election of 24 May 1921, which returned MPs (and TDs) for both the Assemblies – the British proposed to open in Dublin and Belfast in July – that paved the way for peace negotiations. The unsettled political situation made a contested election impossible. Apart from the four Dublin University MPs, Sinn Féin 'won' 124 seats unopposed. Sir Hamar Greenwood's objection aside, the truce terms advanced the previous December now proved acceptable to both parties and it was eventually agreed to end hostilities on 11 July 1921.

Ironically, the last engagement of the war took place near Castleisland on 10/11 July, resulting in the death of three British soldiers and the wounding of two others. Among the five IRA killed in the attack was John Flynn, one of the men involved in the Gortatlea attack of April 1918.

3

FROM THE TRUCE TO THE TREATY

The implementation of the ceasefire and accompanying truce from noon on Monday, 11 July 1921 took the rank and file IRA volunteers by surprise. They had not been consulted in advance and were presented with a *fait accompli* by GHQ. Many welcomed a temporary respite from the conflict, but did not believe the agreement would last. Michael Collins had mixed feelings. Following the Custom House operation in Dublin in May, his trump card had been thrown in at de Valera's behest. And as the British began to gauge, evaluate and identify the IRA's strengths and weaknesses (and key personnel) at local level, it would be, he argued, 'extermination for us if the truce should fail'.[1]

Jeremiah Murphy, from Kilquane, near Rathmore, put the changes the agreement produced in more human terms:

> The truce brought about much needed rest for many harassed IRA men and a little relaxation was indulged in. Some who had not been home for a year were able to see their families again, for they had not been operating in their native territory. They were either too well-known, or the districts might have been largely pro-British, or the terrain was very unsuitable for guerrilla warfare. But the majority of the men were able to be at home most of the time and didn't suffer from the worries of the wanted men in the flying columns.[2]

And yet there was a niggling suspicion that Sinn Féin's politicians would compromise and do a deal with the British and surrender the ideals that the IRA (the inheritors of the 1916 'flame') had fought so hard to achieve. After all it was their willingness to bear arms against the crown and risk their lives to achieve freedom that had brought Lloyd George to the negotiating table. Florence O'Donoghue, a leading Cork republican, who would later adopt an anti-Treaty stance in 1922, articulated the fears of many of his comrades in the flying columns of both Cork and Kerry when he observed: 'We'll wake up some morning … members or the civil population … with peace made. And our occupation and our power gone. I'll go back to the poorhouse.'[3]

The truce had another effect: people queued up to join the IRA, which swelled from a ceasefire strength of 3,000 (in July) to over 70,000 by year's end. The latter-day recruits – known disdainfully as 'Trucileers' by *bona fide* War of Independence activists – were driven in the main by the prospect of careers in a post-independent Ireland.

In the meantime there was the delicate matter of negotiating a settlement that would be acceptable to both the British and Irish governments and to public opinion. Lloyd George, in consultation with Balfour and Chamberlain, offered a twenty-six county dominion-type status, where Ireland would have an army but no navy. Britain would have port facilities in time of war, and Dublin's parliament would recognise the powers and *de jure* rights of its Northern Ireland counterpart. By 19 July, scarcely a week into talks in London, de Valera was writing to Collins advising him of the imminent collapse of negotiations.

During August/September 1921 letter and telegraphic

communiqués criss-crossed the Irish Sea, to-ing and fro-ing between Lloyd George's and de Valera's offices. When a significant offer, or stance, was put forward by the British, the Dáil was convened and informed of progress and the rationales of both parties.

In late September the British invited an Irish delegation to London to attend a conference on 11 October, where 'the association of Ireland with the community of nations known as the British Empire may best be recognised with Irish national aspirations'. Removing the bones from the sinews of diplomatic niceties, Britain's offer precluded the granting of an Irish republic (or its equivalent) even as an opening position.

Given the subsequent fallout surrounding the Treaty negotiations (the 11 October meeting was the start of formal negotiations) and charges of a 'sell out' of the republic by the plenipotentiaries, the very fact that the Irish agreed to attend the conference at all signified a willingness to compromise (on de Valera's part, in particular). All that remained to be decided was the composition of the delegation – a topic that even now (eight decades later) can lead to heated arguments – especially if alcohol fuels the discussion.

As president of the Dáil, Éamon de Valera was the sole channel of communication with London between July and September, and it was assumed he would be the chief negotiator in any delegation that would attend the conference. Arthur Griffith, Michael Collins and W. T. Cosgrave, three members of the cabinet (which comprised seven members), took it for granted that this would be the case.

De Valera was equally adamant that he should not be present at the Downing Street negotiations. Cathal Brugha and Austin

Stack, along with Robert Barton, supported de Valera's stance, who crucially had the casting vote. Both Brugha and Stack were asked if they wanted to act as delegates. Both men rejected the offer, as did Michael Collins when he was canvassed on the subject. Collins argued he was temperamentally unsuited to negotiations; he was a soldier, not a politician. While he had the IRB man's innate distaste for politics, Collins felt he had no patience for poring over documents, posturing, studying the minutiae of constitutions and treatises.

De Valera, as president of the Dáil, was head of 'government'. And as he was by training a mathematician, he was, Collins argued, used to formulae, breaking a problem down into its component parts and a stickler for protocol – skills that made him the 'natural' choice as leader of the team Dáil Éireann was sending to London. However, de Valera felt himself above politics, as regards brokering deals. A complicated individual, he complemented Collins' skills during the 1919–21 struggle for independence. His self image was that he was a symbol of the republic, and (I believe) the fact that he was spared an execution for his part in the 1916 Rebellion (on account of being an American citizen) led him to assume the mantle of the conscience of the signatories of the Proclamation.

Both Collins and de Valera wanted to avoid having to sup from the poisoned chalice. In the end Collins agreed to go to London, though he sensed Brugha, Stack and de Valera had colluded to restrict his options. Collins was not being modest when he stated he wasn't a politician, but he was being disingenuous. As director of intelligence, his use of terror was based in part on the expectation of a particular politico-military response by the British to an 'atrocity' that wouldn't alienate moderate public opinion (both in Britain and Ireland) from the IRA campaign. His war was a 'political' one. The clichés about politics being 'the art of the possible' and war being the 'continuation of diplomacy by other means' retain their currency because they contain a kernel of truth about the range of policy options followed by the state, or nations aspiring to statehood. Failing an outright military victory by the IRA, and the unconditional surrender by British forces the best the Irish could hope for was that the IRA campaign would wear down Whitehall/Westminster's enthusiasm for a military solution in favour of resolving the conflict around the conference table.

In the final analysis Michael Collins probably felt that having succeeded in bringing the British to the table he had a duty to pull up a chair and face his adversaries, even though he felt de Valera had better negotiating skills and was more at ease in a political and conciliatory environment than he was.

The Irish delegation that attended the London conference, on Tuesday, 11 October 1921, was headed by Arthur Griffith and included Michael Collins, Robert Barton, Charles Gavin Duffy and Éamon Duggan as plenipotentiaries 'who … given a free hand in such negotiations … duly report to the Dáil'. Erskine Childers was the official secretary to the delegation. Fionán Lynch, a native of Caherciveen and TD for South Kerry, served as one of the two assistant secretaries on the negotiating team.

The British were represented by David Lloyd George, Lord Birkenhead, Austin Chamberlain and Winston Churchill. Sir Gordon Hewart, the attorney general, and Sir Hamar Greenwood, the chief secretary for Ireland, were part of the back-up team serving the crown. Steeped in parliamentary and administrative procedures, the British had the experience of the Versailles peace conference under their belts and were a formidable negotiating team. Lloyd George, prime minister and leader of the Liberal Party, headed a coalition government where the Tories held 338 of the government's 484 seats. Natural allies of the Ulster Unionists, the Conservatives restricted Lloyd George's room for manoeuvre.

Between 11 and 24 October seven plenary sessions took place. Many of the practical 'positions', however, were teased out at sub-conference level, which focused on defence, finance and Treaty violations. On a defence proposal submitted on 13 October by Erskine Childers in Collins' and Winston Churchill's presence, Collins was stunned when Childers said: 'I mean to demonstrate that Ireland is not only no source of danger to England, but from the military standpoint is virtually useless.'[4]

While negotiating for peace, Collins continued to keep the military options open if – or when – talks failed. Following Childers' unsolicited admission of Ireland's comparative weak position militarily, Collins wanted to marginalise him, and saw him as a 'spy' sending weekly messages to de Valera in Dublin. Arthur Griffith's dislike of Childers was even more pronounced, and he and Collins had little difficulty in persuading both Lloyd George and Chamberlain to adopt the smaller sub-conference format in future deliberations, thereby excluding both Childers (whom the British regarded as too doctrinaire) and Sir Hamar Greenwood (whom Collins despised) from any effective role in the Treaty negotiations.

In Kerry the IRA availed of intensive training and technical instruction. Jeremiah Murphy recalled the east Kerry column's preparations:

Behind all this veneer of peace, the IRA leaders were cautious and pessimistic and used the respite to plan strategy in the event of a recurrence of hostilities. A large-scale programme of training was planned and carried out. The battalion and company officers of East Kerry were located at a place west of Greevegulla in 'F' Company area. The high point of the proceedings was a full parade and sham battle of the 5th Battalion which was held on a warm Saturday in September. It consisted of over 600 men. They were instructed to show up with any and all arms. Some even came from our company with dummy guns which had been made for training purposes.[5]

The negotiations on Northern Ireland – or rather the six north-eastern counties that were already excluded from the state territory Griffith and Collins were being offered – were broached initially by Arthur Griffith. The founder of Sinn Féin and Apostle of 'go it alone' abstentionism, Griffith was not an ideological republican so the oath was not a matter of conscience for him, as indeed it was not for a sizeable number of Sinn Féin's electoral base.

It was decided to advance the status of Northern Ireland in tandem with constitutional issues, i.e. recognition of the crown and membership of the Commonwealth and the formula of words that would be acceptable to both British and Irish political elites and public opinions. In return for 'essential' unity – an all-Ireland parliament with Northern Ireland retaining its six-county territorial area – the plenipotentiaries would recommend that the Dáil approve free partnership in the Commonwealth as a form of association and would pledge recognition of the king in his capacity as head of the association.

In politics timing is everything. The Ulster Unionist leader, James Craig, was canvassed on the 'unity' issue by Lloyd George on 5 November to see if he was willing to consider participating in an all-Ireland parliament. As the Unionist annual conference was being held in Liverpool on 17 November, advisors like Sir Henry Wilson and Sir Lamington Worthington-Evans, the Conservative Secretary for War, recommended non-participation. Lloyd George informed Griffith of the meeting's outcome on 12 November.

Collins proposed a boundary commission as an alternative approach to the problem. If Belfast demanded self-determination for the six counties, it could hardly refuse the same rights to the nationalist population within its boundaries, when proportionately the nationalist community in Northern Ireland was larger than the unionist constituency (that opted out) on the island as a whole. Lloyd George agreed in principle to the establishment of the commission. Collins reported the British response to Dublin where de Valera and the cabinet endorsed the proposal on 13 November 1921.

Collins and most of the Sinn Féin TDs anticipated a series of referenda or plebiscites on a county basis. As it was taken for granted that most of Tyrone and Fermanagh, Derry city and parts of Derry, Armagh and Down would opt to join the Free State (at the expense of the 'Orange' Free State), few southern nationalists believed partition was a permanent state of affairs. In fact a rump 'state' based on Antrim and Down and the city of Belfast, Sinn Féin argued, was too small to be economically viable. Once the unionists saw it was in their economic interests, they would come on board and voluntarily join with Dublin as part of a single island administration.

On 22 November both British and Irish delegations met to discuss proposals on dominion status within the empire, the oath of allegiance to the king and guarantees on defence.

The British stipulated that failure to recognise the crown would mean war. As a concession to Irish sensitivities Birkenhead agreed to Griffith's proposal that the title Irish Free State would go into the Treaty. At this juncture Griffith and Collins returned to Dublin to consult with their cabinet colleagues. The cabinet agreed unanimously that Ireland 'should recognise the British Crown for the purposes of Association, as symbol and accepted head of the combination of associated states'. At this point Michael Collins accepted dominion status represented the only possibility of compromise between the crown and the republic. He did not see it as an ideal solution, or as an end in itself. Rather, it was a starting point, the Hibernian equivalent of the Confucian adage that 'the journey of one thousand miles begins with the first step'. Lloyd George's assertion that the Irish could insert 'any phrase they liked which would ensure that the position of the Crown in Ireland should be no more in practice than it was in Canada or any other Dominion reinforced Collins' argument.

The British published a draft treaty on 30 November 1921, in which it was proposed:

> The Irish Free State would have Dominion status in law and practice. Defence of Ireland's coastal waters would be Britain's responsibility and four ports were to be provided for Royal Navy use. Each member of Parliament would swear an oath of allegiance to: The Constitution of the Irish Free State; the Community of nations known as the British Commonwealth; and the King as Head of State and of Empire. Fleeting recognition was also given to Irish unity and a Boundary Commission.

On 1 December Downing Street was a flurry of activity as every aspect of the document was scrutinised to fine tune or tweak concessions from the Treaty. It was stipulated that allegiance to the crown was only as 'Head of State and Empire', and that naval defence would only be an exclusively British prerogative until the Free State could safeguard and enforce her own coastal defence.

The cabinet met in full session at the Mansion House, Dublin on 3–4 December to hear the deliberations of the plenipotentiaries on the 'final' deal Britain was prepared to offer. Amazingly, no proper minutes of the meeting were taken by an impartial reporter. Individual contributors kept notes as an *aide-memoire*, or to clarify points of law, opinion or fact. But no verbatim report of the most important political discussions in twentieth-century nationalist history exists. Perhaps this was the norm for the cabinet in its 'underground' years, but a bizarre oversight given that its words would, in fullness of time, be as lethal as bullets, and destroy lives as much as reputations.

From the outset de Valera found the provisions on Ulster and the oath unacceptable. He suggested amendments, without which Ireland would not budge, even if the consequences led to a resumption of the war. Griffith admitted the document was flawed, but he did not think it was dishonourable. It delivered a virtual republic. If it were to be rejected the people were entitled to know what alternative solution was on offer. He would not recommend acceptance by the government, but felt the plenipotentiaries should sign and leave it to the president (de Valera) and Dáil Éireann to decide the issues. The meeting instructed the plenipotentiaries to return to London to convey the message that the existing oath could not be subscribed to, even if non-compliance led to renewal of the war. Griffith was instructed to withdraw his pledges on the boundary commission and secure a promise from James Craig in relation to 'essential unity'.

Lloyd George put it to the Irish delegates that if they agreed to sign the document – accepting the terms of the Treaty – he would do everything in his power (in reality Lloyd George had very little leverage over either Craig or his backers in the Conservative Party) to get the Ulster Unionists to accept 'essential unity'. Collins wanted written acceptance from Craig before signing any agreement, whereupon Lloyd George produced a letter that Arthur Griffith had assented to a month previously, stating that he would sign without prior agreement from Craig. Michael Collins was dumbfounded but remained poker-faced. Griffith told Lloyd George that he would personally sign the terms of the agreement, but said it would be unfair to expect the other delegates to sign without knowing Craig's final position on the 'unity question'.

Addressing his remarks to both Barton and Collins, Lloyd George said that those who were not for peace 'must take full responsibility for the war that would immediately follow refusal by any delegate to sign the Articles of Agreement'. On their way back to their accommodation, Barton was astounded by Collins' admission that he would sign. If war restarted, the IRA would be defeated, Collins argued, and he didn't want their deaths on his conscience. It changed Barton's mind. Returning to Downing Street the Irish delegation agreed to sign the terms of the agreement at 2.30 a.m. on Tuesday, 6 December 1921.

4

A HOUSE DIVIDED

When Collins and Griffith arrived back in Dun Laoghaire *en route* to the cabinet meeting they were met by an IRB delegation. Collins took advantage of the opportunity to ask Tom Cullen what the IRB thought about the proposals. He replied: 'What is good enough for you is good enough for them.'[1] It was at this level, a personal loyalty to the protagonist's point of view, rather than in the realms of abstract issues, that the question of whether a person went pro- or anti-Treaty was determined The de Valera/Collins fissure was at the apex of the pyramid, but other local figures reinforced the national trend. In Kerry, for example, Austin Stack's trenchant opposition to the terms of the Treaty would have been the decisive factor in swaying most political activists and IRA men to oppose it. Within a column, battalion or company an IRA commander from the War of Independence could, if he chose to force the issue, bring his men to take up arms against the Provisional Government, adopt a neutral stance (i.e. oppose the Treaty, but not offer military resistance) or join the government's army.

Arthur Griffith had agreed that he would refer back to de Valera before signing any agreement on the Treaty. The delegates signed without informing de Valera, who first learned of the *fait accompli* when Austin Stack showed him a copy of the *Evening Mail*. Not surprisingly de Valera was incandescent with rage at what he regarded as both a personal slight – a betrayal of trust – and an insult to his status as president of Dáil Éireann. Next morning he summoned a cabinet meeting to announce he was seeking the resignations of Collins, Barton and Griffith. This was music to Stack's and Brugha's ears, but W. T. Cosgrave dissented, arguing that the three men had a right to state their case. On 8 December 1921, a full cabinet meeting was held at the Mansion House in Dublin. Ironically, more attention was given to the circumstances in which the Treaty was signed than to the terms the delegates had accepted. Robert Barton, to de Valera's surprise, blamed him both for vacillation and for refusing to go to London as part of the negotiation team. When the vote was taken on whether to refer the Treaty terms to the Dáil, Barton, Griffith, Cosgrave and Collins voted in favour, tilting the balance four–three in support of the motion, with de Valera, Stack and Brugha in the minority.

Advised by many senior members within Sinn Féin not to oppose the cabinet majority decision publicly because of the consequences that would follow, de Valera deliberately took a provocative course, determined to get his retaliation in first. In a press release he stated:

> The terms of this agreement are in violent conflict with the wishes of the majority of this nation, as expressed freely in successive elections during the past three years. I feel it is my duty to inform you immediately that I cannot recommend the acceptance of this Treaty either to Dáil Éireann or to the country. In this attitude I am supported by the Ministers of Home Affairs and Defence. The greatest test of our people has come. Let us face it worthily without bitterness, and above all, without recrimination. There is a definite constitutional way of resolving our political differences – let us not depart from it.[2]

The speech is a world away from de Valera s 'maiden' speech delivered at the East Clare by-election in 1917, when he proclaimed: 'We want an Irish Republic – but if the Irish people want another form of Government, so long as it is an Irish Government, I would not put a word against it.'[3] It is a truism to say that de Valera saw himself as a medium, who only had to look into his own heart to know what the Irish people wanted. This political Shamanism was combined and reinforced by a familiarity with *The Prince*, Machiavelli's guide to statecraft and 'political spin'. The majority of the nation was not (to invert and misquote de Valera's comments) 'in violent conflict with the terms of the agreement'. In fact, most people were willing to give the advocates of the Treaty some breathing space to prove it could deliver the terms they claimed it contained. In the 1918 general election the bulk of those who voted for Sinn Féin did so on the basis that the party would not take their seats in Westminster, and instead set up an independent Dáil in Dublin. It did not endorse a republic as the absolute (or sole) expression of Irish nationalism, no more than it gave the IRA an electoral mandate for Soloheadbeg. The second Dáil, elected without a contest in May 1921, represented Sinn Féin rather than the national electorate. On a country-wide basis political violence prevented normal campaigning and polling, while a degree of harassment of the Parliamentary and Unionist Party candidates ensured that Sinn Féin nominees were the only names on the voting list.

Éamon de Valera had hoped to scuttle the Treaty at cabinet level if the terms were not to his liking. Falling at that hurdle he decided to adopt a two-pronged approach in the Dáil. Firstly, he would present his own document as an alternative Treaty, and secondly, he would argue that the delegates had exceeded their authority in agreeing to sign the document without referring back to Dublin. The nature of the oath of allegiance to the British monarch and dominion status were the main sources of division on the Treaty, in an assembly that hardly broached the issue of partition during the debate. The division of the island was an issue, but in a myopic manner, as neither pro- nor anti-Treaty factions envisioned the northern state having a long-term future once the boundary commission deliberated on the demographic distribution of Catholics and Protestants within the six counties. Apart from Brugha and Stack, de Valera's most vocal support came from the cohort of female deputies in the Dáil – Countess Markievicz, Kathleen Clarke (Tom Clarke's widow), Margaret Pearse (Patrick Pearse's mother) and Mary MacSwiney (Terence MacSwiney's sister) – and Erskine Childers – who spewed vitriolic abuse, on Collins in particular, on behalf of their dead relatives, and were dubbed by Dublin wits 'the women and Childers party'.

From the outset of the debate both Griffith and Collins pointed out that, as early as July 1921, Éamon de Valera (and Brugha and Stack) knew that an Irish republic would not be acceptable to the British, so some form of compromise was inevitable. Collins also criticised de Valera for not participating in the London conference, comparing his contribution to that of a captain who sent his crew to sea and tried to direct operations from dry land. The alternative document de Valera proposed did not contain an oath of allegiance to the crown, but neither did it contain the word 'republic'. The articles relating to partition were virtually identical to those contained in the Treaty. The general public couldn't see what all the fuss was about. In his concluding address before the Christmas recess on 22 December Michael Collins recommended that the Dáil vote in favour of the agreement because:

> In my opinion it gives us freedom, not the ultimate freedom that all nations desire and develop to, but the freedom to achieve it … we have stated we would not coerce the North East. We have stated it officially. I stated it publicly in Armagh and nobody has found fault with me. What is the use of talking big phrases about not agreeing to the partition of our country? Surely we recognise that the North-East corner does exist, and surely our intention was that we should take such steps as would lead to mutual understanding. The Treaty has made an effort … to deal with it on lines that will lead very rapidly to goodwill and the entry of the North-East under the Irish Parliament.[4]

During the recess, which lasted until 3 January, W. T. Cosgrave, Minister for Local Government, worked assiduously, persuading no less than twenty county councils to pass resolutions in favour of the Treaty. The *Cork Examiner* of 5 January 1922 contained the following 'straw poll' indicating tacit support for the Treaty across a wide range of public bodies and organisations:

County Councils	20
Urban/Rural District Councils	75
Corporations	3
Town Commissioners	9
Boards of Guardians	23
Sinn Féin Executives	31
Sinn Féin Clubs	32
Farmers' Associations	53
Labour Bodies	11
Miscellaneous	66

Table 2: Public Bodies' support for the Treaty

The paper's editorial accompanying the poll results was well timed, showing the deputies about to vote on the Treaty that there were many other democratic fora in the country that had voices and represented the wider Irish people's wishes and aspirations as validly as the Second Dáil. There were some dissenting voices in the *Examiner*'s survey, however; both Bantry and Caherciveen rural district councils urged the Dáil to reject the Treaty.[5]

On Sunday, 1 January prayers were asked for at all masses in Tralee parish churches for the ratification of the Treaty; while in Saint Mary's cathedral and the Franciscan church in Killarney, the congregations were told that the Treaty may be rejected and the country 'plunged into strife and warfare'. The bishop's pastoral concluded: 'While fully recognising the exalted motives and untarnished patriotism of the members of a Dáil who are opposed to the ratification, we are compelled to take issue with them ... and assert our right to influence this issue of vital importance.'[6]

The next day, Monday, 2 January, as Paddy Cahill, TD and Fionán Lynch, TD arrived at Tralee railway station to catch the midday train to Dublin to resume the Treaty debate, they were met on the platform by Fianna boys in uniform, Cumann na mBan, and several young men bearing flags and placards: 'Young Ireland is at heart Republican. No Partition', and 'The bones of the dead republicans will rattle in your ears, Mr Lynch'.[7] Fionán Lynch in a letter to the *Cork Examiner* challenged the paper's account of 'a remarkable demonstration' which, he claimed, consisted of 'eight men, four boys and two women. Tralee ... is not the constituency that returned me, but the constituency of one of the outstanding opponents of the Treaty. The enthusiasm was not spontaneous.'[8]

The figure Lynch did not mention was Austin Stack, TD,

whose power base was centred in Tralee. The exchange of views between Stack and Michael Collins – as recorded by Ryle Dwyer – on the day of the cabinet 'split', 8 December 1921, is illuminating. 'You have signed and undertaken to recommend the document to the Dáil,' Stack said. 'Well, recommend it. Your duty stops there. You are not supposed to throw all your influence onto the scale.'[9] The fact that Stack proposed such a course of action as a practical strategy (for both Collins and the pro-Treaty faction) indicates that Stack didn't really understand parliamentary politics any better than he understood Collins' motivation.

THE DÁIL DEBATE

The Dáil began debating the terms of the Treaty on 14 December 1921 at the UCD buildings on Earlsfort Terrace (now the National Concert Hall) as the Mansion House was hosting a Christmas fair. The composition of the Dáil's representatives was inauspicious from the outset for a calm, measured debate on the nuances, merits and the constitutional potential contained in the Treaty. When selecting candidates for the 1921 general election, no fewer than forty-seven of the nominees were IRA volunteers serving jail sentences, while a further fifty-two were either wanted by the police, 'on the run', or both. At Collins' behest the slogan 'Put them in (parliament) to get them out (of prison)' was the strategy used to get the leading militants back into the IRA ranks. At that point Collins had little time for politicians whom he regarded as the 'bargaining type', a term of disdain on a par with Napoleon's description of the English as a nation of shopkeepers, which meant individuals who had no principles, and would buy and sell anything – if the price were right. Individually and collectively many of the 'May TDs' bowed to the notion that force of arms rather than force of argument had brought Lloyd George to the negotiating table. Instinctively many would have felt that Collins had been outsmarted in London; the more extreme may even have regarded him as a traitor. Of course such was Collins' prestige that a pro-Treaty Dáil majority would probably never have been achieved without his urging and cajoling.

At the initial stages of the debate, the Labour Party – though not represented in the Dáil – suggested an interim peace formula. De Valera would serve as president of the Dáil, but the Provisional Government would be permitted to function, deriving its authority from the Dáil. On 4 January a group of nine pro- and anti-Treaty TDs met to fine tune the Labour Party proposals. De Valera refused to accept the terms of the accord, no doubt encouraged in his rejection of the deal by the fact that the plan was acceptable to both Griffith and Collins. Though nearly forty, de Valera's behaviour during the Treaty debate was akin to a spoilt child who always got its own way, complete with temper tantrums and table-thumping outbursts directed at those who dared challenge his position. On 6 January, the penultimate day of the debate, he delivered a long speech outlining his unique role in the independence struggle, emphasising he had always been a conciliating and unifying force within Sinn Féin. All of this was by way of an introduction to Document No. 2, an alternative to the terms accepted by the plenipotentiaries in December. The alternative rested on two amendments:

1. Members of the Dáil would not swear an oath of allegiance to the British monarch.
2. Ireland would not be a member of the Commonwealth. It would, however, agree to external association.

In a theatrical flourish de Valera offered to resign as president of the Dáil if his proposals were not given attention, thus precipitating a crisis whereby the entire cabinet would have to be re-elected with both the 'agreed' version of the Treaty and de Valera's version being resubmitted on an equal footing. It transpired that it was relatively easy to persuade de Valera to withdraw his offer of resignation. He was convinced that if the Dáil rejected the terms of the Treaty Britain would not resume the Anglo-Irish War. At the same time he knew that many Tory MPs were appalled by the concessions that Lloyd George had given the plenipotentiaries. A majority of the Conservative Party and a substantial part of the Liberal Party – 'Liberal/Imperialists' – could not accept an agreement whereby Ireland would not acknowledge either the crown or the empire, and were as doctrinaire in their royalism as militants like Rory O'Connor were in not deviating an inch from the republic. Had the Dáil endorsed de Valera's proposals it is probable that not only would they have not formed the basis of a solution acceptable to the British, but they would not even have been acceptable as an opening gambit with which to recommence bilateral negotiations. On the other side of the House many pro-Treaty deputies – not least of them Collins and Kevin O'Higgins – had serious reservations about some of the terms. Even so, they were willing to accept it as a foundation upon which a more acceptable – in the longer term – Irish government could be based, leading to an eventual re-integration (they hoped) of the six north-eastern counties into the Free State.

Kerry/West Limerick constituency returned eight TDs (unopposed) on the Sinn Féin ticket in the 1921 general election. All members of the Dáil were entitled to outline their reasons why they voted the way they did on the Treaty issue. Only two Kerry TDs – Austin Stack and Fionán Lynch, representing opposite sides of the argument – elaborated and explained their positions. Austin Stack alluded to his Fenian heritage and the fact that his father had served time in an English jail for his republican ideal as reasons enough to reject the Treaty. He also personalised his stance from a sense of loyalty to Éamon de Valera. Fionán Lynch approved the terms because it gave Ireland an army, enabling the British army to withdraw from Ireland, and gave the state control over its own financial and educational system. The fact that Michael Collins was willing to accept the Treaty was sufficient reason to support it, Lynch argued. The remaining Kerry TDs did not contribute to the debate, but Thomas O'Donoghue and Paddy J. Cahill joined Austin Stack in the 'no' lobby, while Piaras Beaslaí and James Crowley voted in favour, carrying a pro-Treaty majority of sixty-four votes to fifty-seven.

5

Things Fall Apart

When the results of the vote became known around the streets of Dublin there was a general sense of relief among the public at large. Some even cheered at the news. Within the Dáil, however, there was little to cheer about. Both sides were emotionally drained and personally traumatised following three weeks of debate that was corrosive, bitter and acrimonious and left the Sinn Féin movement broken. De Valera resigned as president of the Dáil. On 10 January the Assembly reconvened to elect a new leader. Arthur Griffith won, securing sixty votes to de Valera's fifty eight, whereupon de Valera and his supporters left the Dáil. On 14 January the sixty pro-Treaty TDs and four Unionist MPs returned by Dublin University (Trinity) formed a Provisional Government that would hold the reins of power until a 'Free State'(based on parliamentary elections) was established.

Michael Collins became chairman (prime minister) of the Provisional Government consisting of eight ministers, including Kerryman Fionán Lynch as Minister for Education. Kevin O'Higgins would later encapsulate (*circa* 1924) fairly graphically the tasks and circumstances facing the new government: 'Simply eight young men in City Hall standing amid the ruins of one administration, with the foundations of another not yet laid, and with wild men screaming through the keyhole.'[1] Following Cathal Brugha's resignation as defence minister on 10 January, Richard Mulcahy assumed responsibility for the IRA and its relationship with both the Dáil and the Provisional Government. The next day IRA leaders such as Rory O'Connor, Liam Mellows, Oscar Traynor and Liam Lynch demanded that Mulcahy should hold an army convention on 5 February to ascertain the army's position on the Treaty. The writ sent the Provisional Government a mixed message; on the one hand it gave Mulcahy *de facto* recognition as a government representative, but proclaimed that the IRA's loyalty to the Provisional Government (and the terms it accepted from the British) could not be taken for granted. Mulcahy managed to secure an extension of one month on the army convention; in the interim a watchdog group (two members from each wing of the IRA) would monitor developments. The 11 January meeting papered over the cracks in the IRA, preserving the myth of army unity. This was an essential prerequisite for the British, and from this point onwards British military, paramilitary and police forces began to evacuate their barracks and other installations and hand them over to local IRA units, in the process giving anti-Treaty forces control of substantial parts of the country. In practice the British began evacuating the smaller and more remote areas of the country first, retaining strategic installations in the country's major cities until the end of the process. There were still British troop concentrations in Dublin, for example, in June 1922 even as Free State forces began shelling the Four Courts:

> January 11: Crown Forces evacuate the Lansdowne Arms hotel and the Carnegie Library, Kenmare.
> January 20: Five hundred Royal Fusiliers leave the Great Southern hotel, and the new Great Southern hotel, Killarney, their Head-

quarters for three years. The remainder will leave by two trains on Saturday, 28 January.

January 28: Barbed wire entanglements and Radio installation removed from Kenmare RIC Station.

February 9: Military Garrison stationed at Tralee march to Fenit. Humphrey Murphy accepts the handover of Ballymullen Barracks.

February 18: Ballybunion and Ballylongford RIC Barracks taken over by James Sugrue and Cornelius Dee of Listowel.

February 18: The force of twenty Black and Tans stationed in Caherciveen RIC Barracks leave town.

February 20: RIC leave the New hotel, Killarney.

March 4: RIC Barracks, Day Place, Tralee taken over by units of the Irish Army.

Table 3: The withdrawal of crown forces in Kerry, spring 1922

For Collins, British military withdrawal was crucial. He was worried that anti-Treaty groups would attack crown forces as a way of reopening hostilities in the Anglo-Irish War. The Provisional Government didn't yet have an army to confront (nor did they want to confront) their former comrades, so by postponing a decision the new government could consolidate its position, and in so doing could win over more people in the anti-Treaty camp to at least a 'neutral' position (i.e. opposed to the Treaty, but not taking up arms against the government). Time, it seemed, was on Collins' side. It would have been to the government's advantage to hold an election on the Treaty issue sooner rather than later, as Griffith argued, but Collins postponed a decision on the electoral front. In the spring of 1922 it was more important to him to preserve Sinn Féin and IRA 'unity' than obtain a popular mandate for the Treaty and secure a mandate for the Provisional/Free State government.

Even before the Dáil voted on the issue all the brigade commanders in Kerry declared to the men under their jurisdiction that they would not support, or argue for acceptance of, the terms of the Treaty. To an extent their statement was a declaration of solidarity with the line taken by Austin Stack. And by the same token it was a rebuff to the overhaul GHQ had imposed on the Kerry IRA over the summer of 1921, culminating in the suspension of Paddy Cahill as O/C of Kerry No. 1 brigade. Among themselves, officers as diverse as Tom O'Connor of Kenmare and Billy Mullins of Tralee would admit that it was only in the closing months of the War of Independence that their units were beginning to achieve their full potential in both the scale and levels of success in their attacks on the British. Local pride was hurt when the national organisation (GHQ) tried to reorganise Kerry No. 2 brigade. Andy Cooney, a Tipperary man, was ostracised as he attempted – with some success –to improve the brigade's performance. In June 1921 Cooney transferred to Kerry No. 1 brigade, where Paddy Cahill had been suspended as O/C. The close association between Cahill and Austin Stack had wider implications (at national level) as it overflowed into and exacerbated the power struggle and personality clash between Collins/Mulcahy and Brugha/Stack. For most of the officers in Kerry No. 1, GHQ's humiliation of Cahill was perceived as a rebuff to Stack. Consequently no one was willing to accept the appointment as Cahill's successor. Ironically, Cooney – against his wishes – was placed in command of the brigade. The problem was 'solved' in the longer term by transferring Humphrey Murphy to Kerry No. 1 brigade and appointing John Joe Rice as O/C of Kerry No. 2. As a face-saving exercise, Paddy Cahill was given command of the 9th battalion, an 'autonomous' unit within Kerry No. 1 brigade.[2]

From the point of view of the Civil War, the GHQ intervention and the Cahill affair had a profound effect on the Kerry IRA. They had been found wanting, and judged as under-performers in the War of Independence, at a point when they (subjectively) saw their success levels take an upward turn. For many within the organisation, if an opportunity arose to challenge GHQ's assessment 'on the ground' in Kerry, there would be a 'no holds barred' approach to any incursion, if and when Collins and Mulcahy sent troops to the Kingdom.

As 1921 drew to a close, Éamon Coogan, who worked in the Dáil's Department of Local Government, in a report penned in Killarney, noted: 'The county [Kerry] abounded in cliques and factions ... the people, liars, blackmailers and masters of intrigues. Some of our warriors in Kerry would wish to set up a Mexico here ... free to continue their noble profession of arms.' To put these comments in context, it would be absurd to take Coogan's comparison with Mexico – where over a million people died in a series of conflicts between 1911 and 1920 – at face value. He is using it as a metaphor for lawlessness. In Kerry – as in Ireland in general – the campaigns of civil disobedience that evolved from the anti-conscription campaign, and the subsequent Sinn Féin party and IRA policy of undermining both the British police (RIC), courts and wider judicial system led to an acceptance of anarchy (in the sense of a lack of respect for any form of government or control mechanism) among substantial sections of the local community. Ratepayers in Kerry, for example, would not contribute to local government coffers, as local authorities assumed responsibility for processing malicious injuries and property damages claims (by default) because central government would not accept or acknowledge the 'conflict' as a war. In the popular imagination ratepayers saw themselves as carrying the can for acts of 'vandalism' perpetrated by either the Black and Tans or the IRA. Consequently it served as an excuse for widespread non payment of local charges, to the extent that Kerry County Council was owed £74,000 in rates arrears to the year ending March 1921.[3] In an era when local government had far more significance and relevance in people's lives than central government, and raised most of its finances locally, any large-scale loss of income (£74,000 was a vast sum in the 1920s) seriously undermined the effectiveness of the local administration.

While it was a grand gesture for brigade commanders to reject the Treaty terms, unless their rank and file troops took a similar view they would be generals without an army. In *Listowel and its Vicinity*, Anthony Gaughan provides interesting insights into the way local IRA units split on the Treaty issue. From a total strength of twenty-three Volunteers during the War of Independence, No. 3 battalion lost two men during that conflict. The remaining veterans split three ways; ten opted for the Free State, six supported the republican line, while five remained non-aligned. Four members of the 6th battalion's original eighteen Volunteers were killed during 1920–21, the remainder divided six to eight in favour of the Free State and the republic respectively:[4]

LISTOWEL DISTRICT: IRA division, early 1922

Pro-Treaty	Neutral	Anti-Treaty	Total
16 (45.7%)	5 (14.3%)	14 (40%)	35 (100%)

These figures represent a spectrum – and a fluidity – of opinion even within the most committed nationalists (or extremists, depending on one's point of view), those willing to kill or sacrifice their lives for their country's independence. It is not possible to superimpose the Listowel unit's divisions as valid for anywhere else in Kerry. However, local and regional press reports during January and February suggest that a narrow enough margin (possibly 10–15 per cent of Sinn Féin/IRA members) tipped the balance between a pro- and anti-Treaty majority in most Kerry districts. In late January, the *Kerry People* newspaper reported that the Killarney Sinn Féin club had unanimously declared against the Treaty. The 4 February edition of the paper contained a correction from the chairman of the Killarney club, stating that a final decision had not yet been resolved. In Waterville, as far geographically from Killarney as Killarney was from Listowel, the Sinn Féin club declared itself by fifty-two votes to thirty-eight in favour of de Valera's position on the Treaty.[5] The Sinn Féin clubs and the IRA columns were very much a political 'elite' who saw themselves as the vanguard of the revolution, who knew better than the ordinary person what was good for them. A republican need not be a democrat; indeed the canon of physical force nationalism was (to quote Mao Tse Tsung) that all political power came from the barrel of a gun. In many ways the core issues on the Treaty that led to the Civil War were seen by the general public as hair splitting, having no practical relevance to the 'bread and butter' concerns of the ordinary citizen.

In practical terms, Florence O'Donoghue, a Corkman and deputy leader of the 1st southern division, estimated that the Kerry IRA at full strength could draw from a pool of 8,750 volunteers from their three brigade areas, broken down as follows:

Kerry No. 1 brigade	4,000
Kerry No. 2 brigade	3,400
Kerry No. 3 brigade	1,350[6]

Effectively about a thousand of the Kerry IRA would take up arms against the Provisional Government, and work to undermine and overthrow the regime it would impose on Kerry and Ireland. By late March 1922 anti-Treaty manpower and weaponry in the south and west of the country – where republicans were the dominant faction – numbered 12,900 troops who had an arsenal of 6,780 rifles.

From January 1922 onwards local IRA units in Kerry began to take a more active role in day-to-day policing. Sometimes their methods could approach vigilante-style tactics. The *Cork Examiner* reported: 'Sensation was caused in Tralee last evening when a motor car pulled up into Denny Street and a manacled young man with his hair removed was placed against a lamp post and chained. Placards stated he "Collected money on behalf of the IRA"; unauthorised Republican Police did this as an example to others.'[7] It was a brave, or foolhardy, confidence trickster who would carry out what was effectively a payroll robbery on police wages, without being prepared to accept the consequences of his actions. Unlike their Volunteer predecessors (1914–16) who wore a uniform, the War of Independence IRA wore civilian clothes – as a camouflage – to make them indistinguishable from the wider population; so it would be relatively easy to masquerade as a member. Presumably levies were collected at household level within the IRA company area on a weekly basis. It seems the deterrent effect of being 'put in stocks' worked, as there were no further reports of similar incidents in Kerry. In many ways the incident is symptomatic of the level of disaffection that existed towards any form of legitimate authority. In this instance, ironically, the victim was the local face of a movement that itself refused to accept the legitimacy of the Provisional Government, seeing the interim regime that accepted the reins of power in Dublin Castle on 16 January as a 'quisling' government beholden to the British.

Increasingly, people were prepared to take the law into their own hands on a wide range of issues from cattle driving (rustling) to property disputes, safe in the knowledge that there would be no sanction (or punishment) from a force that was gearing itself up for another war, and re-honing its military capabilities to the detriment of its police duties. The country had enough real – economic and social – problems to tackle in the spring of 1922 without inventing additional, constitutional ones. Unemployment was widespread on the island as a whole; 109,786 were on the register at the end of December 1921, very probably an underestimation of the real levels of those who were without jobs – and this a workforce for whom there was little or no form of social welfare provision.[8] The disruption caused by the 1919–21 conflict only exacerbated the already sharp drop in agricultural incomes and prices that followed the end of the 1914–18 war. If any real gains were to be realised in a newly independent Ireland, peace and stability were essential to enable the infant state to tackle the real problems that needed immediate attention. One example is Kerry County Council, the largest single employer in Kerry, certainly in the area of unskilled/casual work. The loss of income incurred as a result of the non-payment of rates was of such a magnitude that by the end of December 1921 the local authority could only afford to retain fifty men on the payroll of its road maintenance division where once it employed 480 staff on a full-time basis.[9]

On the night of Monday, 16 January a party of uniformed men went on a shooting spree on William Street, Listowel. Windows were smashed and a horse belonging to a man named Hogan from Finuge was shot dead. Apart from property damage, however, there were no serious injuries or loss of life. In a separate, but related, incident later that night a Black and Tan was shot and wounded. Local people must have been bemused – and fearful – when they contrasted the peaceful handover of power between the viceroy, Lord FitzAlan and Michael Collins in the upper castle yard, Dublin Castle earlier that morning, and what they had experienced at the close of day in Listowel.

Later that same week, Friday, 20 January at 5 p.m. shots rang out at Benner's motor garage on Edward Street, Tralee. A local man was wounded. The incident occurred when three IRA men spotted a Black and Tan truck in for repair and saw the opportunity of acquiring a vehicle for their unit. One of the Black and Tans opened fire, wounding one of his own men and an IRA man, Percy Hanafin, who died from his wounds a few days later. The next night about 9 p.m. several car loads of police armed with rifles and revolvers converged on Denny Street determined to leave Tralee with a bang rather than a whimper. In Kerry – as elsewhere – the Anglo-Irish War was an intensely 'personal' conflict, almost to the point of being a blood feud. On previous occasions, such as the 'reign of terror' known as the siege of Tralee, or the violence following the McKinnion assassination, the Black and Tans had the upper hand. On Saturday, 21 January 1922 IRA units fought a three-and-a-half-hour gun battle, forcing their old enemy out of successive streets and back to their barracks at Ballymullen, where they tended to the wounds of the five men injured in the engagement.[10] In reality neither the Listowel nor the Tralee clashes were intended to re-ignite hostilities (Collins' worst case scenario) between the IRA and crown forces; rather they were the parting shots of two adversaries who hated each other's guts. Earlier that same evening a group of armed men held up the station master at Rathmore railway station and stole £80, a substantial sum at a time when the average weekly wage for a Great Southern and Western Railway Company (GS & WR) employee was £3.[11] It is not clear if the robbery was a criminal act or a fundraising effort on behalf of the local IRA. As spring unfolded, and the number and frequency of armed raids on both post offices and GS & WR cash outlets grew, it became increasingly difficult for the public at large to differentiate between IRA (both pro- and anti-Treaty) and criminal activity.

As January drew to a close Michael Collins engaged in a series of three meetings (24 January, 27 January and 2 February) with his northern counterpart, Sir James Craig. At the inaugural session, held in London, both parties agreed to establish a conference of elected representatives from all of Ireland to draw up a constitution and guarantee northern autonomy. Instead of a boundary commission a case-by-case review of the territorial claims would be presided over by both Collins and Craig. In relation to nationalists/Catholics who had been driven from their jobs and homes during the 1920–21 period, Craig promised to address/redress their problems in return for a cessation of the (southern-inspired) Belfast boycott. The two leaders even broached the thorny issue of republican prisoners held in northern jails. It seemed that Collins' stepping stone argument had potential, after all. Collins may have taken solace from an earlier conference, at Buckingham Palace in July 1914, when John Redmond managed to prise three of Ulster's traditional nine counties from Craig's predecessor, Sir Edward Carson. But the fact that Donegal, Cavan and Monaghan were negotiable was driven by political expediency. After disposing of the three majority nationalist counties, the remaining six constituted a far more cohesive unionist core that would have an inbuilt Protestant/unionist majority.

At the London meeting (27 January) and the follow-up conference in Dublin on 2 February, all the promise contained in the leaders' initial contact unravelled and turned sour. Collins' expectation that, following plebiscites, Tyrone and Fermanagh, and possibly parts of other 'border' counties, would be restored to the south evaporated as the meeting broke down in the face of stringent opposition from both the unionists and the British. Even so Collins had no intention of either leaving the issue aside or abandoning the northern nationalists to their fate. Within the cabinet, however, apart from some support from Mulcahy, Collins was very much in the minority. In common with the bulk of public opinion in the twenty-six counties, Griffith, O'Higgins, MacNeill, Cosgrave and others favoured consolidating the southern state, their immediate priority to confront and crush the anti-Treatyites before they became too powerful. On 1 February 1922 the first unit of the Provisional Government's army – a company of forty-six men drawn mainly from the Dublin brigade, under the command of Captain Paddy O'Daly, a veteran of the 1916 Rising and the O/C of Collins' Squad during the War of Independence – resplendent in their new uniforms marched past City Hall (where Collins took the salute) *en route* to Beggars Bush barracks, the national army's new headquarters. This unit would grow and evolve into the Dublin Guard regiment, which by the outbreak of hostilities in June/July would consist of two battalions (900–1,000 men) under Brigadier General O'Daly. Apart from the Squad (with its culture of assassination and personal loyalty to Collins), the Dublin Guard had a substantial number of pro-Treaty northern division men from Donegal, Monaghan and Belfast among its officers and other ranks, as well as raw recruits – predominantly Dubliners – who saw the army as a refuge (on 3/6 a day, for a few months at least) from unemployment.

In Kerry another army was making preparations for another conflict, and taking a longer view in a raid that – superficially at least – was the Civil War equivalent of the Gortatlea raid of 1918. At 9 p.m. on Saturday, 11 February, thirty armed men marched on Castleisland barracks, which was occupied by twelve constables. Locking the policemen in the guard room, they took rifles, revolvers, arms, ammunition and grenades.[12] It is almost certain that Tom McEllistrim's column carried out the raid to make provision for what they believed was inevitable confrontation if and when the Provisional Government tried to impose its writ on Kerry.

Due to its unique politico-sectarian fault lines, the War of Independence was far less evident in the loyalist heartlands of Ulster than was the case in the rest of nationalist Ireland. Nevertheless, unionists viewed the increased killing of policemen – from the summer of 1920 onwards – and IRA attacks on isolated Protestant homes during their campaign in the south as proof of what Protestants in Ulster could expect if they were subsumed into an independent papist/Sinn Féin republic.

Inter-communal relations between Protestants and Catholics were far more acute in Northern Ireland – where the sectarian split was nearer to 60/40 per cent – than in the rest of Ireland, where Catholics outnumbered Protestants (mostly Anglicans) by a ratio of ten to one. The confrontation and rivalry between both groups in north-east Ulster was centuries old, but was stirred up each year during the 'marching season' (a combination of triumphalism and coat trailing) which usually led to communal violence that only exacerbated the pre-existing economic, social, political and territorial grievances that existed on both sides of the sectarian divide.

It was economic factors – competition for jobs – that initiated the period of unrest that would become known as the 'Belfast pogroms' in northern nationalist folk memory. During the First World War Protestant workers joined the British army in vast numbers; in their absence the jobs they'd held were filled by Catholics. By the summer of 1920 thousands of ex-servicemen, many pre-war UVF, were out of work. Their solution to their predicament was brutally simple – and sectarian: they were entitled to reclaim 'Protestant' jobs. During July and August a massive campaign of intimidation orchestrated by the Belfast Protestant Association saw thousands of Catholics forced from their jobs. The scale of unemployment would remain inordinately high in Belfast throughout 1921 and 1922. To compare Belfast to Dublin, both cities had similar populations (the 1911 Census recorded their respective populations as 398,235 and 386,794), yet by late December 1921 Belfast's unemployed outnumbered Dublin's by a ratio of 3 to 1, namely 36,886 to 11,986.[13] Sinn Féin's response to the mass expulsions was to organise a retaliatory 'boycott' of Protestant businesses in

Belfast. Initially, banks and financial institutions bore the brunt of the campaign, but by early 1921 its scope was cast much wider. And by April of that year four northern counties and over a dozen in the south were involved in the embargo which was enforced by the IRA and whose effects were particularly detrimental to imports of northern whiskey and textiles.

During the War of Independence IRA attacks on the security forces in Northern Ireland were usually accompanied by a major outbreak of sectarian violence in Belfast where Catholic civilians made up a disproportionate number of the dead and injured in the flare-up of violence. On Wednesday, 23 June, King George V formally opened the Northern Ireland parliament in Belfast. Later that same evening, the train taking the 10th Hussars (the cavalry regiment that 'trooped the colour' at the formal opening of Northern Ireland's new parliament at City Hall in Belfast) was attacked by the IRA near Bessbrooke, leaving four soldiers dead and a further twenty wounded. In the ensuing riots in Belfast – a mixture of 'sporadic' acts performed in the heat of the moment and premeditated killings – fourteen lives were lost and dozens were injured. Ironically, the truce that brought the War of Independence to a close occurred over the night of 10/11 July, the eve of 12 July, the most sacred date in the 'Orange' calendar. To loyalists the truce would have been seen as a 'Fenian' victory, and the twelfth an opportunity to 'teach the Taigs a lesson' as to who was still 'on top'. In the week following the truce twenty people were killed and over seventy were injured. On the worst day sixteen people (eleven Catholics and five Protestants) lost their lives. The emergence of the Provisional Government in Dublin and the boundary commission that accompanied it, claiming – as it did – substantial parts of Northern Ireland's territory, increased tensions and heightened the feelings of insecurity among the unionist community. The breakdown in the Craig–Collins talks threw the frosty relations between the two states into sharp focus. In such a charged atmosphere, any brinkmanship along the border could easily lead to violence directed against Catholics/nationalists in Belfast, who were seen as both fifth columnists for the IRA and the major beneficiaries of their actions and activities.

In mid-January 1922, police detained the Monaghan football team (which included several armed IRA men) *en route* to the Ulster championship in Derry on the suspicion that some of the 'players' intended to 'spring' three IRA prisoners awaiting execution in Derry city jail. On 7 February, the day after the date Collins had requested Craig approve the prisoners' release, IRA units, acting on Collins' orders, kidnapped forty-two prominent Orangemen and brought their hostages across the border. A patrol of fifteen special constabulary acting as a search party came under fire from the IRA near Clones, County Monaghan; four officers died and nine others were wounded. When news of the deaths reached Belfast, the killing spree that followed extended over five days (12 to 16 February) and left thirty-one dead and ninety-one injured. On 22 February Collins set up the 'Belfast Guard' – a cohort of seventy-two officers and men – in response to the desperate plight of the nationalist communities. For Collins, a man steeped in the IRB tradition, citing Wolfe Tone 'republicanism', one of whose principal tenets was the cultivation of a non-sectarian definition of 'Irishness', the day-to-day reality in Belfast was that the 'traditional' northern Catholic response – 'defenderism' – hadn't been surpassed, or been made redundant, by a form of 'republicanism' that Tone would have recognised.

On 18 February Commander Thomas Malone of the mid-Limerick division declared for the republic, and repudiated GHQ's claim to speak for the IRA. The move had serious implications for the government's two provincial enclaves, Michael Brennan's 1st Westerns in Clare and Seán MacEoin's power base in Athlone, which could potentially be isolated and overwhelmed by concerted attacks by anti-Treaty forces. Following Ernie O'Malley's raid on the Clonmel police depot, republican units in the mid-west acquired 293 rifles, 273 revolvers, three Lewis guns and 324,000 rounds of ammunition, as well as eleven motor cars, making the mid-Limerick division one of the best equipped autonomous military groups in the country.[14] It gave O'Malley huge leverage and he threw down the gauntlet to the Dublin brigade and the 1st Westerns that GHQ had sent to Limerick to buttress up the small pro-government garrison, calling on them to leave the city. During late February and early March both sides brought in reinforcements, bringing the two groups up to parity with about 700 men on each side. At this point GHQ seized the initiative and Mulcahy summoned Liam Lynch and Oscar Traynor to Beggars Bush barracks in Dublin to defuse the situation. They persuaded O'Malley to back down. The resolution was a diplomatic victory for Mulcahy, who learned a lot more from the experience than his anti-Treaty rivals. Following what was in effect a regional coup attempt, Mulcahy took measures to give the Provisional Government a military presence in Munster, setting up garrisons at Skibbereen and Listowel. The Listowel unit consisted of about 250 men, mostly raw recruits, with

NCOs and officers drawn from the War of Independence veterans who had declared themselves pro-Treaty at the start of the year. Under the command of Thomas J. Kennelly, who led the North Kerry flying column during the War of Independence, the 'Kerry brigade' was billeted in Listowel workhouse. It was a well equipped force, receiving 200 rifles, four Lewis machine-guns, large quantities of ammunition, new uniforms and a Crossley tender lorry from GHQ on 3 March 1922.[15]

At a wider level, on 15 March Mulcahy cancelled the IRA army convention, which had been due to take place in Dublin on 26 March. In tandem with the proscription, all GHQ financing of the brigades and divisions unwilling to acknowledge its authority was suspended. The result was a massive surge of armed robberies at local level by anti-Treaty IRA. Between 23 March and 19 April there were 331 post office robberies, and between 1 March and 22 April over 319 GS & WR railway station cash offices were raided.[16] Nationally the IRA carried out several spectacular bank robberies in the country's principal cities and large provincial towns, which did a lot to alienate moderate public opinion against the republicans. The fifteenth of March was also the day Éamon de Valera set up Cumann na Poblachta, a new political party that aimed to articulate the republican viewpoint in the forthcoming elections due to be held in June. Following the party's Dublin launch de Valera set off on a week-long speaking tour which concentrated on the republican heartland of Munster, including meetings in Dungarvan, Thurles, Carrick on Suir, Tralee and Killarney. The tour might have been billed as 'tonic for the troops' as de Valera's talks were attended by and intended for the IRA, especially the venues in Tipperary. At Thurles, on Saint Patrick's day, de Valera told his audience, many of whom carried rifles: 'If the Volunteers of the future tried to complete the work of the Volunteers of the last four years, they … would have to wade through Irish blood, the blood of the soldiers of the Irish government, perhaps the blood of some members of the Irish government in order to get Irish freedom.'[17]

The 'elasticity' of de Valera's rhetoric was such that his words could be taken as a warning as to what might happen; to many of his listeners, who were as drunk on their own sense of power as they may have been on the 'festive' whiskey, he was urging them to take up arms against the Provisional Government. How many Irish lives would be lost, either in a 'government' uniform or in an IRA trench coat, because de Valera's March speeches were taken at face value by impressionable people for whom de Valera was a republican icon, and who naively assumed that what he'd said and what they'd heard were the same thing? While de Valera's words may have swayed many rank and file IRA volunteers to take up arms against the government, he was increasingly a marginal figure as far as people such as Rory O'Connor were concerned. To use the sporting parlance of his native New York, de Valera's role was more akin to a cheerleader on the sidelines than the team coach whose 'time out' pep talk could seriously influence (and alter) the way the team approached the rest of the match.

On 22 March Rory O'Connor held a press conference where he proclaimed that he represented over 80 per cent of the army, and that in ignoring the wishes of the majority of the Volunteers, GHQ was itself smothering the democratic wishes of the IRA. A total of 223 delegates went to the Dublin meeting, which was not attended by any GHQ representatives. The 1st and 2nd southern divisions sent fifty-four and twenty-eight delegates respectively, while the four western divisions had sixty-nine representatives. O'Connor would claim the allegiance of twelve of the country's sixteen IRA divisions at a conference that was attended by fifty-two out of the seventy-three War of Independence brigades. The convention elected a sixteen-member executive, in which O'Connor, Liam Mellows and Ernie O'Malley were the principal spokesmen. The *Freeman's Journal* published a highly critical editorial, focusing on O'Connor's comments on the possibility of setting up a military dictatorship. Press freedom was not a priority for the 'executive', and on the night of 29 March the IRA burned down the newspaper's Dublin headquarters. The phoenix that would rise from the ashes would become a fierce critic of the anti-Treaty military campaign and one of the most trenchant supporters of the government's repressive measures adopted against the republicans.

In a highly symbolic gesture, members of Dublin No. 1 brigade seized the Four Courts over the night of 13/14 April (Holy Thursday/Good Friday) in a move that reclaimed the mantle of the 1916 Rebellion, and threw down the gauntlet to the Provisional Government. Liam Mellows, as secretary of the executive, read out the group's demands. No elections could be held while British occupation of the country continued. The civic guards should be disbanded, and any further recruitment into the Provisional Government's army should cease. The Dáil should reinstate and continue to pay all the executive's financial and operating expenses. While high on symbolism, the emotionally charged act was not accompanied by any coherent military strategy. The 200 men in the garrison, for instance, made no attempts to fortify the vast complex of buildings at any point between the initial seizure and the eventual government assault almost two and a half months later. O'Connor and Mellows' plan – insofar as such a strategy existed – was to provoke a resumption of hostilities with the British (who still had sizeable troop concentrations in Dublin) and in the process the *de facto* 'Free State' forces would have no choice but to stand shoulder to shoulder with their estranged comrades and together challenge the traditional enemy. At this point de Valera offered his considerable political prestige (the only surviving 1916 'leader' and former president of the Dáil) to legitimise and lend credibility to the acts of the self-styled 'executive'.

Events in Dublin were viewed with a mixture of bemusement and bewilderment by both the mandarins and their political masters in Whitehall. The Irish had finally won the 800 year struggle against British rule on the island, and within four months of their 'victory' they were squaring up to fight each other. The developments at the Four Courts reinforced British prejudices about the Irish being incapable of self government. Churchill doubted if anyone in the Provisional Government was willing to fight for the new regime given their apparent reluctance to confront opponents who challenged their political and military authority. It wasn't cricket. But, at that point, Collins was content to play his hurling from the ditch. The sectarian conflict in Northern Ireland, particularly in Belfast – to some extent an undeclared, yet a real civil war – preoccupied him more than the 'declared' conflict that wasn't happening in Dublin.

In Kerry many small Protestant communities were worried, not so much for their own personal safety but that their property or businesses might be damaged by individuals acting on the basis that attacks on the minority in the north justified retaliatory actions in the south's own Protestant communities. At 11 p.m. on Saturday, 1 April 'stones were thrown through the windows of Smith's residence, the Mill and Farm Manager for Latchford. He strongly condemned atrocities carried out in Ulster on numerous occasions in the past.'[18] It seems the attack was sectarian, but it appears to have been a 'once off' incident. Nevertheless, it generated concern among many of Kerry's Church of Ireland parishes. The *Cork Examiner* of 11 April included a statement from Killiney Protestants expressing their 'abhorrence, shared with Christians of all denominations, of the loss of life in Belfast and the Northern Province of both Roman Catholics and Protestants brutally taking each other's lives'. The 13 April edition of the same paper contained a similar condemnation from the Ballymacelligott and Ballyseedy parish council, signed by the rector, George Maxwell, and his colleagues William Blennerhassett, John Groves and Charlie Mansfield.

By the end of April a further thirty-five names would be added to an already grisly catalogue of murders and 'tit for tat' killings, claiming the lives of twenty-four Catholics and eleven Protestants. May was even bloodier, with sixty-three deaths in Belfast alone, forty Catholic and twenty-three Protestant. To put these figures in context, the May death toll was only two fewer than the number killed in Dublin (sixty-five) during the week of fighting following the fall of the Four Courts at the start of the Civil War.

In Kerry there is no evidence of republicans actively involved in sectarian harassment of Kerry's minority communities. The same forebearance, however, was not evident in their sense of political pluralism, or the rights of freedom of speech, association and assembly for those advocating a pro-Treaty point of view. John O'Hara, a son of James O'Hara, secretary of Tralee races committee, was arrested by the local republican 'police' in Killorglin while engaged in organising a pro-Treaty meeting in the town, and was, for his efforts, incarcerated in Ballymullen barracks, where he went on hunger strike against unjust imprisonment.[19] John Scannell, an employee of Slattery's bacon store, Tralee, found the republicans in his native town adopting a more 'hands on' approach than their Killorglin counterparts when they beat him until he lost consciousness.[20] Local activists brave (or foolhardy) enough to encourage recruitment into the national army could find themselves under lock and key. On Monday, 17 April John Linehan and David Crowley from Rathmore went to Kenmare to encourage local youths to enlist in the 'Free State' army. Placed under arrest, their immediate response was to go on hunger strike. They were released three days later.[21] On matters of 'criminal activity' not connected to politics, the republican police provided an impartial and efficient enough service. W. F. Beatty, a commercial traveller for Musgrave brothers, Tralee, was held up by armed men near Caherciveen on Tuesday, 19 April and relieved of £100, which was mostly cheques. Caherciveen police (IRA) arrested three men on 21 April (identified as Clifford, Sweeney and Moriarty) and recovered most of the stolen money.[22]

Given the level of harassment experienced by local pro-Treaty activists at the hands of their political opponents, it was inevitable that the republicans would adopt a hard-line approach to the two public meetings that Michael Collins was to address in Killarney and Tralee over the weekend of 22/23 April 1922. Notices were put up in and around Killarney proscribing the rally, advising those attending that republicans could not guarantee their safety if they attended. The platform erected for the meeting was burnt to the ground. When Collins and his entourage, Kevin O'Higgins, Seán MacEoin, Fionán Lynch and a twelve-man security detail under Joe Dolan's command arrived on the platform of Killarney railway station on Saturday afternoon they were met by a heavily armed (Thompson submachine-guns) anti-Treaty force. The confrontation was defused by the intervention of the local Franciscan abbot, who offered the friary grounds as a venue, providing Collins with a 'brake' (trailer) as a platform. The meeting went ahead, though with a much reduced attendance.

Tralee republicans surpassed their Killarney counterparts in their efforts to undermine the staging of a pro–Treaty meeting in their town. Special trains laid on to transport government supporters from Kenmare, Killarney and Newcastle West were unable to travel because sections of the line were taken up; only the 'special' from Dingle reached Tralee. The gates on railway level crossings were opened across the road and chained shut, making an effective barricade for all road traffic. Following the Killarney stand off, it was deemed necessary to reinforce Joe Dolan's force, and a further twenty-four men under the control of Denny Galvin of Knocknagoshel were drafted in to provide assistance.

After the rally ten pro-Treaty security stewards had their rifles seized by republicans. Ordered by Seán MacEoin to take a similar number of weapons from republicans, Galvin exceeded his orders and also arrested them. When Humphrey Murphy heard this he was furious, and protested to Seán MacEoin, whereupon the 'blacksmith of Ballinalee' hurled Murphy down a flight of stairs, jumped on him and began pummelling him repeatedly with his fists. Collins broke up the fight, and persuaded MacEoin to apologise to Murphy. Galvin's captives were released and both sides agreed to confine their troops to barracks (Ballymullen and the hotel on Denny Street) until the meeting was over.[23]

During his address, in which he emphasised that the Treaty terms weren't worth fighting a civil war over, Collins' words were punctuated by random shots of gunfire on the perimeter of the crowd. It is not so much what Collins said at the meetings in Tralee and Killarney that is newsworthy, but the fact that both meetings took place at all given the republican determination to prevent them. An estimated 4,000 people attended the Tralee meeting in spite of all the measures the republicans used to disrupt the gathering, an indication there was a substantial audience in Kerry at least willing to listen to Collins' 'stepping stone' argument in favour of accepting the Treaty.

By late April armed clashes between government troops and republicans became more frequent as the national army began to openly challenge the 'Irregulars'. Confrontations in Mullingar, and in early May at Burtonport and Buncrana in Donegal, left dead and wounded on both sides. At Buncrana, in a 'shoot out' surrounding a bank robbery, five civilians were also wounded. There had been a national army garrison (250 men) in Listowel since early March. As April passed into May, 150 troops drawn from both Kerry No. 1 and No. 2 brigades billeted themselves in the Listowel Arms hotel, Maguire's, the Provincial bank, and Carroll's shop, on the Square. Mulvihil's shop, Scanlon's and Walshe's corner houses entering Market Street, which led to the workhouse, the strongly fortified Free State HQ, were also taken over.[24] Townspeople waited anxiously for the impending military confrontation. Ironically, neither side, especially Tom Kennelly, the Free State commander, wanted to start shooting, and both hoped for a peaceful solution. However, Listowel was on a war footing for almost two months in a situation reminiscent of the Cold War stand-off of a later era. Sometimes the methods used to avoid confrontation could be comical; rival patrols could do an 'about turn' simultaneously once they saw another patrol approach. The town's civilian population must have been on tenterhooks the entire time, waiting for the inevitable clash.

In the wake of the republicans' arrival in Listowel there were two robberies (or attempted robberies) in the town. The 2 May edition of the *Cork Examiner* noted: 'A party of uniformed men entered the Bank of Ireland and demanded £10,000 from the Manager, Mr McQuaid. Once he told them the notes had been cancelled the previous night, the men left.' This would seem to be a pre-emptive strike by the Free State authorities in Listowel to block any attempt by anti-Treatyites to take money from the bank. Nevertheless, a few days later a party of seven men armed with revolvers took £450, the only uncancelled notes remaining in the bank, leaving a note reading 'by the authority of headquarters'. As republican promissory notes were usually signed with 'executive' authorisation, it would seem the cash was seized by pro-government sources. It is hard to be certain. Not all government troops had uniforms at this point and republicans often stole uniforms as it made it easier to challenge (and infiltrate) government security measures and obtain arms and ammunition.

In the void left by any form of civil authority people began to take the law into their own hands, especially in the matter of grievances over land in north Kerry. In the space of a week or so the *Cork Examiner* contained three separate reports on rural social unrest. Significantly, neither pro- nor anti-Treaty factions, despite their irrevocable differences on constitutional matters, politicised the issue for short-term sectional advantage. This is because, other than radicalism on the issue of the 'republic', both sides in the Civil War held shared (conservative) views on social and economic matters. In one instance, cattle grazing on the estate of A. V. Mountcoal were driven off his land and given to him at his residence at Ballyhorgan. It was surmised that the people who removed the livestock intended to occupy and partition the land among themselves.[25] On the night of Monday, 15 May the home of William Blennerhassett of Cullenagh Beg (Beaufort parish, near Killarney) was attacked by a number of armed and masked men who fired shots. The *Cork Examiner* noted: 'It will be remembered that some time ago Mr Blennerhassett was evicted, and the farm was put in the possession of Mr Murphy, who claimed his family once held the land and were evicted for non payment of rent. Blennerhassett had been reinstated by the IRA. Mr Blennerhassett agreed to have the dispute over the farm put before Davit, B. L. ; Mr. Murphy would not accept this.'[26] On Friday, 19 May 'a cattle drive took place on the lands of the late Mr Cook, Tawnaralla, whose unoccupied residence was burned down two years ago. Shots were fired into cottages on the land, which incurred the visit of a fully armed Company of GHQ troops from Listowel.'[27] Interestingly, both the police forces provided by the Provisional Government (the army, effectively) and local IRA units (anti-Treaty) were extremely uncomfortable when called upon to provide a civil police function, especially when it involved property disputes or quarrels between neighbours.

6

FROM THE BALLOT TO THE BULLET

In late April a group of senior IRB men suggested an 'agreed' election, combined with the establishment of a joint army council as the best way to maintain both unity in the Sinn Féin party and the IRA and prevent the outbreak of a civil war. On 2 May a pro-Treaty delegation, which included Michael Collins, Richard Mulcahy, Eoin O'Duffy and Gearoid O'Sullivan, met Dan Breen, Seán Moylan, Florry O'Donoghue, Tom Hales and Humphrey Murphy to hammer out an agenda, on the basis that the majority of the people accepted the Treaty and did not want a civil war. Over the subsequent two weeks the two groups met to put flesh on the bones. An electoral pact that reflected both the ratio of seats and the number of deputies that each faction held when the Dáil voted on the Treaty were to be maintained without contesting the issue electorally. Once the joint parties formed a coalition government, cabinet portfolios would be divided between pro- and anti-Treaty factions in a ratio of five to four. On the military front an eight-man army council would be established with four representatives from either side. The defence minister would be a pro-Treaty appointment, while his chief of staff would be chosen from the republican ranks. Both groups would hold frequent meetings and inspections to verify their rivals' *bona fides* and pacific intents. In reality both groups were deeply suspicious of each other and used the visits and meetings to gather intelligence on their rivals' military strengths and weaknesses as well as trying to gain maximum leverage at their opponents' expense.

While many of Collins' cabinet colleagues were unhappy and deeply suspicious of the concessions he had given to his political opponents on the one hand, and his indifference to the serious flaws in a deal that would seriously compromise a fair and representative poll of the popular vote on the other, they agreed to let the negotiations continue. Collins argued that unless an agreed election took place, no election would take place at all, as the anti-Treaty IRA would intimidate, harass and interfere with both candidates and voters, and possibly burn or destroy ballot boxes once the polls closed. On the military front Collins' analysis was that the more extreme elements on the Four Courts executive, O'Connor, Mellows, and O'Malley in particular, were so far apart ideologically, politically and militarily from their more moderate (though far more numerous) colleagues in Southern Command that even if there was a 'flare up' in Dublin it would not lead either to a civil war or a national conflict. Éamon de Valera, the leading player (the only player) politically on the anti-Treaty side also wanted to avoid having to face the electorate. As he saw it, both his own party, Cumann na Poblachta, and Sinn Féin would lose seats on a grand scale if they had to face an open vote. Despite his bellicose 'militant' and 'militarist' rhetoric, de Valera believed in politics (compromise) and it was because of this that he had no influence on his militarist colleagues who dealt in absolutes.

Over a three-day period (18–20 May) Collins and de Valera conferred in camera in UCD to finalise the electoral arrangements for the 16 June poll. The meeting successfully concluded, Collins returned to his cabinet colleagues and presented them with a *fait accompli* on the deal. Arthur Griffith, W. T. Cosgrave, Ernest Blythe and Kevin O'Higgins were appalled both by the concessions that Collins had given to his political opponents and the cavalier way he was willing to short circuit the democratic process in a deal that combined vote rigging and a national gerrymander between the two wings of Sinn Féin, but at least permitted 'non party' candidates (other than Sinn Féin) to participate in an electoral contest in which their prospects were seriously compromised. To be fair to Collins he was adamant that other-party and independent candidates should – and would – participate in the election that many republicans (who saw themselves as being more politically perceptive) felt need only reflect the existing Dáil strengths as determined in the 7 January poll and that it would be a truly democratic exercise.

The fact that the second Dáil, returned in May 1921 without referring to the electorate, was the national parliament indicates a level of arrogance and indifference by both wings of Sinn Féin towards securing a real democratic mandate to govern Ireland in a way that would reflect public opinion. Collins himself was not immune to this mindset; his willingness to appease 'hard line' republicans seemingly superseded his willingness to share responsibility with his cabinet colleagues and permit the electorate a truly free choice in deciding the issue. Had Collins survived the Béal na mBláth assassination, it is open to question if any administration presided over by him would have delivered an open, transparent and accountable government ultimately responsible to both executive (cabinet) and legislative (Dáil) scrutiny for all its actions.

On 23 May a special Sinn Féin Árd Fheis endorsed the Collins–de Valera pact, while Collins set to work drafting a constitution that would reflect 'republican' values (i.e. the Treaty and the oath of allegiance would not be mentioned in the document) and serve as a joint programme for (coalition) government, that might be in place in the wake of the 16 June election. In his enthusiasm to progress with his revised constitution, Collins seems to have lost focus on his international obligations – the fact that both Lloyd George and Churchill would scrutinise every article and amendment that Collins proposed, to ensure his document for government matched the agreement that he and Griffith had signed in Whitehall the previous December.

The commencement of the northern campaign on 18/19 May was viewed by many within the nationalist community with a deep sense of foreboding; a substantial section of Catholic/nationalist opinion – especially those living in isolated enclaves – felt the IRA offensive actually worsened their plight rather than alleviating it. Reprisal killing of policemen or cold-blooded sectarian murders of Protestants at their place of work achieved nothing, as the IRA didn't have enough weapons or manpower to cordon off Catholic neighbourhoods from vigilante attacks by the Ulster Protestant Association, a core group of about one hundred activists, many of them ex-servicemen with a sprinkling of off-duty policemen. Heeding nationalist public opinion, the IRA focused on bombing and arson attacks on economic and commercial targets as well as the homes of unionist politicians and businessmen, on the assumption that this would result in fewer reprisals against the minority community. In the course of a fortnight, the IRA carried out forty-one arson attacks on flax and linen mills, bonded warehouses, railway stations and signal installations, causing over £500,000 worth of damages.[1] On 22 May the IRA assassinated William J. Twaddle, Unionist MP for Woodvale, on Garfield Street, Belfast. Craig's response was swift; operating on fairly accurate police intelligence, he interned about 200 IRA and Sinn Féin activists without implementing any corresponding measures against their loyalist equivalents.[2] By early June 1922 Collins decided to bring the curtain down on his northern campaign. It was probably around this time that orders were issued (probably by Collins himself) to IRA agents in London to assassinate Sir Henry Wilson, the chief security advisor to the Northern Ireland government.

A natural conspirator, Collins had a core of agents and an ability to compartmentalise people and problem solving in such a way that two or three associates could be following mutually exclusive – contradictory – objectives while being blissfully unaware of any divergence. Apart from the Belfast Guard, Collins was arming and directing both pro- and anti-Treaty factions of the IRA to undermine the northern state – in total violation of his Treaty obligations – while convincing both his own cabinet colleagues and the British government in Whitehall that the Four Courts executive was behind the entire campaign.

Leaving the northern question to one side, in early June 1922 Collins' twin preoccupations were the forthcoming 16 June election and putting the final touches to his revised constitution. The prospect of a 'one size fits all' constitution, leastwise a 'garment' that could stretch all the way from Whitehall to the Four Courts, was a non-starter. But Collins had to persist with the myth that he was working assiduously to have the document ready for the eve of polling day, as if he were to have revealed his hand and published the document it would have handed his coalition partners, the anti-Treaty wing, a massive propaganda coup with which to challenge the pro-Treaty lobby. The fact that the elections were, for the first time, being held under a proportional representation (PR) system meant that voters could choose to vote for each and all of the candidates on the ballot paper. In theory, once any other candidates put their names on the list of nominees to contest the election, the Sinn Féin panel agreement was dead in the water. Consequently, the anti-Treaty grouping and their electoral workers (local IRA in many cases) engaged in widespread intimidation and harassment of non-panel candidates and their electoral workers to persuade them to withdraw from the campaign (as had worked against the Irish Parliamentary Party and Unionists, etc., in 1918) or, failing that, prevent them from getting their message across to a public eager to vote in a 'free' election that offered a real choice of candidates. Collins and many of his pro-Treaty panel colleagues and candidates were uncomfortable with this aspect of the anti-Treaty campaign and increasingly began to distance themselves from joint canvases with their erstwhile election partners.

On Saturday, 3 June the Kerry Farmers' Union held an electoral convention in Tralee to select candidates for the forthcoming election. The meeting, presided over by John T. O'Neill, began with a motion from the floor that, 'In the interests of national unity no contest should be held'. This motion was proposed by John Maher, Loughlin, Killarney, who argued: 'A contested election would endanger the Agreement [de Valera–Collins] in many ways. Farmers not alone in Kerry – but Ireland – should not put forward candidates.' Michael Murphy, Castlemaine, seconded the proposal, adding that, 'This parliament would be short lived and would cease to function in December. It would be ill advised to contest such a short term Assembly.' The motion was defeated by forty votes to sixteen. The assembled group (which represented larger/commercial farmers) selected Denis Brosnan of Kilflynn, John Mangan, the Kerries, and Jeremiah O'Carroll, Droumcloughlit, Listowel as Farmer Party candidates for the Kerry/West Limerick constituency.[3] In many ways the dissenting voice is more interesting for being articulated, even though the consensus would appear to overrule the minority view. Maher and Murphy's contributions seem to assume that if the panel candidates got a good representation in the new Dáil it would make a resolution of the 'split' in Sinn Féin more likely and award them a democratic mandate (without having to contest an election). Not having to deal with mere sectional interests (Labour, Independents, Farmers), Sinn Féin would close ranks and bring about national reconciliation to avoid a civil war.

It would seem the minority faction were more devious, better organised, or both than the wider party as they seem to have 'short circuited' the notification of a full membership for the meeting on the nomination day (6 June) when the Kerry Farmers' Union decided by fourteen votes to ten not to contest the election. The Labour Party in Kerry also decided not to put forward any candidates.[4] Thus on 9 June 1922, as the sitting candidates were the only nominees on the 'ballot', the existing eight TDs were returned unopposed. In fact Kerry wasn't all that unusual. Nationally, seven of the twenty-eight Dáil constituencies (Limerick East; Clare; Mayo North West; Mayo/South Roscommon; Leitrim/North Roscommon; Kerry/Limerick West and Donegal) returned thirty-four TDs without a contest, a sizeable enough number given the total tally for the Dáil was 128 seats. This meant that there were seventeen pro- and seventeen anti-Treaty TDs alongside the forty-one pro-Treaty and the nineteen anti-Treaty TDs elected by popular mandate on 16 June 1922. The following chart represents the number, and the percentage, of first-preference votes, the main electoral blocs received, and the number of seats obtained by each party in the 16 June poll:[5]

Electoral Group	1st Pref	No. of TDs	% 1st Pref	% of TDs
Non Panel	247,276	*34	38.30%	26 %
Pro-Treaty	239,193	58	37 %	46%
Anti-Treaty	153,864	36	24. 70 %	28 %

(Labour 17; Farmers 7; Independents 6; Unionists 4)

The high number of votes for non-panel candidates (over 38 per cent of first-preference votes) was a protest against both wings of Sinn Féin (especially the anti-Treaty) for their arrogance and intransigence in postponing an election, combined with their obsession with purely national(ist)/constitutional issues to the detriment of focusing on the country's social and economic problems. Comparing the electoral strength of the two Sinn Féin parties in January, when the Dáil divided sixty-four to fifty-seven (pro-/anti-Treaty) with their post-electoral strengths in June of fifty-eight and thirty-six TDs respectively (a loss of six pro-Treaty and twenty-one anti-Treaty politicians), it is apparent that the electorate was less than satisfied with their performance during their first six months at the helm; though the level of impatience directed at the anti-Treaty grouping was far more pronounced.

The Collins–de Valera electoral pact was a success to the

extent that it facilitated anti-Treaty participation in the election. While the Sinn Féin panel returned ninety-four TDs to the third Dáil compared to a total of thirty-four non-panel candidates, the Sinn Féin panel was a political eunuch because the anti-Treaty partner could not consummate the relationship as they were ideologically opposed to taking the oath of allegiance to the British monarch, which was a prerequisite for entering the Dáil. The remaining non-panel candidates had no such ideological objection, fully accepted the Dáil as the legitimate national assembly for an independent Ireland and were totally committed to participating in its deliberations. Thus the reality of the 16 June election was that the greater part of the electorate returned ninety-two TDs who accepted the legitimacy of the new state and its parliament, as against thirty-six members who refused to recognise it as a legitimate manifestation of the independence that they had fought for between 1919 and 1921.

The British authorities were pleased with the result of the election. The Provisional Government had finally received a popular mandate from the electorate. As seen from Whitehall, Collins no longer had any reason to defer to, or put up with, the Four Courts military junta that had deliberately challenged and flouted his authority for over two months. Now was the time to act and assert his authority and that of a democratically elected government over a handful of gunmen and extremists totally out of line with the wishes of the majority of the Irish people. Collins still treated the issue with kid gloves and was extremely reluctant to take pre-emptive action or force the issue.

On the same day as the election, 16 June 1922, the 'Kerry land case' came before the High Court in Dublin. The background to the case was as follows: 'Mr William Blennerhassett, a Protestant farmer from Culleneghy Beg, Beaufort, County Kerry, had an order restraining Mr John Murphy and James and Phillip Scully. On April 9th last, Mr Blennerhassett, his wife and seven children were evicted by a band of masked armed men and the defendant, Mr Murphy, who claimed his relatives were tenants to the place prior to 1880. On the following day Blennerhassett was reinstated by Battalion Commander Allman. On the 13th May, the premises was again attacked. The IRA was unable to offer protection. A three day siege ensued during which Blennerhassett was wounded twice and his fifteen year old son was wounded in the face. On May 17th Blennerhassett surrendered.'[6] The court ruled in favour of Blennerhassett's right of possession and ownership. It may seem strange that a dispute that reverted back to the 'Land War' of the 1880s was still a live issue, at least as far as the Murphy family were concerned.

Significantly, the local IRA, in their capacity as a police force, washed their hands of the issue. During the Civil War, in late December 1922, Beaufort republican activists would intervene on behalf of the Murphy faction. The 'land' issue was complicated by the fact that the Blennerhassett family was Protestant, which probably increased the IRA's reluctance to tackle an issue that could be perceived as sectarian.

Around the same time as the Blennerhassett ruling, a number of Protestants and their families from Tralee and surrounding areas were ordered to leave the locality or suffer the consequences. On informing the authorities of the intimidation and threats to their safety, the local republican police advised them to stay in the county. Every effort would be made to discover the identity of the people who issued the threats, the republican police asserted, and they would be caught and punished.[7]

On 18 June, two days after election, the IRA convention supported a motion submitted by Tom Barry that unless the British army withdrew from Dublin within seventy-two hours the IRA should launch an immediate attack. Both the moderate wing, as represented by Liam Lynch of Southern Command, and the more extreme militarists in the executive (Rory O'Connor and Liam Mellows) were taken aback by the rank and file willingness to approve a course of action that they both considered too radical. Barry's motion was withdrawn from the convention's agenda on a technicality and reworded using more moderate language; on its second reading, Barry's motion was defeated by a narrow margin.

On 22 June 1922 Sir Henry Wilson, the military advisor to the Northern Ireland government, was assassinated in London in what was seen as a 'bolt from the blue' action from the Four Courts executive, though it was more than likely carried out by IRA agents acting on Michael Collins' orders. Winston Churchill, already frustrated at Collins' unwillingness to confront the Four Courts garrison, was considering taking unilateral action against the perpetrators (as he saw it) of the Wilson assassination over the heads of the Provisional Government. Wiser counsel prevailed, with the British government agreeing to hold its fire, but forcing Collins' hand, offering him the choice of bringing the anti-Treatyite occupation of the Four Courts to an end using his own forces. The British military still stationed in Dublin provided artillery pieces, though not the actual gunners, to the Provisional Government's troops, who reluctantly fired the opening salvoes of an artillery barrage against the Four Courts garrison on 28 June 1922. At the outset of hostilities Collins resigned from the civilian government to assume the role of commander-in-chief of the army. W. T. Cosgrave became head of the council of state (prime minister), thereby creating a separation of power between the military and civilian branches of government. This was a course of action that virtually put the conduct of the war outside civic political scrutiny and gave Michael Collins *carte blanche* as the Provisional Government's supreme warlord. It was a high-risk strategy for Collins, as any military setbacks the government forces might suffer would be laid at his door. As he knew all his adversaries personally from the War of Independence days, Collins reckoned once the Four Courts garrison put up their symbolic resistance, before being forced to concede defeat, the more moderate republicans in the 1st Southern division, as represented by Liam Lynch and Liam Deasy, would not continue to oppose the Provisional Government. In short, Collins was convinced that he could win the war, a conflict which at most would last a couple of weeks.

During the course of a week of fighting in Dublin, stretching from Wednesday, 28 June to Thursday, 6 July, the Provisional Government armed forces (about two thousand men) successfully defeated both the Four Courts garrison and the outposts the Dublin brigade had set up in and around O'Connell Street. Like their 1916 predecessors the anti-Treaty IRA locked themselves into static positions that allowed them no room for manoeuvre and surrendered the initiative to their enemies who successfully isolated each strong-point, using armoured cars and artillery to negate the spurious protection offered to the republicans even by partially fortified buildings. Had the republicans adopted a more mobile approach to the conflict, sniping at the gun crews bombarding the Four Courts, for example, and launching assaults on the troops surrounding and laying siege to the large complex of buildings at the Four Courts, the outcome of the Dublin fighting and the subsequent Civil War might have been very different. Of course, it is worth pointing out that a republican victory would have had as its prize a resumption of the war against the British, whose intervention might have come midway through the Dublin fighting if the Provisional Government's armed forces weren't up to the task. Faced with a choice of siding with their former War of Independence comrades or standing shoulder to shoulder with the British army against the Dublin brigade and the Four Courts garrison, the government forces would have been in a very awkward position. The military and political fallout from such a dilemma would have been hard to call.

CASUALTIES DURING THE DUBLIN FIGHTING
28 June – 6 July, 1922[8]

Date	Killed	Wounded
June 28	15	40
June 29	14	29
June 30	10	107
July 1/2	11	22
July 3	3	24
July 4	3	38
July 5	5	13
July 6	1	3
Total	**62**	**276**

These figures represent the total killed and wounded during a week of fighting and include Provisional Government troops (19 killed, 122 wounded),[9] civilians (at least 22 killed,

40 wounded to Saturday, 1 July)[10] and republicans (precise figures not available). Compared to the loss of life in Dublin during Easter 1916 – about 500 deaths, more than half of them civilians – the opening week of the Civil War was comparatively restrained and far less bloody than the campaign waged by the British in 1916. Following the surrender of the Four Courts garrison, 130 prisoners were taken, including senior members of the executive, among them Rory O'Connor and Liam Mellows. The most senior republican casualty, Cathal Brugha, emerged from the Granville hotel in O'Connell Street brandishing a revolver in each hand. Anxious to capture Brugha alive, the Free State officer ordered his men to shoot at his legs, but one of the shots severed a femoral artery, causing Brugha to bleed to death. Among the dead on the government side was a soldier named Connolly from Kerry, serving with the Dublin Guard, who was killed on Moore Street on Tuesday, 4 July. He had put in for a transfer to the 1st Southern division (an anti-Treaty unit) a few days before the outbreak of hostilities but decided to wait until after the Dublin fighting ended, and then return to Munster.[11] Private Connolly, however, was not the first Kerry soldier to lose his life in the Civil War.

With the outbreak of hostilities in Dublin, on 28 June the two months' stand-off between the Provisional Government garrison and republicans in Listowel came to an end. On Friday, 30 June at 8.30 a.m. republicans opened fire on Free State troops billeted in T. J. Walsh's drapery shop on Market Street, while soldiers based in the Listowel Arms hotel on the Square came under fire from republicans located in R. M. Danagher's shop on the opposite side of the Square. Private Edward Sheehy, a twenty-year-old serving with the government force,

whose father was an insurance broker in the town, was killed
and Dónalín O'Grady was wounded. Tom Kennelly, the Free
State commander, was anxious to bring the conflict to an end,
and avoid any further loss of life on either side.[12] Fr Charles
Troy, a native of Listowel, then a postgraduate student studying in Maynooth, though serving in Dublin archdiocese, put
himself forward as an intermediary and successfully brokered
a ceasefire.[13] At 5 p.m. the Free State garrison surrendered
to the republicans, Tom Kennelly, O/C Listowel garrison and
Humphrey Murphy, O/C Kerry No. 1 brigade issuing a joint
statement to the effect that as Kerrymen neither side wanted
to fight each other in a Civil War.

The *Republican Bulletin* in the *Cork Examiner* reported that
the republican forces at Listowel captured an armoured car, two
Lewis guns, 150 rifles and several private cars. Fifty members
of the captured garrison threw in their lot with the republicans,
opting to join with them and go to the front in Limerick.
The remaining 200 prisoners were transferred to Ballymullen
barracks in Tralee.[14] Republicans in west Cork took comparable
action to the Kerry brigades, launching an attack on the Free
State garrison in Skibbereen early in July, and neutralised
Mulcahy's second outpost in Munster. The *Republican Bulletin*'s
account of events in Listowel was accurate, except for the
fact that the garrison didn't have an armoured car, a piece of
equipment far too rare and valuable to assign to a provincial
outpost in early March when the Listowel garrison was first
established. The British only began supplying armoured vehicles
and artillery in critical numbers to the Provisional Government
when hostilities commenced in Dublin. This information was
included exclusively for propaganda purposes – aimed at a

civilian audience, as the military authorities in Dublin knew the Listowel garrison didn't have an armoured car. The loss of 20 per cent of the garrison (fifty men) who defected to the republican side on surrender was true, and a much more worrying trend. An army that could not depend either politically or militarily on its own troops in a conflict had a major problem.

The only fatality of the Listowel conflict, twenty-year-old Private Edward Sheehy, was buried at Saul cemetery, Listowel, on Sunday, 2 July. According to the *Cork Examiner* '… the most pathetic feature was when his comrades in uniform, but without equipment, formed a firing party, carrying rifles lent to them by Republicans. Saint Patrick's Brass Band led the funeral march. Several Republican soldiers attended the funeral of the dead Free State soldier.'[15]

Having secured victory in the capital, and learning of republican plans to launch a counter attack on Dublin from Blessington, the government dispatched a large force (upwards of a thousand men with armoured cars and artillery support) which caused the republicans to abort their plans and scatter to avoid encirclement. Meanwhile, Liam Lynch and Liam Deasy, the two senior commanders of the 1st Southern division, with Mulcahy's approval were allowed to return to Munster, where both Collins and Mulcahy anticipated they would be a moderating influence and do their utmost to avoid continuing the conflict. The government miscalculated on this assessment; as far as Lynch was concerned the die was cast when Collins ordered his troops to shell the Four Courts, thereby commencing (if not actually declaring) war on not just the executive headquarters, but on the entire republican/anti-Treaty military organisation. Liam Lynch was in charge of a substantial second front in Munster. On paper the front line stretched from Limerick city to Waterford city, both port towns and substantial military assets, from which a successful holding action – as a prelude to launching a counterattack against the metropolitan army – could be directed.

On Thursday, 7 July 1922 two creameries owned by the Manchester Co-operative Society in Kerry were destroyed by fire. Their premises at Chapeltown were burned down at about 1 a.m., with a fire at Ballymacquin beginning two hours later. No motive was assigned by locals for either arson attack as the company was described as 'a most popular institution in Tralee District with a turn over of £20,000 and a big employer of labour. In terms of wages the Society leads the way with employees happy with both the hours of work and the conditions of pay.'[16] The double attack echoed (and surpassed) the Black and Tans' tactics during the War of Independence of focusing on the destruction of a creamery as the most effective way of inflicting economic suffering on an entire rural community. Not only was a creamery the sole source of non-farm employment, but its loss affected the entire agricultural community as virtually all farmers were involved in dairying to some extent and would be poorer because they no longer had any means of processing their milk.

Though no one suggested a motive, it is possible the actions were politically motivated. As the parent company was English (Manchester based) a maverick republican group might have seen the attacks as a blow against continued British economic presence in Kerry. The closeness of the attack to 11 July, the first anniversary of the truce in the War of Independence, may also have been a factor. This date had additional significance in Kerry; on 11 July 1921 five republicans and three British soldiers lost their lives in the Castleisland ambush, which by a pure coincidence turned out to be the last military action of the conflict nationally. The symbolic importance of this event to Kerry republicans cannot be underestimated.

On Monday, 11 July 1922 the commemoration of the first anniversary was turned into a major political rally, preparing Kerry republicans for the coming conflict with the Provisional Government's forces. According to the *Cork Examiner:*

> Captain Richard Shanahan, Lieutenant John Flynn and NCO John Prendeville led the procession to Castleisland cemetery, which was reviewed by Diarmuid O'Leary O/C and attended by over 1,000 Volunteers, Cumann na mBan and Fianna Éireann who marched in military formation to the republican plot. Rev. Fr Myles Allman, CC addressed the gathering. They [the men killed in the Castleisland ambush] believed in the argument of physical force and went light-heartedly into battle against superior number of forces … Today, being laid to rest the former Minister of Defence, Cathal Brugha … his body riddled with bullets of an alien enemy. Acceptance of a Treaty and a Constitution will ensure that Irishmen will deprive Irishmen of their place among the nations of the world.[17]

Father Allman, from a staunchly republican family (his brother Dan was killed during the Headford ambush in March 1921), had no doubts about the continuity between the War of Independence and the Civil War, and the path that the Kerry IRA would have to follow to achieve the republic proclaimed in 1916. A similar – though a much smaller – commemoration was held at Rath cemetery in Tralee. At this point the two addresses were being used to motivate the troops, as various IRA units in Kerry were already preparing to send contingents to the front in Limerick city and county.

In mid-July 1922 about 400 members of the 1st Westerns under the command of Michael Brennan were based in Limerick city where they faced a republican force of around 700 men. Brennan, conscious of the inadequacy of his force compared to the republicans and cut off from communications with GHQ in Dublin, began to enter into negotiations with Liam Lynch to avoid a military confrontation. In Dublin, GHQ viewed his actions with bewilderment, and his efforts to buy time for his garrison until Dublin sent reinforcements were misunderstood as going over to the enemy. Once the lines of communication were re-established, additional troops equipped with armoured cars and much needed artillery were dispatched to Limerick. Dublin Guard units under Brigadier Paddy O'Daly assisted Brennan's forces when the assault was finally launched on republican positions in the city on Wednesday, 19 July. Over the subsequent three days artillery proved the crucial factor in undermining republican strong-points in the city such as the Strand barracks (now Clancy's Strand). At the cessation of hostilities on Friday, 21 July government troop losses were reported as eight dead and twenty wounded. Estimates of the republican casualties were between twenty and thirty dead. Volunteer Patrick Foran (twenty) of Lisellton, County Kerry was among the wounded. He subsequently died of his injuries on 26 July, thereby becoming the first Kerry republican killed in the Civil War.[18]

Following the fall of Limerick city, evacuating republicans converged on an existing republican strong-point based around Bruree, Bruff and Kilmallock in east Limerick where the major road and rail links between Dublin, Cork and Limerick cities converged. The front line in east Limerick was the nearest the

Civil War came to conventional warfare and as such favoured the support structures of a conventionally organised army rather than a force like the War of Independence IRA who operated what might be described as a 'hit and run' policy, where surprise and the ability to inflict a lot of injuries on a lot of men in a short period of time was the core of their military experience, and not really suited to the conduct of conventional warfare. Kerry units were also active in the fighting in east Limerick. Charles Hanlon of Listowel was wounded in Bruree on 26 July, dying of his wounds on 4 August 1922.[19]

Already public opinion in Kerry began to focus on the worrying speed at which hostilities (ignoring the brief flashpoint at Listowel on 30 June) had catapulted from Dublin a month earlier and were now in their own back yard. On the evening of Monday, 24 July the Kerry Farmers' Union organised a public meeting at Tralee courthouse. Representatives of the labour movement and commercial interests were also present at the meeting, which was presided over by John T. O'Neill, president of the Kerry Farmers' Union, who called on members of Dáil Éireann for Kerry and west Limerick to press for the immediate summoning of the Dáil to hold a meeting to bring about peace.

Humphrey Murphy, O/C Kerry No. 1 brigade IRA, addressed the meeting, outlining events as he saw them evolving if the government chose to continue a war policy:

> If the Provisional Government continue to fight with English guns, English bullets and shells, English Armoured Cars and the ex-soldiers of the English Army ... I am certain they are going to fail as the Black and Tans failed, because the war did not come properly until it came to Cork and Kerry. We will defend every town to the last. You will have towns in ruins and famine finishing

those who have escaped the bullet. We will stop at nothing, and we are going to win even if it takes years.[20]

Murphy's blood-curdling rhetoric must have made the hair stand on the back of the necks of the audience who listened to the twenty-eight-year-old former national schoolteacher from Currow elaborating on the fate he had in store for both the army of the newly elected government and – by default – the civilian population of Kerry once hostilities began in the county. Of course it is important to realise that Murphy's comments weren't delivered just for the benefit of his immediate audience. He was also speaking in the aftermath of the fall of Limerick, a major military setback for the republican cause in Munster. And in this context he needed to both boost the morale of his own troops and issue a warning to his adversaries still drunk on the euphoria of victory.

Initially the Dáil elected on 16 June was scheduled to assemble in Dublin on 30 June, but the outbreak of hostilities in the capital on the 28th made the opening of parliament far too dangerous and a threat to the safety of any TD who travelled from the provinces to the capital. And once ensconced in the city the possibility of being taken prisoner by republicans was a real one. To avoid these risks, the government, at Collins' behest, postponed the opening of the third Dáil until 15 July, which because of ongoing hostilities was further extended to 30 July. While Michael Collins' concerns about the safety of his parliamentarians was genuine, he was also happy to be able to determine the conduct of the war without having to expose his decisions either to cabinet review or wider parliamentary scrutiny. Ironically, a major contributory factor in the development of the Civil War was the inability of the political representatives of the nationalist movement (Sinn Féin) to control its military wing (IRA); yet, as military leader of a democratically elected government, Collins himself personified this militarist mindset.

Since the split in the IRA on the Treaty issue in mid-January, Collins had done his utmost to appease the republicans, often to the consternation of fellow cabinet colleagues, not least Arthur Griffith, who wanted an early election to endorse the Provisional Government and give them a democratic mandate to challenge the anti-Treatyites militarily. Once the election was out of the way, Collins wasn't unduly worried about confronting the Four Courts garrison until the British government forced his hand following the assassination of Sir Henry Wilson. Even then he calculated that once the militants in the Four Courts had had their '1916 moment', republicans elsewhere (mainly Munster) would not have the stomach for anything more than a token display of arms. As he evaluated the opposition Collins reckoned he had a good idea of both the strength of the IRA and the calibre of their leadership, all of whom he knew intimately. He felt he could win the war, which he anticipated would be over by September.

7

THE FREE STATE ARCHIPELAGO

It was Emmet Dalton who suggested a series of seaborne landings on the Cork and Kerry coasts as a way of foreshortening
and undermining the military cohesion of the Munster republic.
Born in Dublin in 1897, Dalton was the most experienced professional soldier in the Provisional Government's armed forces.
From a Redmondite family, he took the Woodenbridge route, as
advocated by John Redmond, and joined the Royal Dublin Fusiliers as a private (aged seventeen) in 1914. He showed a good
deal of initiative and was soon promoted to corporal. Rallying
his men when their officer was killed, his success in repelling an
attack by a more numerous German force earned him a commission. He was awarded the Military Medal on the Somme.
By the war's end Dalton had attained the rank of major, ironically serving as the aide-de-camp for Field Marshal Sir Henry
Wilson, whose assassination in June 1922 precipitated the attack on the Four Courts that started the Civil War.

It was his younger brother, Charlie – who was in the Dublin
brigade (IRA) – who facilitated Emmet Dalton's introduction
to Michael Collins, who valued his military expertise not only
for its own sake but also because of the invaluable insights Dalton had into the mindset of the upper echelon 'top brass' that
constituted the core of the chief imperial general staff. Dur-

ing the Treaty negotiations in London, Dalton played a central role in organising the Irish delegation's security measures, including having an aeroplane 'on stand by' in case the team had to leave London at short notice if the talks failed. In the early months of 1922, Dalton, aided by J. J. 'Ginger' O'Connell, who had served in the US army, tried to train a professional army; not an easy task as none of the IRA who stayed on board with the pro-Treaty army had much in the way of conventional military skills or training. In common with their anti-Treaty adversaries, most of their War of Independence experience involved engagements that were opportunistic attacks and ambushes that took place at a local level and on a small scale without any sense of a wider tactical or strategic pattern or template. Circumstances and practical considerations would have made any other campaign impossible.

Dalton's First World War experience and his arguments for invasion were compelling. If government troops landed behind enemy lines, Cork and Kerry contingents – some of the most experienced and battle-hardened troops on the anti-Treaty side – would be forced to abandon the front line in favour of returning home to defend their own areas. Not only would the Limerick–Waterford line collapse like a folded umbrella, but avoiding having to face costly and protracted rearguard actions by republicans at every crossroads and hillock across west Limerick, north Cork and east Kerry would save the lives of scores of government troops.

We are fortunate to have an excellent first-hand account of the preparation and execution of the Free State army's task force that landed in Fenit in early August 1922. Niall Harrington, a twenty-one-year-old trainee pharmacist from Dublin joined the Army Medical Service (AMS) as a medical assistant, holding the rank of corporal, and was seconded to the Dublin Guard, to whom Collins had assigned the task of establishing a government military enclave in Kerry. From a distinguished home rule/Redmondite family, Harrington was no stranger to Kerry. His father, Timothy Harrington, was first elected MP for Dublin in the Parnellite landslide election of 1885. Alongside his brother, Edward (an MP for Kerry), Timothy Harrington was one of the chief architects of the 'plan of campaign' during the Land War, and later served as lord mayor of Dublin. Another brother, Dan, was the owner and editor of the *Kerry Sentinel* newspaper, which vindicated the Land League/home rule position in Kerry between 1879 and 1913 and served as a journalistic foil to the unionist *Kerry Evening Post*. Following his father's death in 1910, Niall Harrington made several visits to Tralee, where his uncle Dan still lived (he died in 1913), and was more familiar with Tralee and its surroundings than most of the others on board the *Lady Wicklow*.

The Provisional Government chartered the 262-foot *Lady Wicklow* to serve as troop transport, bringing a task force of 450 men to Fenit. The ship's master, John Theodore Rogers, was not at all happy to have his vessel requisitioned for military purposes, given the fate of the previous expedition that had headed for Tralee. The *Aud*'s commander was intercepted by the royal navy and ended up having to scuttle his ship (and its contents) *en route* to Cork. Rogers would have been well aware of the possibility of his ship coming under hostile fire as it approached the Kerry coast. Arriving at the ship's embarkation point at 10.30 p.m. on Monday, 31 July, Harrington learned that the departure was delayed awaiting the arrival of eighty additional troops.

In addition to its complement of men the cargo included an 'eighteen-pounder' field gun and a Rolls Royce 'whippet' type armoured car with a rotating tower and Vickers machine-guns. It was the first armoured car that the army had received from the British and was nicknamed the 'ex-mutineer' as it had been commandeered by republicans at the time of the assault on the Four Courts but was recaptured during the course of the Free State victory.[1] In spite of its complement of armour and artillery, however, it was still the ordinary soldier with his rifle who would have to bear the brunt of the campaign against the republicans in Kerry, so the cliché 'the poor bloody infantry' still applied. However, the advantage of having these additional weapons gave the Free State army the upper hand in many encounters during the course of the war and saved many lives in Kerry during the ten-month campaign.

Brigadier Paddy O'Daly, O/C the Dublin Guard who had the ultimate responsibility for the delivery of a successful landing, was assisted by Commandant James Dempsey and Vice-Commandant Jim McGuinness. An indication of the seriousness Collins placed on a swift, successful campaign in Kerry was the inclusion of two of his most effective intelligence officers from the War of Independence days, James McNamara and David Neligan. Leaving Dublin at midday on 1 August, the *Lady Wicklow* approached the Kerry coast at first light on Wednesday, 2 August. Niall Harrington was roused from his sleep by Commandant David Neligan with the news that the force's senior commander, Paddy O'Daly, wanted to talk to him. Daly was poring over some maps of Tralee and its hinterland and asked Harrington's opinion on the various routes he might use to capture Ballymullen barracks and other key military installations. Interestingly, the young corporal's innovative suggestion, that he delay the landing until after dark and thereby take the objectives and their garrisons in a surprise attack, was overruled by O'Daly, who explained that he was under orders to capture Tralee by 12.30 p.m. that day. As their conversation drew to a close, Harrington asked O'Daly if he could transfer from the Army Medical Service to the Dublin Guard. O'Daly granted his request.

The plan of attack, as outlined by Harrington, was that the force would land in Fenit and advance to Spa, where it would split and form a pincer movement; a column under Captain Billy McClean would advance along Strand Road, encircling the town via Blennerville and Ballyard, and, hopefully, neutralise and capture any republican resistance it met on its way. Meanwhile, the main body of the army would enter Tralee at Pembroke Street, where some of the men, under Dempsey's command, would advance along the railway line and head for the workhouse and Ballymullen barracks; while the remaining troops under O'Daly and McGuinness would progress via Rock Street and rejoin with McClean's column in the Square/Bridge Street. At this point, assuming everything had gone according to plan, they would advance towards Moyderwell Cross, capture the 'staff' barracks, re-unite with Dempsey's column and surround and take Ballymullen barracks.[2]

Though he didn't know it at the time of the invasion, Harrington would later learn that O'Daly had no intelligence on the strength, disposition or defences of the republican forces he would encounter as the troops under his command set foot on Kerry soil. Apart from the fact that he knew that all three Kerry brigades were staunchly anti-Treaty, he wasn't aware that many of the 'flower' of those same brigades – possibly as many as 250–300 of Kerry's most experienced fighting men – were in service on the front line of the 'Munster republic', principally in east Limerick. When Niall Harrington suggested an invasion under the cover of darkness, he didn't realise the irony that the daylight attack was taking place almost totally in the dark.

When Napoleon was told of a potential commander, 'He's a good general, sir', he replied: 'Yes, but is he lucky?' This quip was very apt. Paddy O'Daly and the men under his command were very lucky as the expedition didn't even carry any form of bridging equipment as a contingency, if circumstances as they evolved at Fenit prevented an actual landing at the pier. Amazingly, there was no qualified doctor accompanying the Dublin Guard to Kerry; the most senior medical orderly on board was Sergeant Ted (T. J.) Keating from Dundalk, County Louth. Given the numbers of men who served in the Dublin Fusiliers during the First World War it is inconceivable that there were no military surgeons who could have been recruited to accompany the Dublin Guard expedition.

The defensive measures that awaited O'Daly's force at Fenit were mainly the result of Paddy Cahill's suspicion that the Free State might land troops in Kerry. If they did so, he believed that Fenit, Tarbert and (possibly) Dingle would be the most likely landing areas. Even though Cahill was demoted as O/C of Kerry No. 1 brigade, his precautionary measures – had they been heeded and properly implemented – would have posed a serious challenge to the Dublin Guard, both at the initial landings at Fenit and later at the approaches to Tralee town. In his capacity as commander of the 9th battalion, Cahill asked John Joe Sheehy to draw up a defensive plan both for Fenit pier and the north-western approaches to Tralee town. In the event Humphrey Murphy took the Cahill–Sheehy plan on board on 15 July when a small garrison of twenty men drawn from the 1st battalion (Tralee) and the 7th battalion (Castleisland) under Tony Sheehy and Seamus O'Connor was installed at the coastguard station at Fenit, which gave them an unrivalled view of the pier and the 700-foot wooden causeway that joined it to the mainland. A landmine strategically located at the centre of the causeway served as the lynchpin of the defences. It would be detonated on the arrival of a suspicious vessel, isolating the invading force on the pier and allowing the garrison to pin down government troops until their own reinforcements ar- rived. In Tralee town, Sheehy recommended placing sniper units in Latchford's Mills, a four-storey warehouse on Nel- son (Ashe) Street, where their field of fire would cover Ashe Street, Castle Street and the GS & WR railway station. An additional small force located in the GS & WR goods depot on Edward Street would widen the scope to cover the Dingle railway station and yards and the 'new line'. If these posts had been manned, the entire area could have become a lethal killing ground for many of the troops as they entered Tralee.

The arrival of the coastguard 'garrison' was viewed with a mixture of suspicion and foreboding by many of the fishermen and Harbour Commissioner staff working out of Fenit, who quickly realised the landmine's potential to destroy the port, and in the process their livelihoods, leaving them without work for long after both belligerents had left the area. As time moved on the more observant noticed that the garrison did not examine the landmine on anything like a regular basis. On Thursday, 27 July at 4 a.m. two employees of the Harbour Commissioners, acting without any political motivation other than to preserve their jobs, disconnected the cable attaching the explosives to the detonator.[3]

Shortly before 10 a.m. on Wednesday, 2 August the *Lady Wicklow* approached Fenit. As there was no prior notification of any vessel docking that morning, and as the tide was unsuitable for an immediate landing, John Fitzgerald, the harbour pilot, got his two sons to row him out to the mystery vessel. As soon as he was on board he noticed the armoured car under the tarpaulin, but as his sons were already on their way back to shore he had little option but to assist the berthing of the ship, which proved difficult because of the tidal conditions. Sergeant Jack Lydon (aged twenty-eight) from James' Street, Tralee, a senior NCO with the Dublin Guard, provided invaluable assistance and so the *Lady Wicklow* was successfully berthed at Fenit pier at 10.30 a.m. From his vantage point on shore, almost a thousand yards away, Johnny Sheehan could make out uniformed men on the deck of the ship that had just docked. He rushed off to alert the garrison and warn the villagers that a landing was imminent.

As soon as the commander got word he flicked the switch that would detonate the landmine, but nothing happened. Repeated attempts proved equally futile. Meanwhile some of the troops were already descending onto the pier, from where a long line of railway wagons stretching the length of the causeway provided fortuitous cover. Nevertheless a number of defenders on the republican side fired at the ship, managing to wound some of the soldiers as they descended the gangplank, whereupon the armoured car still strapped to the deck opened up with a massive volley of machine-gun fire. It would have been suicidal for any of the garrison to even attempt resistance; indeed, the *Republican Bulletin*, a mixture of fact, misinformation, and downright propaganda that was published daily in the *Cork Examiner* while the republicans still held the city (Cork fell on 11 August), recorded that a British navy sloop bombarded Fenit, successfully assisting the Free State landing.[4]

Unfortunately for the republicans there was no telephone contact out of Fenit to inform their other units of the landing, because Mrs Kelly, the local postmistress, became hysterical once the shooting began and was preoccupied with saying the rosary.[5] Denis Keane went to Spa RIC barracks, from where he phoned Ballymullen barracks via the GPO in Edward Street. Meanwhile the Free State force was advancing towards Spa, suffering their first fatality (Private Patrick Quinn) at Kilfenora. The republicans tried to implement a holding action at Sammy's Rock, a 100-foot crag near Spa, resulting in the death of one Free State soldier (Private Edward Byrne) and the loss of John O'Sullivan of Castlegregory on the republican side, bringing their total losses to two as Tom Flynn had been killed earlier on the beach near Fenit.

At this point both John Joe Sheehy and Mike McGlynn had travelled out to assess the strength of the force arraigned against them. It was decided the best they could do was to hold off the advance long enough to enable them to burn and destroy Ballymullen barracks to deny the government army use of the principal military base in Kerry. Even here the fates were against them; no sooner had they set fire to one of the blocks than it became apparent that some of their own men were still sleeping in it (off guard duty), and frantic measures had to be taken to rescue them. By 1.30 p.m. the main Free State column under O'Daly had reached the Rock Street/Pembroke Street junction. Armed with a Lewis machine-gun, Michael Fitzgerald and Johnny O'Connor took up a firing position on the roof of Shamrock Mills and sprayed the advancing column with gunfire, wounding several soldiers. AMS stretcher bearers, wearing large Red Cross armbands, came under continuing fire while attempting to tend the wounded. Without any concern for his own safety, O'Daly grabbed a large Red Cross flag and began waving it vigorously in the vain hope it would bring a cessation in firing.

In the end orders were given to storm the post, which were successfully executed, by which time O'Connor and Fitzgerald had escaped. The Rock Street encounter, which claimed the lives of six Dublin Guards and one medical orderly, would prove to be the largest single death toll the Free State army suffered during the entire conflict in Kerry. At Corporal Niall Harrington's suggestion the remaining troops moved along Nelson Street, passing by Latchford's Mills, which by a stroke of luck had not been garrisoned in the manner John Joe Sheehy had suggested. Had it been, the resulting casualty levels to government troops might well have been dozens (both killed and wounded), given the Rock Street experience. By late afternoon the vanguard of the Free State force was approaching Moyderwell barracks, where they chose to use rifle grenades to force the garrison to evacuate their positions, leaving the road open to their final objective, the capture of Ballymullen barracks.

The *Republican Bulletin* went into overdrive on the 7 August edition of the *Cork Examiner*, describing the heroic efforts of the single republican armoured car as it gallantly offered resistance to the two armoured cars at Moyderwell Cross to prevent them advancing on Ballymullen barracks. The report was pure

fiction, resembling more the American Civil War battle between the 'ironclads' (battleships) in the opening stages of that
war than any actual confrontation in suburban Tralee during
August 1922. The press release was equally wide of the mark in
its report of the level of casualties inflicted on the government
force by the republicans: thirty-one dead and over one hundred
wounded.[6]

While the fire at Ballymullen had done some damage to
the officers' mess, the most impressive building in the barracks,
a lot of the other facilities were left unscathed and were quickly
utilised by incoming troops. From a practical point of view the
army set up over a dozen smaller posts in and around Tralee:
at the Jeffers Institute, Day Place; at the corner of the Mall
and Ashe Street; at the post office, Edward Street; in several
locations on both Rock and Pembroke Streets; and at Ballyard
and Boherbee to ensure that they had effective 'on the ground'
control over most of Tralee's urban area, as well as Ballymullen
barracks.

At 3 a.m. on Thursday, 3 August the *Corona* and three smaller boats left Kilrush, County Clare bound for Tarbert. On
board were 240 men drawn from the 1st Western division under
the command of Colonel Michael Hogan.[7] The 1st Westerns
evolved from the East Clare brigade of the IRA following its re-
organisation in the summer of 1921, and were ultimately under
the command of Michael Brennan, a twenty-five-year-old from
Meelick on the Clare/Limerick border. The bulk of the force was
from west Clare, but it also contained a sizeable contingent from
south Galway. The unit played a significant role in the 'stand
off' with Ernie O'Malley in Limerick in March 1922 when a
number of Limerick pro-Treaty troops joined its ranks. The 1st

Westerns were regarded, along with the Dublin Guard, as one of the most militarily effective – and politically reliable – units in the government's army, and the dispatch of both to Kerry is an indication of the importance Collins placed on bringing hostilities to a swift conclusion there.

Michael Hogan, a native of Kilfrikle, Loughrea, County Galway, was the son of a civil servant with the Land Commission, who farmed 270 acres in east Galway. From a gifted family academically, Hogan's elder brother, James, served as intelligence officer of the East Clare brigade during the War of Independence, a role he would hold in the national army for the duration of the Civil War, before taking up an appointment as professor of history at UCC at the end of hostilities. In January 1922, Patrick Hogan, the eldest in the family (and a solicitor by training), was appointed Minister for Agriculture, a portfolio he retained until the Cumann na nGaedheal government left office in 1932.

Arriving in Tarbert, Hogan found the anti-Treaty garrison had left town, leaving the charred ruins of the coastguard station in their wake, to deprive the incoming force of accommodation and a headquarters. Leaving twenty-five troops under the command of Captain Brian O'Grady and Lieutenant Egan billeted in the RIC barracks, the unit moved on to Ballylongford, where they took six republican prisoners and captured their arms and ammunition. The main force entered Listowel at 5.30 p.m. without firing a shot to find the republicans had gone, leaving the workhouse, the courthouse and the RIC barracks as burnt-out shells. An additional fifty troops were billeted in the town, which combined with the earlier deployment in Tarbert represented more than a quarter of the original force (75 out of a total of 240 troops) that was tied down to static positions.

The civilian population of Listowel were glad to see the troops enter their town, as their arrival brought to an end months of virtual isolation, which had seriously reduced the levels of trade and commerce between the town and its rural hinterland. A local resident, writing to the *Cork Examiner* in early September, recalled:

> Many happenings have taken place in Listowel and district during the last month ... due to the stoppage of train services (on all sides), as well as the dislocation of telegraph wires and telephone apparatus, no means of communication was to be had with the outside world. To complete our misery, all roads leading to the town were destroyed by trenches, making it impossible for farmers to carry on their usual avocations to the town. As a result, no fairs or markets took place, traders could have to all intent and purposes closed down. The strike on the wage question ... and disruption of rail added to our distress ... e. g. numerous bridges were destroyed. At Gale, Ballybunion road, Tralee road, Gortnadromgouna cross, Ballyhorgan cross, Ballyhorgan railway metal bridge, and the bridge between Duagh and Abbeydorney. Just a few days before our isolation ended, anti-Treatyites burned the Workhouse, the police barracks and the Courthouse.[8]

By nightfall the remainder of Hogan's column had arrived in Ballymullen barracks. At the end of day two almost 700 government troops were *in situ* in north Kerry and Tralee in what might be described as a political and military vacuum, and with very little local knowledge. On 4 August Éamon Horan began a recruitment campaign to enlist a 'Kerry brigade' to serve and broaden the government's military presence in Kerry. The majority of the new recruits had no military experience, were still in civilian clothes, and awaiting the issue of uniforms and weapons. On their first day in the army, under the direction of Horan and Captain Jack Harpur, who would later become director of prisons, Kerry, they assisted in a round-up of known republicans, which brought the number of detainees in government hands to around a hundred, including the forty or so captured on the first day of fighting. The *Lady Wicklow* left Tralee on 4 August bound for Dublin, carrying the bodies of the troops who had been killed capturing the town. Michael Collins was among the attendance at their state funeral on 8 August. In a short letter to his fiancée, Kitty Kiernan, he wrote:

> The scenes at mass were really heartbreaking. The poor women weeping and almost shrieking (some of them) for their dead sons. Sisters, and one wife were there too, and a few small children. It makes one feel I tell you.[9]

By this time the *Lady Wicklow* and the *Avaronia* were on their way to Cork where they would land troops at Union Hall (100), Youghal (200) and Passage West (500) as part of a highly successful series of coastal incursions on the 'rebel county' over 8 and 9 August. The only concerted republican resistance occurred at Rochestown (leaving nine Free State soldiers and seven republicans dead), only postponing the capture of the southern capital by one day, leaving it in government hands by 11 August 1922. On 10 August, in spite of a well organised protest campaign by commercial and municipal leaders on the impact its destruction would have on the local economy, republicans blew up a section of the Blackwater viaduct at Mallow, thereby severing rail contact between Cork city and the south west and the rest of the country.

Taking advantage of the arrival of reinforcements, Paddy O'Daly decided to extend the area under the government's control. In this regard he was following the strategy that Collins and Mulcahy had outlined for undermining the Munster republic. During the War of Independence GHQ realised that the IRA did not have to win every time to appear victorious; all they had to do was disrupt the life of the country so that the government couldn't function. As poacher turned game-keeper, Collins saw that an immediate overwhelming defeat of the republicans was unlikely; a practical strategy, however, was to establish a military presence in the principal towns in the area. As the army presence expanded incrementally so too would popular support for the new regime in the areas control-led by government troops. Gradually the republican heartland would shrink, and the pro-government enclave would expand from the inside out. Early on Saturday, 5 August, a combined force of the Dublin Guard and the 1st Westerns commanded by James Dempsey and Jim McGuinness left Tralee. Unsure of what levels of resistance they would encounter, the force included their eighteen-pounder field gun – which had been nicknamed the 'Rose of Tralee' – in their arsenal. Their arrival took the local garrison at Farranfore totally by surprise. The Free State troops would later recall jokingly that the republi-cans not only abandoned their arms and ammunition in their haste to avoid capture but left their half-eaten beef dinners on the table. Unable to find any 'Irregulars' in the follow-up search, the Free State troops returned to the deserted head-quarters and duly ate the abandoned dinners.[10]

The republican outpost on the approaches to Castleisland offered more stubborn resistance, but the discharge of a number of shells from the eighteen-pounder proved the decisive factor. The use of artillery was as much a psychological strike (and a warning salvo to future enemy encounters) as a military necessity. In practical terms the republicans – or the 'Irregulars' as the government and the press increasingly dubbed them – had abandoned both Farranfore and Castleisland, and both towns were in government hands by 12.30 p.m. From a republican perspective, the local garrisons were too small and had insufficient quantities of ammunition to offer a credible resistance that would inflict serious casualties on the attacking troops. In the face of a much stronger force, to stand and fight would ultimately involve being surrounded and captured and removed from the equation for the remainder of the conflict.

The army established their Castleisland headquarters at Hartnett's hotel. Though much smaller in terms of population than Castleisland, Farranfore represented a key strategic asset due to its pivotal position in the county's rail and road network. Lying midway between Tralee and Killarney, with 'spur' lines to Castleisland and Valentia, it carried the promise of swift lines of communication into central Kerry and the mountain vastness of the Iveragh peninsula. In early twentieth century Ireland the rail network was vastly superior both in terms of standards of construction and speed of service than any comparable communications by road. For the duration of the conflict the GS & WR and, to a lesser extent, the Tralee and Dingle Railway Company would see their rail tracks, bridges, signalling equipment, rolling stock, locomotives and stations constantly – and repeatedly – sabotaged and destroyed by republicans so as to deprive the national army of a transport network that reached virtually every important population centre in Kerry. In the process the civilian population of the county was deprived of a cheap, speedy and efficient means of public transport with all the repercussions that its absence implied in the commercial, economic and social life of the community. It became more difficult to bring agricultural produce to the weekly market; basic foodstuffs – tea, sugar, salt, etc. – were not delivered to local shops; postal deliveries were suspended; all of which combined to increase people's sense of isolation and make their daily lives a misery. Of course the republicans did not consider the discomfort their campaign caused to the wider community, as they were by and large as contemptuous of them as they were immune from public criticism. On the other hand, the actual conflict rarely impacted on the ordinary person's sense of personal safety. Unlike other civil conflicts such as the Mexican Revolution, or the Spanish Civil War, where popular support for both protagonists was widespread and ran very deep, most of the civilian population were largely indifferent to the ideological fault lines of Free State versus republic.

The positive side of this non-alignment was an almost total absence of any attacks or atrocities perpetrated against civilians by either side. On the rare occasions when innocent bystanders were either killed or wounded, it was usually the result of being caught in crossfire or an ambush and firefight between the two belligerents. Generally speaking republican attacks were episodic and opportunistic, with troop movements being under constant – but covert – surveillance by IRA scouts in rural areas; in towns, the younger Fianna Éireann or Cumann na mBan members passed on information which could see a sniper or one or two men with revolvers open fire on the foot patrol or the vehicle on its return journey. Individual sentries and soldiers entering and leaving the relative safety of buildings had to be wary of snipers; while patrolling their districts, a felled tree on the road could be a prelude to an ambush or be booby-trapped to kill or maim the soldier as he tried to remove the obstacle. As most of the government troops in Kerry were either serving in Dublin or Clare units they had none of the local knowledge that their republican opponents had of the terrain or the locations the local IRA had used to their advantage in the war against the British little more than a year earlier.

It has often been stated that neighbour was reluctant to shoot neighbour, and this probably caused many ambushes to be aborted, resulting in low casualty levels in the Civil War. Indeed, some authorities cite the 'outside' factor – the fact that the bulk of the national troops came from outside Kerry – as one of the chief reasons the conflict was so bitter in the county. A valid point, certainly, but if anything the Civil War was a conflict that bred maverick actions driven by the intensity of a vendetta. On 5 August three individual Kerrymen would lose their lives in incidents that were in many ways typical of the conflict in the county. The actual details surrounding the death of Private Michael Purcell of 2, Lower Abbey Street, Tralee are scant. He enlisted in the Kerry brigade the previous day as part of Éamon Horan's recruitment drive. In a staunchly republican town like Tralee the fact that he joined the hated Free State army was enough – in some people's eyes – to justify his death, which probably came from a sniper's bullet. For republicans, watching and besetting troop movements was not risk-free either. Michael Reidy, a seventeen-year-old Fianna member from Ballymacelligott, was observing an army patrol somewhere in the vicinity of the Earl of Desmond hotel in Ballyseedy that Saturday when, unbeknownst to him, he was spotted by one of the soldiers and summarily shot dead. Most probably Michael Reidy was unarmed when he was killed.[11]

The development of scattered outposts necessitated a supply network to deliver food and ammunition to the garrisons, as well as facilitating the changing of the guard on a regular basis. A supply lorry was ambushed at Knockeen Cross, on the way to Castleisland, resulting in the death of Captain Brian Houlihan of the Dublin Guard and the wounding of three others, two of whom would subsequently die of wounds inflicted by the dumdum-type mauser bullets, which fragmented on hitting a bone, creating hideous shrapnel-type internal injuries. A native of Kenmare and a veteran of the 1916 Rising and the War of Independence, Brian Houlihan, who had travelled to Kerry on board the *Lady Wicklow*, was the first of seventeen troops who would die in Kerry while engaged in convoy and protection duties, either delivering supplies to isolated army posts or escorting humanitarian deliveries of basic foodstuffs to aid the hard-pressed civilian population in Tralee and Killarney. It is unclear if Houlihan was the principal target of the ambush, or if his death was purely a matter of chance in a random attack.

In a curious twist to the conflict, the *New York Times* carried a report of an explosion that damaged the transatlantic cable link at Waterville. The rationale for this action is hard to fathom, unless the installation was seen as a British-owned business and a reminder of the imperial presence. This would echo the two arson attacks that the republicans carried out on British-owned creameries in early July. While the republicans held Cork they retained editorial control over the *Cork Examiner* and used their position to publish the *Republican Bulletin*, which provided illustrious accounts of the encounters between their forces and the Free State army. The information they provided on their casualties at Fenit (one dead, one wounded and four prisoners) was the only accurate part of the report, but at least it was a source of information. From 14 August onwards accurate information on republican casualties is extremely difficult to substantiate, even more so the identity of the individual volunteers who lost their lives. The *Kerry People*, an eight-page weekly newspaper owned and edited by Maurice Ryle, whose journalistic experience included stints at both the *Dublin Evening Mail* and the *Kerry Sentinel*, was the only local newspaper still in operation in the county at the start of the Civil War. The newspaper provided accurate and balanced coverage of the conflict, but its independent editorial line did not endear it to republicans. National Dublin-based newspapers such as the *Freeman's Journal*, the *Irish Independent* and the *Irish Times*, which were read by few people in Kerry at the best of times, would have become unavailable once the conflict cut off rail and other means of communications between Dublin and the provinces.

The *Army Bulletin*, an 'official' source of information (subject to both time delays and military censorship) provided details of the progress of the war to a press and public eager for news of a conflict that they hoped would be over sooner rather than later. More often than not the figures it provided on both the size of the 'Irregular' force the army encountered and the casualties they inflicted on their adversaries are grossly exaggerated. The army's report on the Tralee operations, quoted in the *Irish Times*, noted that of, 'seventy-five Irregulars, thirty – a certainty – were killed during the capture of the town, while eleven National troops were killed and 114 wounded during the same action.'[12] It is highly improbable that the figures on the wounded (114 would represent over a quarter of O'Daly's entire force) are accurate. Niall Harrington, writing in *Kerry*

Landing, estimated twenty to thirty (at most) were wounded during the capture of Tralee, figures that correspond to Paddy Cahill's field report (on the republican side) to Kerry No. 1 brigade.

On 10 August General Dermot McManus arranged to have two vessels – the *Mermaid* and the *Margaret* – at the dockside in Limerick city to transport Brigadier Tom O'Connor Scarteen and the 200 men under his command to Kenmare. Most of the men in O'Connor's force were raw recruits, the bulk of them from Cork and Kerry, it seems, with a sprinkling of men from the more experienced Northern division, and included a younger brother of Kevin O'Higgins, the Provisional Government's justice minister. Tom O'Connor was the only commander of any significance in Kerry from the War of Independence days to adopt a pro-Treaty position. Bertie Scully of Glenbeigh suggests it was a stance taken due to the fact that he (O'Connor) had been passed over as brigade engineer when the IRA was reorganised over the summer of 1921.[13] Whether this was the case or not, O'Connor was a formidable addition to the government's military force, given both his knowledge of his adversaries (and former comrades) in Kerry No. 2 and No. 3 brigades and his familiarity with the topography of south Kerry, which with its wild coastal and mountain terrain could be described as ideal ambush country.

During the voyage down from Limerick, McManus, a Mayo man and a graduate of Sandhurst military academy, who had served with the Royal Enniskillen Fusiliers at Gallipoli, was not impressed by either the calibre or the discipline of the men on board, recalling, '… even on the ship I had a good deal of friction with those young fellows.' As they approached the entrance to the Kenmare river at dawn on 11 August, Mc-Manus advised the men to take up defensive positions around the perimeter of the town, garrison the barracks properly, and carry out regular patrols of the town. No sooner had they arrived in Kenmare than they went visiting and drinking with their friends. Tom O'Connor returned to his family home over the bakery at No. 5 Main Street without posting a sentry to guard what was in effect the command HQ, while the remaining troops billeted themselves at the workhouse, the Carnegie library and the National bank.

According to the *Cork Examiner*, the troops were given an enthusiastic welcome by the townspeople of Kenmare, and the church parade (Sunday, 13 August) was a spectacle never before seen in Kenmare, and the splendid military bearing was a cause of great celebration and excitement. Archdeacon Patrick Marshall, parish priest of Kenmare, welcomed the troops to the town, and used the occasion to condemn the republicans for the destruction of the coastguard station at Lickeen, the RIC barracks and the fever hospital. The burning of the latter drew particular criticism, as the parish priest pointed out that while the building was not now in use, it might be needed in the future in the event of outbreaks of serious illnesses or diseases that might require isolation to contain their infection of the wider community.[14]

On Saturday, 12 August Michael Collins visited Tralee as part of a wider tour of the south west. Given the fall of Cork city, and the capture of Kenmare the previous day, he must have been pleased how quickly Free State forces had ruptured the hull of the Munster republic. With landings at Tarbert on the Shannon at one end and at Youghal on the

Cork/Waterford border at the other, and at several intermediate points in between over the course of ten days, the idea of a republican heartland in the south seemed delusional to all but the most militaristic and doctrinaire republicans. Collins had prepared the ground for discussion; his chief intelligence officer in Kerry, Colonel David Neligan, had visited the most senior (and influential) republican prisoners in custody in Tralee jail – Tim Kennedy, Billy Mullins and Paddy Paul Fitzgerald – with a view to getting them to act as intermediaries with their colleagues still militarily active to arrange a cessation of hostilities in Kerry.

While in Tralee Collins received news of the death of Arthur Griffith in Dublin and cut short his plans for discussions and instead returned to the capital. The rapid capture of several key towns in Kerry within a few days of Collins' visit suggests that. his instructions were pretty specific – continue to expand the area in Kerry under the government's military control. And yet it was extremely premature to dismiss republican resistance in Kerry as a spent force. At 4 p.m. on 12 August a twenty-five-man foot patrol was marching along a particularly exposed stretch of road at Bedford, about two miles from Listowel, when they came under fire from republicans. John Quayne from Meelick in Clare was killed and two others wounded, before the sound of gunfire drew the armoured car, the 'ex-mutineer', to the scene where it focused concentrated machine-gun fire on the republicans according to the *Cork Examiner*.[15] This proved the decisive factor in that it allowed the troops to take cover, and in the process seriously reduced the casualty levels that would have otherwise occurred. Interestingly, the *Freeman's Journal*'s coverage of the same attack recorded that the patrol consisted of four lorries, unusual given that their information probably came from the same source, the *Army Bulletin*.

Free State troops – predominantly Dublin Guard, commanded by James Dempsey and Jim McGuinness – must have felt a degree of trepidation on Sunday 13 August, as they approached Killarney. If they were to believe their own propaganda, as reported in the *Irish Times*, the town was occupied by a force of over 500 'Irregulars' commanded by Erskine Childers.[16] On the face of it, the idea that such a large concentration of republicans – virtually half of all the IRA active in Kerry – would offer stiff resistance and risk being surrounded and captured *en masse* in Killarney is absurd, and goes against the grain of all the previous tactics adopted by the IRA both in Kerry and elsewhere. Republican strongholds such as Limerick and Cork cities were abandoned without any serious attempts being made to use a coherent evacuation of an urban centre as a way of inflicting maximum casualties on the national army.

On the other hand, Killarney, as headquarters of Kerry No. 2 brigade, might be expected to defend their town more robustly than Kerry No. 1 brigade had done at Tralee ten days earlier. On that occasion national troops had the advantage of a surprise attack; nevertheless a single Lewis gun had inflicted relatively high casualties on the Dublin Guard in the Pembroke/Rock Street area of the town. In the interim towns like Listowel and Castleisland had been taken without any serious fighting, but if Kerry republicans wanted a major confrontation, Killarney had time to prepare its defences and absorb the Kerry contingents who were returning from the Limerick front to rejoin their local units. Finally, the presence of Erskine Childers as commander would help galvanise the defending garrison.

Childers – in many ways a *bête noir* to the Free State army – was portrayed as a military genius. True, he had served in the Boer War and had written a highly acclaimed book on guerrilla warfare based on those experiences as well as the prophetic novel *Riddle of the Sands*, a *Boy's Own*-type adventure warning of the dangers of the German naval build-up in the North Sea, before turning full circle and using his yacht, the *Asgard* to smuggle German rifles into Howth in 1914 to arm the Irish Volunteers. And yet Childers' reputation as military leader was based as much on his ability to hold a pen as to shoulder a rifle; indeed his principal role during the Civil War was to return good copy as a propagandist in the pro-republican *War News*.

In war, as in all other areas of human activity, what people believe to be true is as important as the actual truth in determining their actions. And so the final advance on Killarney took place under the cover of darkness so as to reduce the number of potential casualties the national army might have to incur in capturing the town. In the event government troops occupied Killarney at 11 p.m. on Sunday only to discover that only about sixty of the original force (estimated at between 400 and 700) remained in the town. This figure was probably near to the real strength of the garrison. As they abandoned the town the republicans burned down the RIC barracks and the 'new' Great Southern hotel (built in 1907 to cater for those who could not afford the more luxurious older establishment), so as to deprive the incoming troops of accommodation. The older part of the hotel, opened in 1854 and consisting of over a hundred bedrooms, was spared destruction thanks to the intervention of Seán Moylan, the republican 'director of operations', who appreciated the Great Southern was the lynchpin of Killarney's tourist industry, and the subsequent – wanton – destruction of such a facility would take the town years, if not decades, to recover from and which would result in the loss of a quarter of the town's most deluxe accommodation.[17] According to a report in the *Kerry People*, the townspeople of Killarney declared Monday, 14 August a bank holiday to mark their 'liberation'. Interestingly, neither the local press nor any of the national dailies had any reports of casualties on anything like the scale that both sides issued regarding the numbers of killed and wounded they had inflicted on the enemy during the capture of Tralee.

On Tuesday, 15 August a detachment of the Dublin Guard left Killarney bound for Rathmore. There they found the republicans had abandoned the town leaving their customary 'burnt offering' – the charred remains of the RIC barracks – for the incoming troops. The local courthouse was used as temporary accommodation, and troops were also billeted in a number of private houses. On the same day about 100 men from the 1st Westerns left Tralee. *En route* to Killorglin they set up an outpost at Castlemaine, before moving on to Milltown. The column encountered some resistance near Kilderry, between Milltown and Killorglin, but it was half-hearted, and the government force took six republicans prisoner, capturing their arms and ammunition. Arriving in Killorglin, the seventy-man force commanded by Captain Dan Lehane (aged twenty-four) of Lahinch, County Clare was cordially received and cheered by townspeople. Lehane divided his force in three, selecting Morris' hotel as his principal headquarters, primarily because of its proximity to Saint James' church (Church of Ireland) whose square tower (accessible independently of the church building) provided an ideal observation point/machine-gun post which gave commanding views of both the town and the rail and road approaches from Tralee and Killarney. The remaining troops, commanded by Lieutenants O'Callaghan and Corry, took over the town's RIC barracks – which had been partially damaged by a landmine detonated by the evacuating garrison – and the Carnegie library, which also served as the town's secondary school.

At this point, the Dublin Guard assumed responsibility for the Kerry No. 2 brigade area in the eastern part of the county, while the 1st Westerns presided over north Kerry and the rural areas of Kerry No. 1 brigade. Both units had a presence in Ballymullen barracks and patrolled both the Tralee urban area and its hinterland. By mid-August the Free State army did not yet have any foothold on the Dingle peninsula, but anticipating Dingle would be next on their list the local republican garrison burned down both the town's RIC barracks and coastguard station.

From his base in Kenmare, Tom O'Connor-Scarteen and his second-in-command, Captain Dick O'Sullivan, commandeered a meal and flour boat (which regularly landed at Kenmare) and, with 100 men on board, sailed along the coast to Reenard Point. As the force disembarked they came under fire and suffered some casualties, both killed and wounded. Approaching Caherciveen, O'Connor anticipated that the republicans would use the town's hillside location to maximum advantage and offer stiff resistance. In contrast to his expectations Caherciveen offered no resistance and, posting some men to hold the town, O'Connor requisitioned a number of cars and drove on to Waterville where he billeted a number of troops at the Butler Arms hotel. Even though O'Connor-Scarteen used his personal popularity to recruit some additional troops across south Kerry it was apparent to him that his force was too small even to be able to maintain a presence in – much less control over – the Kerry No. 3 brigade area.

While abandoning the main population centres to national troops, the republicans mounted a concerted campaign aimed at destroying rail communications in the county so as to force all military traffic on to the roads, thus enabling the anti-Treaty side to have much greater freedom in deciding ambush locations. In early August rails were taken up between Tralee and Farranfore and at several points on the thirty-nine-mile Farranfore–Valentia line, while bridges were blown up at Ballycarthy and Ballyseedy, and burned at Headford junction and near Kenmare. A landmine detonated under a moving train derailed a locomotive and some carriages between Ballyhar and Farranfore. There were more subtle ways of undermining the rail network – sabotage. During the War of Independence many rail employees mounted a non-cooperation campaign, refusing to handle any military traffic including both men and materials. This solidarity continued in Kerry, manifesting itself during the early stages of the Civil War in support of the republican cause. For example GS & WR employees dismantled fourteen railway engines in Tralee station. In follow-up measures eight rail workers were arrested by the army who replaced the crucial parts of the locomotives that had been removed.[18]

As the campaign progressed republicans took a more aggressive approach. On Tuesday, 15 August at 5 p.m. republicans ambushed a train at Curran's Bridge near Farranfore. A small landmine detonated on the line in front of the train brought the train to a halt, whereupon rifle fire concentrated on the locomotive wounded both the driver, Denis O'Keeffe, and the guard, Daniel Linehan, as well as the soldier 'riding shotgun', twenty-year-old Joseph Berry of Clifton, County Galway. Among the passengers on the train were the government's most senior military men in Kerry, Paddy Daly and Jim McGuinness, and a couple of American journalists, for whom the encounter must have contained echoes of the 'wild west'. The train also included a machine-gun post, and once the gunner identified the source of the rifle fire he concentrated his fire on that area, which caused the ambush to be aborted. In the follow-up search, an anti-Treaty volunteer named O'Connor was captured, and 600 yards of cable, three landmines and three detonators were seized.[19]

The next day, Wednesday, 16 August 1922, republicans held up a breakdown train returning from Killarney to Tralee, where the team had repaired damaged track and the rail bridge at Killan, where they were fired upon by anti-Treatyites and forced to destroy the repairs. On the return journey the train, a locomotive and two carriages, slowed down at Ballymacthomas, about five miles from Tralee, to allow a GS & WR employee to get off the train. As he did so, Carroll, the permanent way inspector, the driver and the fireman were held at gunpoint and ordered to drive at full speed to Tralee. All three refused to carry out the republicans' command. As it turned out one of the republicans – a former GS & WR employee – who knew how to operate the locomotive commandeered the train and proceeded towards Tralee at speeds of between fifty and sixty miles per hour. As it approached the station, disaster was averted thanks to the swift response of Johnny O'Connor, who manually switched the tracks, thereby diverting the train from the main station. The train smashed into a buffer, crashed into three stationary goods wagons and ploughed through two solid masonry walls before plunging across the Listowel Road where the boiler ruptured and reduced the two wagons to matchwood close to houses occupied by the railway workers.[20] Fortunately there was no one either in the railway station or on the Listowel Road when the locomotive exploded, which was initially assumed to be a bomb explosion.

Public opinion was appalled by the recklessness of the republican actions, while it prompted the GS & WR to suspend all rail services, effective from Friday, 18 August. Two days later the company announced it would pay off its entire permanent staff indefinitely (including clerical grades), effective from 22 August. This involved substantial job losses across the county, as the GS & WR employed sixty-four staff in Tralee district, nine in Killarney and thirty-eight in Caherciveen.[21] For the Great Southern and Western Railway, a private company, it must be added, it was a black week. The loss of the new Great Southern hotel and the destruction of the locomotive cost the company £30,000 and £15,000 respectively. Viewed from a strictly military perspective the republican campaign on the Great Southern and Western front was a great success.

Ironically, due to the conflict the only guests the company was likely to have in the Great Southern hotel were the Free State army. For the troops lucky enough to be billeted in the hotel – with its high Victorian décor echoing Georgian influences, and its Corinthian-columned dining room – their immediate surroundings were a world away from most army accommodation and must have added a surreal quality to their experience of Killarney. For the hotel staff, there must have been a sense of *déjà vu* as it was little more than six months since the British army – over 500 members of the Royal Fusiliers regiment – had vacated the premises after a residency spanning two years. Of course to republicans the fact that a green uniform replaced a khaki one made little difference, many referring to the national army as 'Green and Tans' – a term of contempt. As they saw it the Provisional Government was only a puppet administration beholden to Lloyd George, and its army a barely concealed repackaging of the recently disbanded 'Irish' regiments of the British army.[22]

On, Thursday, 17 August two medical orderlies, Privates Cecil Fitzgerald and John O'Meara from Gort and Galway city, had a day off and decided to walk to Ross castle. Aged sixteen and twenty respectively and wearing their army uniforms with a large Red Cross badge on their upper arms, they asked Robert Roberts, a local boatman, to ferry them out to Innisfallen island. As the two medics reached the pier at Innisfallen they were shot dead by a sniper firing from the island. Fearing for his own life, Roberts dived for cover, and later returned to the mainland where he alerted the military authorities to what had happened. The army carried out a thorough search of Innisfallen, but those responsible for the double killing had long since left the island.[23]

People in Killarney were shocked by the deaths of the two soldiers, both because of the men's relative youth and the fact that they were unarmed and on a tourist trip to the lake at the time of their deaths. Father Jarlath, speaking at mass in the Franciscan friary later that evening, was unequivocal in his condemnation of the republican attack, in which he described '… the brutality and callousness of a foul deed … not justified in lawful warfare, and considering the Irish Bishops' pronouncement on armed resistance to the supreme authority of the will of the Irish people. The commission of such a crime ... would not be tolerated ... or carried out even by uncivilised tribes.' He finished his homily by telling the congregation that, at the request of the people of Killarney, 7 a.m. masses at the Franciscan friary for the next two weeks would be offered for the repose of the souls of Fitzgerald and O'Meara.[24]

On Friday, 18 August, a large motorised column left Killarney for Rathmore with the twin aims of consolidating the foothold they had established there three days earlier and carrying out a wider reconnaissance of the east Kerry area. The importance of the patrol to the national army was reflected by the fact that the convoy was commanded both by Brigadier Paddy O'Daly and Colonel James McGuinness, the two most senior officers in the Dublin Guard, and included both an armoured car and an eighteen-pounder field gun in its arsenal as contingency in the event of a major confrontation with the enemy. The republicans decided to ambush the convoy, seeing it as the thin edge of the wedge, and reckoning a strong assault would be the best way to deter further incursions into a salient that was for them a safe area. In fact, the sinewy roads that wound around the Clydagh valley and along the edges of the Derrynasaggart mountains were part of a republican enclave that stretched from east Kerry across the Cork border as far east as Ballyvourney and Macroom, which would remain a no-go area for the Free State army even up to the end of hostilities in May 1923.

We are fortunate to have a first-hand account of the ambush from a republican perspective as well as the pro-government newspaper coverage provided by the army. Jeremiah Murphy, fighting on the republican side, noted the ambush party consisted of seventy riflemen.[25] As the total pool of active republicans in east Kerry at this time was about one hundred members, an attack of this strength represented a no-holds-barred assault, with every available rifle being committed to the fray.

The convoy reached Barraduff about 3 p.m. and divided in two, with part of the column – which included marching troops under O'Daly's command – continuing on towards Rathmore, while a touring car with Red Cross markings (indicating that it was designated as an ambulance) followed by several lorries drove in the direction of Headford. Anticipating the convoy would cross Droum bridge, the republicans hastily began work on a trench that would halt the column at a point that provided the best target, while the riflemen took up positions along the hillside at points between 200 and 600 yards above the road. Time constraints meant that two of the republicans, Jerry Kennedy and Tim Daly, were putting the final touches to the trench when the touring car (with Colonel James McGuinness among its passengers) stopped and troops got out and began filling in the trench.

At this point Kennedy and Daly (senior officers in east Kerry) inadvertently walked out in front of the troops filling in the trench, and were fired upon on the assumption they were leading an attack. The republicans returned fire and wounded four soldiers, including Colonel James McGuinness, who was hit in the head and was bleeding profusely. He was pulled to safety by Lieutenant Reddy, who completed filling in the trench. Meanwhile, Daly and Kennedy, carrying the rifles they had captured from wounded men, returned to their own lines, forcing their men to hold their fire at a point that was very opportune for the government troops. Hearing the gunfire from the Rathmore Road, O'Daly's troops arrived on the scene, and all hell broke loose as Kennedy and Daly were out of the line of fire. Amid the din and confusion twenty-one-year-old Corporal Niall Harrington held his nerve and correctly identified the source of the gunfire, an action that would see him promoted from corporal to second lieutenant, one of a few occasions that a field promotion occurred in Kerry during the Civil War.[26]

The armoured car's Vickers machine-gun concentrated fire on the areas pinpointed by Harrington, while the eighteen-pounder discharged a few shells in the same direction. According to Jeremiah Murphy the republicans suffered no casualties, but their attack was stopped in its tracks by 'superior numbers and armaments'. Murphy took a degree of satisfaction from the fact that the Droum ambush was the only occasion that the field gun was used in east Kerry, in itself a compliment of sorts to the seventy riflemen. As they left the scene the Free State column abandoned two lorries, which the republicans duly burned. This seems a very short-sighted response, as retaining the lorries for their own use would have given the republicans much needed mobility in their campaign at a time when motorised transport was both a scarce and valuable commodity.

More often than not, a small-scale exchange of fire could prove more lethal than a 'firefight' as big as the one in east Kerry. At 8 p.m. on the same evening as the Droum ambush, four soldiers escorting a prisoner, and travelling between Fenit and Tralee, were challenged by republicans near Dan Lyons' pub in Spa, which was used as an outpost by the national army. Sergeant Jack Lydon, a native of James Street, Tralee was hit in the head and died on the spot. He was twenty-nine years old and had arrived in Tralee with the Dublin Guard on 2 August.

According to Niall Harrington, four republicans took part in the attack, including Jim Walsh of Churchill, who would be killed in the Ballyseedy landmine execution in March 1923, and George Nagle of Ballygamboon, Castlemaine who would die in Derrynafeana, Glencar in one of the last clashes between Free State and republican forces in late April of the same year.[27]

Against the wider backdrop of political violence ordinary crime received scant media coverage and got little attention from the civil authorities. The *Cork Examiner* of 18 August devoted a paragraph to the killing of Michael O'Driscoll of Bannow, Camp, who was shot dead by two men with a rifle, in what (the paper claimed) was believed to be a dispute over land. It is interesting that a rifle rather than a shotgun was used in the murder, suggesting possible republican collusion (a rifle being more associated with military than civilian use), if not actual participation in the killing. Significantly, O'Driscoll's next of kin would later submit a claim for malicious injuries on the basis that his death was a result of the political conflict.

In the vacuum created by the absence of law and order, Tralee in particular experienced a spate of burglaries and armed robberies. A delegation of Tralee merchants, including J.M. Slattery (bacon factory), Samuel Hilfe (R. McCowen & Sons) and A.S. Carlton (O'Donovan & Sons) sought help from the UDC to avert crime in the town. T. Huggard, the municipal solicitor, met the delegation. In their submission the businessmen outlined the security situation in the town prior to the commencement of the current conflict. 'At one time,' the delegation began, 'we had the assistance of the military; then the auxiliaries; lately, the republicans, who had a police force of their own. They gave valuable assistance. People at the military barracks are too busy with the war to provide a police force for the town. Once Tralee had night watchmen, it has none now. If we had six good men, who would each earn £3.0.0 per week, appointed for ten weeks at a cost of £180–200, Mr. Gorman would act as the Head of the Service.'28

One of the deputation mentioned that the military authorities were willing to cooperate by way of patrols, while Samuel Hilfe, anxious to avoid political bias, commented that the republican police had given useful service in their time. Huggard cautioned against joint civilian–military patrols, lest an attack on 'police' might lead to compensation claims against the local authority who would presumably administer the *ad hoc* force until a more stable political environment would allow the deployment of a regular government police force. The proposal to establish the interim force doesn't appear to have survived the scrutiny of the meeting with Huggard. If the patrols operated in tandem with the military (who would be armed) in the volatile political environment the risk to the civilian members would be very high. Even if exclusively civilian in composition, wearing a uniform, especially when on night patrol, would place them at risk of being taken for government troops by republicans. Tralee town and its surroundings were, in August 1922 and for several months afterwards, one of the most dangerous military postings in Kerry. There were over a dozen outposts, and with prisoner escorts, guard changing and the duty (often tedious) of manning static lookout points, there were numerous target opportunities for republicans, either a lone sniper, or two or three men with revolvers and hand grenades. To avoid giving their adversaries clear targets, government troops increasingly used darkness as camouflage. Republicans adapted their tactics accordingly, with a degree of recklessness and often with consequences they hadn't intended.

At midnight on 21 August two soldiers escorting a prisoner between Ballymullen barracks and the county jail at Moyderwell were stalked by republicans. When the republicans threw their grenades they wounded two civilians, John George Foley and Thomas Horan, the latter a cattle dealer from Ballymullen, mistaking them for the military patrol.[29] Later that same morning, about 4 a.m. on Tuesday, 22 August, presumably the same unit that carried out the midnight attack, hearing a lot of talking and the sounds of revving engines at the green near one of the gates at Ballymullen barracks, assumed a large convoy was about to leave the barracks. In conditions of total darkness they lobbed five hand grenades over the wall to initiate the assault, following up the explosions with concentrated rifle and revolver fire. The number of casualties ensuing from the rifle fire was reduced as a consequence of Captain James Burke and Lieutenant Timothy McMahon shouting to both soldiers and prisoners alike to dive to the ground so as to reduce their profile as a target. Ironically both James Burke and Timothy McMahon would be dead within a week of the 'green' attack. The bulk of the men (105) in the convoy were republican prisoners, escorted by a relatively small army patrol. Fortunately for all concerned, two of the five grenades failed to explode, but those that did wounded five prisoners and three soldiers. One of the soldiers, Private John Galworthy of Inisboffin, County Galway and a prisoner, Thomas Drummond (twenty-five), a married man with four children, living at 32 Rea Street, Tralee and a labourer at O'Donovan's mills, were seriously injured, suffering multiple shrapnel wounds. Galworthy died at the county infirmary on Thursday, 24 August, Drummond losing his life at the Bon Secour hospital later that same day.[30]

While the margin for error in republican attacks was much greater in Tralee urban area after dark than elsewhere in Kerry, it could not be said with any degree of certainty that it was safe to drive the roads of Kerry even in broad daylight. In mid-August, Edmund Burke, an Irish American who lived in New York but was originally from Miltown Malbay in County Clare, returned to Ireland for the first time in thirty-two years. As he drove over Headley's Bridge he was fired upon by republicans who assumed his Ford was the advance scout car that travelled ahead of a motorised column. Privately owned motor cars were extremely rare in Kerry at this time, and as army officers often used their own vehicles, in nine cases out of ten the assumption that the car was an advance vehicle would be an accurate one. Unfortunately for Edmund Burke he was the exception that proved the rule, and his wounds were serious enough to necessitate amputating his arm; a bystander who stood watching as the car drove by was also slightly wounded in the attack.[31] Commenting on the incident, Colonel Michael Hogan noted he had been fired upon at the same spot a few days earlier, and that the shots were usually used as a signal to the rest of the ambush party to ready themselves for action.

Notwithstanding their setback the previous Friday afternoon, at Droum Bridge, the Free State authorities appear to have acquired accurate intelligence on the republican command structure in east Kerry. Acting on this information, on Tuesday, 22 August, a small patrol commanded by Paddy O'Daly surrounded Michael Fleming's house in Kilcummin, believing it to be the republicans' east Kerry headquarters. O'Daly's challenge to the occupants to surrender solicited a hand grenade by way of a reply, wounding a soldier named Grimes, with O'Daly himself taking a minor shrapnel wound in the thigh. Troops opened fire on the upper floor of the house, wounding a girl who had no political involvement. This focused the occupants to call 'cease fire' and six troops under Captain Conroy stormed the house, taking William Fleming, Con O'Leary, Daniel Mulvihil and Thomas Daly (a first cousin of Dr Charles O'Sullivan, bishop of Kerry) prisoners, as well as a number of other occupants of the house.[32]

During the follow-up search troops confiscated six revolvers with 300 rounds of ammunition, three rifles with 100 rounds, a dozen hand grenades, a Ford car and several documents. As they made their way back to the road, the party came under fire from the very scouts that should have prevented them surrounding the house in the first place. Private Thomas Kavanagh of North Circular Road, Dublin was shot dead and a prisoner named O'Brien was wounded. Later that same evening Captain Peadar O'Brien captured Patrick Allman (a brother of the late Dan Allman, who lost his life at the Headford junction ambush in March 1921) near Farranfore in what was overall a good day for Kerry command.[33]

The Provisional Government lost its most important political and military leader, Michael Collins, as darkness fell over a west Cork bohereen at Béal na mBláth on Tuesday, 22 August 1922. As the small convoy, consisting of an armoured car, a touring car and an assortment of other vehicles, stopped to clear a road block, the escort leader, Emmet Dalton, ordered his men to drive on. Collins, whose judgement was clouded by an intake of alcohol during his tour of west Cork, overruled Dalton, saying, with a sense of bravado, 'No. We'll fight them.' Abandoning the cover provided by the armoured car, Collins initially crawled along the roadside, but unable to get a proper view stood up, and advanced towards the point he thought the firing was coming from. He was hit in the head, possibly from a ricochet bullet, and died at the scene.

Richard Mulcahy succeeded Collins as commander-in-chief of the army, and despite numerous calls for reprisals (against the republican prisoners held in custody) by the more vengeful officers in the Free State army, who idolised Collins, Mulcahy refused to sanction any mass killings. In republican folklore, Mulcahy and Kevin O'Higgins administered the 'murder bill' that led to the execution of seventy-seven republicans. If the more hot-headed officers had had their way scores of republican prisoners would have met their deaths in the wake of the Collins assassination.

George Orwell, who served with an anarchist militia in the Spanish Civil War, a conflict about as far removed ideologically and politically from the Irish Civil War as one can imagine, writing in *Homage to Catalonia* on the ordinary soldier's experience of that conflict and war generally, noted it was 'hours of boredom interspersed by moments of sheer terror'. The effects of boredom, combined with a lack of respect for the lethal nature of the weapons they were dealing with, could lead to pranks or 'play acting' which occasionally had tragic results. The 1st Westerns were responsible for guarding the harbour at the canal basin, Tralee, and a seven-man unit was billeted in a house nearby. A sergeant coming to inspect the post was appalled to see one of the soldiers, John Beatty of Lettermore, County Galway holding a grenade in his hand, from which he had already removed the pin. The NCO shouted at Beatty to throw the grenade in the canal; as he did so the missile exploded, wounding both Beatty and Volunteer Denny Woods from Mountshannon, County Clare. In the days following the incident both men would die of their wounds.[34]

Soldiers could also be at risk as they handled faulty or poor quality ordinance. As a precaution, and to be able to respond to attacks like the ones carried out overnight on 21–2 August, patrols travelling to and from Ballymullen barracks began carrying hand grenades in webbing pouches. On the night of August 25 a four-man patrol *en route* to Moyderwell were unfortunate enough to have a grenade fall out of its webbing. The patrol commander, Lieutenant Timothy McMahon (twenty-five) of Miltown Malbay, dived to the ground to throw the grenade away in case it exploded. The impact of the grenade hitting the ground must have knocked the pin out, and in the subsequent explosion, McMahon and Sergeant Michael Roche (twenty-eight) from Connolly, County Clare were killed and the other two men in the patrol were wounded.[35]

On Friday, 25 August a large force of Dublin Guards commanded by Fionán Lynch, Minister for Education, who held the rank of general in the Free State army, set out for Kenmare with the intention of both relieving and strengthening the garrison that Tom O'Connor-Scarteen had established in south Kerry two weeks earlier. The geographic isolation of the Kenmare military enclave from the rest of the county meant that the troops stationed there could only be contacted and supplied by sea. As the relative deprivation Killarney was experiencing in basic foodstuffs due to the cessation of the rail service deepened, a road link to the harbour on the Kenmare river would have represented a huge advance on several fronts.

Although their predicament as citizens was not a priority for the Provisional Government, the Protestant population of south Kerry, who might be described as from an Anglo-Irish or landed gentry background, found themselves the victims of what approached a pogrom of house burning initiated by republicans over the summer months. Sir Henry Stokes, who lived at Askive, Sneem, writing to his son in Canada, noted:

> The district has been almost entirely isolated since July; no posts, telegrams or newspapers, and no means of communication with the outside world except by casual coasting boats; roads destroyed and bridges blown up; and all means of transport stolen or smashed. The first news ... we learned that Askive was looted and burned early in August; and afterwards that Derriquin was attacked 13 nights in succession, the turret room broken into, sacked, and set on fire, which went out of itself. Colonel Warden was shot at, and the gardens and cottages in the demesne destroyed. On the 28 August, Warden and his wife escaped to Kenmare; on that day and the 29th, the castle was cleared out; and on the 30th it was burnt, and nothing remains but the bare walls. Derreen, Lord Lansdowne's place ... is totally destroyed. What has become of Dromore Castle and Dromquinna is still unknown. Similar things have happened in other parts of Ireland, and are daily reported.[36]

At this point the arson attacks on the property of the minority community or the economic deprivation of the ordinary Kerry household were far down the list of priorities the government had to tackle in Kerry. In the 'Kingdom' (that would be a republic) military and security considerations were paramount.

As Lynch's column advanced along the Killarney–Kilgarvan road, it came under fire from republicans at Filadown, near Glenfesk. This brought the ironic comment from Captain Stan Bishop to Fionán Lynch, TD for the area: 'I believe some of your constituents would like to talk with you.'[37] Reaching a particularly steep rocky cliff face known locally as Robbers Den, the intensity of republican rifle fire increased, wounding eight of the soldiers in the Free State convoy. Even though there was an eighteen-pounder in their arsenal the steep cliffs rendered it useless and as this, combined with the descending darkness, favoured the riflemen, Lynch and his colleagues decided that retreat was the best form of advance, as to drive any further into the ambush would lead to the engulfment of the entire government force. The army issued a statement to the effect that in a follow-up search of the area the next day they discovered twenty bodies.[38] This was purely a face-saving exercise, giving the impression that they had inflicted heavy casualties on the enemy prior to retreating. In reality, the republican tradition honoured the dead with highly symbolic militaristic funeral rituals; dead bodies would not have been abandoned where they fell. In a further press release (presumably focusing on the same incident) in early September the authorities announced that Erskine Childers had been wounded, possibly killed, in an engagement between Killarney and Kenmare.

At 3 a.m. on Sunday, 27 August, twenty-eight-year-old Seán Moriarty was taken from his home at Walpole Lane, Tralee by armed men who wore trench coats, green pants and green leggings, and who, according to his mother (in evidence given to a later enquiry) accused him of being at a recruiting at the barracks, a charge he vociferously denied. At the same time James Healy, a former British soldier, was roused from his bed at No. 11 Cowen's Lane and joined Moriarty on a walk to a field in

Ballonagh, where both men were shot several times and left for dead. Moriarty died of his wounds but Healy survived his injuries by lying as still as possible and by pretending to be dead until the assassins had left the scene of the double killing.[39]

It is unclear why the Squad singled out these two men as suitable candidates for their first *ad hoc* execution in Kerry. It is possible that the military authorities may have obtained information to the effect that Moriarty and Healy had some involvement with the Ballymullen barracks grenade attack of a few evenings earlier. The reality is we will probably never know the real reason for their selection. Whatever the motive, the action crossed the line; and over a four-month period between September and December 1922 Kerry command carried out a further nineteen executions of republican prisoners.[40]

On Monday, 28 August, a column of 1st Westerns under the command of Captain James Burke of Dunmanway, County Cork left Killorglin on a march to Tralee. They came under fire at Steelroe, about two miles outside Killorglin. The ambush party, four men armed with rifles and a Lewis gun, was too small to successfully challenge the column, reputedly consisting of almost one hundred men, and was overwhelmed and captured. The report noted two of the prisoners were from Cork, and there was particular satisfaction in capturing a Lewis gun. The column came under fire for a second time at Castlemaine, in a gun battle that lasted for two and a half hours. Captain James Burke, who was on horseback and at the head of the column, was shot dead near Castlemaine railway bridge. The national army claimed to have killed six and wounded seventeen anti-Treatyites during this engagement, which was the principal ambush in what was a hard march to Tralee. The report contained no details of the column's own casualties apart from Burke's death, and one would be extremely sceptical of the estimates of republican casualties provided by the army. Smaller attacks occurred about a half-mile on the Tralee side of Castlemaine (in what might be described as Humphrey Murphy's own back yard) and near Quills Cross. The final assault, which resulted in the death of Volunteer Connors of Ennistymon, County Clare, occurred towards midnight, as the column entered Ballyseedy wood on the final approaches to Tralee.[41] The multiple ambushes on the column indicate a coordinated campaign of harassment carried out by local republicans and was unique only in the sense that operations on this scale were so rare.

Two soldiers on sentry duty at a checkpoint at the top of High Street, Killarney at 9.30 p.m. the same evening (Monday, 28 August) had a grenade thrown at them. No one was hurt, but a civilian had a narrow escape; the only casualties were two cows belonging to Michael Cronin, who were injured as they grazed in a field on Rock Road. Troops arrested a young fellow named O'Connor, who admitted throwing the bomb. The relative inexperience of O'Connor, the republican volunteer who carried out the attack, reflects the hit-and-miss approach of many IRA assaults on the Free State army carried out in urban areas (Ballymullen, 21/22 August), which suggests a desire to get the attack over as quickly as possible so as to avoid being killed, wounded or captured once the enemy returned fire.

On other occasions, such as shots being fired at GS & WR employees repairing the line at Ballyseedy on Wednesday, 30 August or the rifle fire that wounded four soldiers on board a train at the Deer Park as they returned to Killarney having provided a combined work crew and military escort at the same repair site, shots were primarily fired as a deterrent. The Kerry rail network was constantly under attack. Each time the line was damaged follow-up repairs restored the rails to a serviceable working order. The long-term effect of the disruption of the rail service was more acutely felt by the civilian population. The mental hospital in Killarney, for example, was forced to reduce its daily bread rations from 10oz to 8oz per man, and from 7oz to 6oz per woman. There were also acute shortages of tea, sugar, rice and new milk for 540 patients. Allowances of tea and sugar for inmates of the county home (360), and Killarney hospital (64) were also considerably reduced.[42]

Republicans visited the *Kerry People* print works on 31 August and removed the main printing press, causing the newspaper to cease publication.[43] Maurice Ryle, the owner/editor, would later submit a compensation claim of £1,050 for the loss of the equipment. It would probably be more difficult to put a price on the loss of press freedom.

On Sunday, 3 September, a letter from Dr O'Sullivan, the bishop of Kerry condemning the murder of the two unarmed Red Cross soldiers at Innisfallen was read out at mass by the parish priest, Father Casey, at Curragheen church. An anti-Treaty leader in the congregation blew a whistle, whereupon the IRA left the church *en masse,* and held a meeting outside the church which criticised Fr Casey and challenged his knowledge of politics. The IRA action at Curragheen church was not unique either, as republicans carried out similar walkout protests at churches in Abbeydorney, Ballymacelligott, Clogher and Currow.[44]

In extreme cases, the criticism of individual clergymen precipitated even more direct action. Father Alexander O'Sullivan,

CC, Milltown, a chaplain in the British army during the First World War and described as a vehement supporter of government action, was shot at on Saturday evening, 2 September as he walked along the Milltown–Castlemaine road near the wall of the Godfrey estate. Four shots were fired; Fr O'Sullivan jumped over the wall where he believed the shots originated to pursue the assailant.[45]

More politically astute republicans such as 'Dead Eye' Dave Robinson, a cousin of Erskine Childers from County Tipperary, who served in the tank corps in the British army during the First World War, and who took part in republican assaults on Kenmare and Killorglin that September, was concerned for the safety of clerics such as O'Sullivan. Fr O'Sullivan's actual welfare was not his prime concern, but the propaganda value the death of a priest at the hands of republicans would provide for both the government and pro-government newspapers like the *Freeman's Journal*.[46]

On Saturday, 2 September Colonel Hogan, 1st Western division, commandeered some forty horses and carts, got them loaded in Tralee, and put a convoy of troops to guard them by road as far as Farranfore. Three miles from Tralee, at Ballymacthomas, fire was opened on the convoy. Troops returned fire, but there were no injuries. At Farranfore the supplies were guarded overnight, and next morning they were sent to Killarney by train. This was the first 'humanitarian food convoy' organised by the national army in Kerry. The gesture was as much about satisfying hearts and minds across Kerry as it was about filling mouths and stomachs in Killarney.[47]

John Joe Sheehy had a permanent force of three columns (about 70–75 men) stationed in the Ballymacthomas area, as

Ashill, the point where the Tralee–Killarney road and rail lines converged, provided an ideal ambush location from which to harass the three daily (exclusively military) convoys that travelled each way between Tralee and Killarney.[48] From a republican perspective any convoy guarded by troops was seen as a legitimate military target, in the same way that Red Cross medical orderlies who wore army uniforms – but were unarmed – were seen as an essential part of the enemy war effort.

The practice of ambushing the 'military component' escorting food supplies primarily destined for civilian use reputedly caused dissent within republican ranks. According to an article in the *Cork Examiner* entitled 'Mutiny among the Irregulars', there was '… controversy arising out of the recent ambush of a food convoy between Tralee and Killarney at Farranfore. Tom McEllistrim was opposed to the attack, whereas Humphrey Murphy favoured the tactic. At Farmers Bridge, in an argument over the tactic, blows were exchanged and shots fired. The majority sided with the McEllistrim view. Only a hard core, 40, backed Murphy, who said "he could hold Tralee for three years against any force any Irish Government would sent against him".'[49]

There is no independent source of verification of this report, other than newspaper coverage – the *Cork Examiner* and the *Freeman's Journal* – so we have no way of knowing how many of the details, if any, are factual, and how much is spin issued by army sources. Tom McEllistrim was independent minded, and had a genuine concern for the way the conflict was impacting on the civilian population, as well as the damage intercepting food convoys was causing to the perception of the republican campaign in wider public opinion across Kerry. In reality, each IRA column was an intensely local unit, and more often than not its cohesion was reinforced by a personal loyalty to a charismatic leader. In this context, McEllistrim's men would have supported his stance. In practical terms he could have decided not to participate in similar actions in the future. Realistically the differences of opinion could be more accurately described as dissent rather than mutiny within the ranks. As O/C Kerry No. 1 brigade, Humphrey Murphy was senior to Tom McEllistrim and took a far more militaristic approach to confronting the enemy than McEllistrim. At a later stage in the conflict it was Murphy who declared that any vehicle bearing Red Cross markings would be regarded as an armoured car rather than an ambulance and would be treated accordingly by the men in his command.

If there was a difference of opinion within republican ranks on the morality of attacking food convoys primarily aimed at assisting civilians, the crisis of conscience was short lived, as such attacks continued unabated over the winter and spring of 1922–3. As the sole representatives of the civil power in Kerry, the army had no choice other than provide armed escorts to ensure safe delivery of supplies in a county where both opportunistic criminals commandeered goods and republican columns provisioned their armies by scavenging food from larger farmers or robbing items such as bacon or flour, from the larger wholesalers in Kerry. In early September, the *Cork Examiner* reported the looting of large quantities of butter and twenty bullocks in the Castlemaine district. Given the times that were in it, it is probable that many such crimes were dealt with and resolved locally.

The *Cork Examiner*, in a vociferous editorial addressing the issue of republican interference with food supplies in Kerry, pulled no punches when it stated:

The measures being taken in Killarney in connection with the flour supply (pending the appointment of a flour controller, to be chosen by the people) serve to emphasise the fact that an artificial famine has been created by those who have interrupted the ordinary distribution services. One wonders if those responsible for this temporary hold up of the people's chief article of food in parts of Kerry are proud of this achievement, or do they believe that they are helping Ireland's cause by inflicting loss and inconvenience on the helpless classes? The people of Kerry have always been recognised as the keenest and cleverest in Ireland, and Killarney, which in the past not only fed its own population but provided large numbers of tourists with excellent – even luxurious – fare, is now to all intents and purposes to be rationed because a number of individuals have seen it fit to put the railways out of gear, and to make the roads impassable. What is the meaning of this attack on the people is difficult to understand, but common sense should enable this minority to see that these methods of procedure will neither add to their popularity nor bring a single convert to their views. The present phase is only a passing one, as ample military measures will certainly be adopted to ensure for the different Kerry towns an ample food supply, and steps in this direction have already been taken in Tralee. It is scarcely likely that Killarney, or any other Kerry centre will admit the right of any section to put them on short rations … politics may, and do, create differences of opinion, but to cut down a man's breakfast because he does not agree with him … Even John Bull didn't attempt this. The sad part is, it is old people, sick people, lunatics and growing children are the ones being most put out by short rations. People will remarkably put up with rationing; but they will not surrender indefinitely to outside interference with their daily bread.[50]

Regardless of press criticism, the republican campaign against the railways continued. During the first week in September a railway bridge at Kilmorrna, near Listowel, was blown up. Telegraph lines were cut, and a smaller bridge between Tralee and Ardfert was destroyed. While all these attacks occurred in remote rural areas, well away from any measures the authorities could take to prevent them, a midnight raid on Killarney station on

Wednesday 6 September aimed at burning the signal cabin was successfully beaten off as it occurred virtually on the doorstep of the Great Southern hotel, the national army's Killarney HQ.

On Monday, 4 September it seemed a maritime solution was already in operation to alleviate the acute food shortages caused by the republican disruption of land transport networks in Kerry. A steamer of the Moore and McCormack line had sailed for Kerry the previous week with 2,600 tons of grain and flour on board. According to the *Cork Examiner*, 'the company had established a regular sailing between Cork, Kenmare and Caherciveen, which they intend to maintain. This will be gratifying news to the inhabitants of the county [the report concluded] and do much to relieve the hardship of a sorely tried people.'

The news did not go unnoticed within republican circles in south Kerry either. It seems the republican assault on Saturday, 9 September, which successfully overwhelmed the national army garrison at Kenmare, was initially planned to intercept the cargo carried by the Moore and McCormack vessel, in particular stores of provisions, food and ammunition carried for the benefit of the military billeted in Kenmare. The local garrison had an effective strength of 130 troops when the assault occurred, and about half of the force had been on overnight manoeuvres in Scarteen townland (where the original O'Connor farm was located) and the districts immediately south-west of Kenmare, hoping to encircle the republicans that O'Connor-Scarteen's intelligence network believed were about to sabotage the family farm as a prelude to ambushing the patrol sent to investigate the reports of republican activity in the area. Ironically, a local republican scout, awaiting the arrival of the republican assault force, which approached the town from the east, observed the O'Connor patrol (about sixty to seventy men) returning home scarcely half an hour before the eighty-seven-man force under the command of John Joe Rice had planned to commence their attack on the town, 7 a.m. Had the two forces' paths crossed *en route* to Kenmare that morning, events in the town that Saturday might have taken a very different course, at the very least for the life spans of the O'Connor brothers.

According to Jeremiah Murphy of Barraduff, who took part in the attack, most of the force (about seventy men in all) were drawn from the Loo Bridge (3rd) and Kilgarvan (5th) battalion areas and were mostly riflemen. In order to give the assault a cutting edge – it was the first time republicans had attempted to overwhelm several well fortified military outposts simultaneously in an urban area – John Joe Rice sought thirty men proficient in the use of rifle grenades (the 1920s equivalent of rocket-propelled grenades) from the Ballyvourney battalion area in County Cork.[51] In the event only seventeen turned up, but their input proved decisive, the psychological impact of the grenades on the defending garrison as significant as the physical damage they caused to the buildings.

About a mile outside Kenmare the republican force split into three sections; each group was allocated two local men, who briefed them on the geography of the town and the location and strength of the army positions. The National bank, and some adjacent buildings, the Lansdowne hotel and the Carnegie library were identified by local intelligence (i.e. Kenmare republicans) as the important targets. The Lansdowne hotel was not used by the military at all, whereas the workhouse was, but as it was not included, as soon as the republicans opened fire in the centre of the town the troops stationed there abandoned the building. While the main attack was under way, a maverick force of five men – some wearing Free State uniforms – proceeded to the O'Connor home at No. 5 Main Street, where both Tom O'Connor (twenty) and his older brother, John (twenty-four) were sleeping off the effects of the earlier night patrol. Though it was effectively the command headquarters, no one had seen the need to post armed sentries to control entry to the building.

According to Nora O'Sullivan (aged twelve) and Kathleen Moriarty (aged nineteen), relatives of the family who were both employed as maids in the O'Connor household, John O'Connor was shot twice as he descended the stairwell of the house to see what was causing the commotion at the entrance. His brother Tom was dragged from his bed and shot in the head.[52] The republican version of the event, as recalled by Dan 'Ballagh' Keating of Castlemaine, was that Con Looney and 'Sailor' Dan Healy carried out the shooting: 'They [the O'Connors] were called upon to put up their hands, but instead went to draw their guns. So they were shot dead. They had no other option.'[53]

If the republicans (Looney, Healy *et al.*) shot out of self defence, it would have been possible to wound the O'Connors in both the hands and legs, rendering them immobile and incapable of returning fire. It seems the brothers were regarded as renegades by their former comrades and were summarily executed in a vendetta killing. Throughout the Civil War both sides engaged in reprisal killings almost on a routine 'tit for tat' basis. While the O'Connors lay dying, Jeremiah Murphy's unit was firing on the Carnegie library. The building was well protected, both by sandbags and steel shutters, and small arms fire had virtually no impact, so it was decided to use rifle grenades. Around 8 a.m. the section was summoned to the railway station and ordered to assist the force attacking the National bank – an impressive cut stone building – and the adjacent houses on Main Street, the principal Free State strong-point in Kenmare. Around the same time several national army men converged from the neighbouring houses to join the garrison in the National bank which was coming under concentrated fire (diagonally) from the houses across the street. The republicans had used 'linking' (tunnelling through several houses or an entire street) to devastating effect, seeming to the defending garrison to appear out of nowhere and creating the impression that they were under attack from a much larger force than was actually the case.

'It was pitiful,' Kathleen Moriarty recalled, 'to hear these men calling for Scarteen. They [republicans] tunnelled from a shop – Maybury's – down through Meighans and half a dozen other houses, and right into the sitting room of our own house. And battered their way through into Murphy's opposite the bank.'[54] The proximity of the two forces led to confusion; an incident highlighted by Jeremiah Murphy when his unit broke through a fireplace into an a joining house is worth noting. 'When the occupants [of the house] saw us they thought we were some of their own men and they asked us for ammunition. At first I thought they were our own men, as they were dressed in civilian clothes and I almost gave them some ammunition. The mistake was cleared when they fired through the hole and I got hit by a splinter of a bullet as it ricocheted off a stone.'

Murphy was taken to the adjacent pub to get his wound (to his nose) dressed, and enjoy a local anaesthetic. In the ten-minute interval while he was away the republicans threw an incendiary bomb into the room where the government troops were concentrated, and the occupants surrendered. Among them was the soldier whose shot had wounded Jeremiah Murphy a few moments earlier. 'My pal recognised him, and might have shot him there and then, but I suddenly raised the barrel of his rifle, and the bullet went through the ceiling.'[55]

The incident shows how narrow the line was between life and death in the conflict, and more chillingly how quickly individuals (in this instance a republican) could initiate a reprisal killing. About twenty minutes later the occupants of the National bank surrendered, paving the way for a republican victory in the town centre. The Carnegie library was still holding out and the supply boat docked on the Kenmare river, guarded by a six-man complement, was trapped by a low tide, on the cusp of turning. But the republicans were lucky and captured the vessel and its contents, ironically the initial purpose of a raid which was far more successful than it ought to have been. The inexperience of the defending troops and the vacuum left in the Free State command structure by Tom O'Connor-Scarteen's death at the start of the engagement were crucial factors in the loss of Kenmare. By 2 p.m. the guns finally fell silent in Kenmare, and the republicans who had captured the town found themselves responsible for the welfare of 130 prisoners, including the younger brother of Kevin O'Higgins, TD, the Provisional Government justice minister, although the republicans at that stage don't seem to have been politically astute enough either to see the practical use (as a hostage) or propaganda value of such a high-profile captive. Of course, at such an early point in the conflict, not least because they were in the throes of victory, even brigade commanders such as John Joe

Rice could only see the war strategy in the short and immediate term. Among the prisoners under their control were fourteen wounded, though none of the injuries was life threatening. Interestingly, the *Irish Times* would record the government troops' casualties as four dead and nine wounded.

Local reaction to the fall of Kenmare was mixed. At one level virtually everyone in the area was shocked and appalled by the double murder of the O'Connor brothers. On the other hand there was a degree of admiration and a sense of local pride for the republicans as 'one of our own', i.e. local people/Kerrymen, that even stretched to some government supporters, for the grit and determination they showed in 'putting it up' to the metropolitan army and forcing them to surrender. Barth Houlihan (my mother's uncle), a butcher from Killorglin, was in Kenmare in the wake of the 9 September assault, buying cattle from local smallholders, as livestock fairs had ceased in Kerry since the start of hostilities. The main topic of conversation in town and country was 'the boring of the holes', the term local people used to describe linking.[56] People were amazed that not only were buildings no protection against a determined enemy, but entire streets, if necessary, could be knocked through to obtain the objective.

The capture of such a large number of prisoners placed their would-be jailers in a dilemma. The reality was that the republicans had neither a holding centre to incarcerate the prisoners nor rations to feed them, and as none of the individual units involved in the attack could spare men to guard a prison camp it was decided to march the men under armed escort in the direction of Kilgarvan. After a few miles the prisoners were effectively released and told their best option was to return to Killarney.

The Kenmare victory was not only a huge morale boost for the republican war effort in Kerry but John Joe Rice, O/C Kerry No. 2, found himself in possession of 110 rifles, two Lewis guns, a large quantity of grenades and 20,000 rounds of ammunition, as well as a supply of army uniforms which had never been worn, as the September delivery brought the first supplies to reach Kenmare since 10 August when the O'Connors established a military outpost in the town. The Cork brigades wanted a cut of the Kenmare haul, but Rice was adamant he would not part with a single rifle. He did give ammunition, however; Ballyvourney and Cork No. 5 brigade received 5,000 and 4,000 rounds respectively, while each of the six battalions in Kerry No. 2 was allocated 2,000 rounds.[57] This was a huge boost, as up to that point each man was only given fifteen to twenty rounds per engagement; now they could contemplate much larger exchanges of fire or, alternatively, a series of small ambushes stretching over a period of months.

The Free State authorities admitted that the anti-Treatyites were well armed and that the attack was well planned, involving about five hundred men in all; a highly inflated figure given the actual size of the force (eighty-seven) was almost fifty men below the level of the garrison defending Kenmare. The government press coverage focused particularly on the brutal murder of the O'Connor brothers as proof of the anti-Treatyites' ignominy. In fact, many involved on the republican side at Kenmare were saddened (if not angered) by the double killing. Tom McEllistrim, for example, visited the O'Connor home to offer his condolences to the bereaved and next of kin.[58]

Apart from the capture of military material, the victory at Kenmare brought much by way of booty in the form of general cargo on board the vessels docked at Kenmare pier. Volunteer Jeremiah Murphy recalls the bonanza the ships provided for the ordinary members of the local battalion, who at the best of times had to scavenge for food and provisions, and often as not led a hand-to-mouth existence. 'The next day,' Murphy wrote, 'we rounded up a convoy of horses and carts from Loo Bridge to Clydagh and took them to Kenmare to remove supplies from the ship. Arriving there early in the afternoon we found that another ship, similar to the first, had sailed into the bay and, being ignorant of the situation because it had no radio, was also captured. The activity on the pier was like that around a beehive on a sunny day. As fast as the winches could load them, a long line of horse-drawn carts drove away to our haunts. This was just what we needed – a good haul.'[59]

Below-cost selling by republicans in the wider Kenmare area meant that *bona fide* trade wholesalers could not get orders in the locality:

A commercial traveller from Cork city was selling his product when the shopkeeper told him he got exactly the same quantity of goods at half price from Kenmare. It suddenly dawned on him that trade had been forestalled by those who on capturing the town helped themselves to the cargoes which had just arrived in from Cork, which included a large quantity of the article consigned by his own firm to a Kenmare trader. Capture of two cargoes has brought prices down with a rush in County Kerry. The Traveller, who is not in the Whiskey trade, observed what happened when some barrels of that precious liquid arrived in Kenmare. One was immediately tapped and its contents were taken away in buckets. It would have been a matter of little difficulty to retake the town that night in spite of the presence of five hundred Irregulars in the town. He arrived at Knocknagree. Two soldiers on bicycles were at the head of a column of National troops. A man fired a shot from a doorway, but the bullet lodged between the handle bars. Troops returned fire but the gunman escaped. Three men were arrested, but the Trader noted two women wearing shawls were each able to get away carrying a machine-gun.[60]

The latter part of the account shows the sometimes surreal quality of the conflict in Kerry at the time, but the feature also indicates the invisible hand of the censor, insofar as five hundred was the 'official' (i.e. government estimate) strength of the IRA in Kenmare. By pure coincidence, Saturday, 9 September 1922 was also the inaugural sitting of the third Dáil in Leinster House in Dublin, the first occasion the TDs and the Provisional Government ministers had formally convened since the 16 June general election. Having being deferred on several occasions (at Collins' behest) it was primarily the arrival of W. T. Cosgrave as Collins' successor (on 25 August) that enabled the parliamentarians to be given the right to attend the national assembly. In reality, Michael Collins was happy to have the opportunity to bring the Civil War to a successful conclusion, without having to justify the government's actions on the 'battlefield' or have the executive's actions and policies subject to scrutiny by parliamentarians, before establishing the national parliament. Even though Collins cited the dangerous political situation, and stated the personal safety of individual TDs was his prime concern, it showed an undemocratic – even a 'Bonapartist' – facet to his political profile.

The garrison at Tarbert consisted of twenty-five men drawn from the 1st Westerns. Each Sunday the force in the barracks was diminished by half to enable the troops to attend mass. This took place in the form of a church parade, where twelve men marched – in uniform, but unarmed – from their headquarters to the local church as a unit, leaving a corresponding number of men to hold the barracks. Evidently, local republicans had been monitoring these loopholes as they provided an opportunity to overpower the smaller force and in the process enable them to capture arms and ammunition, which constantly needed to be replenished to enable them to continue and expand their campaign. It is unclear if the news of the republican victory in Kenmare the previous afternoon had reached the republicans (or the garrison) in Tarbert, as it could have been the decisive factor in proceeding with the attack. As the twelve soldiers left Tarbert church after mass they were taken prisoner by the republicans, who proceeded to their barracks and called on the occupants to surrender. The remaining troops refused to do so, whereupon the republican force (which apparently only numbered six or seven men) opened fire on the building. The defenders replied in kind. As the confrontation dragged out for hours, the republicans commandeered the adjacent building and bored a hole through the wall, inserted a metal pipe, pumped petrol into the Free State headquarters and fired incendiary bullets into the building to ignite the fuel. The response of Captain Brian O'Grady and Lieutenant Egan was swift. They used every single pot, pan and container they could find to collect the fuel as it was pumped into the building. Sand bags were ripped open and their contents were spread on the floor to protect the timbers, while coming under heavy fire all the while. The garrison held out until 10 p.m. on Sunday, having no option but to surrender as their supplies of ammunition were exhausted and they could no longer keep the flames at bay. The defenders had two men wounded during the assault.[61]

Press coverage focused on the pluckiness of the defending garrison, as the army had an effective public relations machine.

Nevertheless, on the weekend of 9/10 September, 1922 both Kenmare and Tarbert were disasters for the Free State army in Kerry and were setbacks they could have done without. By the same token, they were a huge morale boost for the anti-Treaty forces in the Kingdom, and gave them the confidence to undertake more ambitious operations such as the attack on Killorglin.

While the reversal in Kenmare was a shock, the military authorities were acutely aware that its geographic isolation from the rest of the Kerry command structure would make it vulnerable to a republican attack. The same could not be said for Tarbert. The 1st Westerns' colonel Michael Hogan was furious at having his men burnt out of their barracks. On Monday, 11 September he set out from Tralee for Listowel at the head of a flying column of 120 men with the aim of capturing as many republicans as he could. The troops captured three prisoners on the first day and arrested ten men in Ballybunion the next. Subsequent sweeps in Finuge/Lixnaw, Tarbert/Ballylongford and Listowel brought in twelve, twelve and fourteen men respectively, including Paddy Landers, O/C Listowel battalion; Dr Roger O'Connor, medical officer and adjutant, Kerry No. 1 brigade; Matthew Finucane, district police inspector, Listowel; and Paddy Mahony. Hogan commented that most of the prisoners who surrendered offered little resistance, but virtually no weapons or ammunition supplies were seized. Nevertheless, he felt, a haul of fifty prisoners was a successful outcome. On 28 September a fourteen-man column surrendered at Doon, near Tralee, handing over seven rifles, two magazines for a Lewis gun and several revolvers. This policy was used widely throughout north Kerry during the course of late 1922.[62]

By mid-September the hidden (and not so hidden) costs of

the war in Kerry were becoming clearer. Kerry County Council estimated that about £118,000 was outstanding in uncollected rates, a local government tax collected primarily during July and August, when most farmers were generally well resourced financially.[63] In Killarney, most shops now only opened two or three days a week, either because they had no commodities on their shelves or because local people had little income in a tourist town without tourists. The bishop of Kerry, Charles O'Sullivan, donated £100 to a relief scheme set up to help the town's poorer and elderly citizens.

All the while republicans continued to disrupt food convoys, as they were a source of much needed supplies for their own columns (and the smallholders who provided them with shelter and accommodation) and the army hadn't the manpower to guard each and every delivery. On Saturday, 16 September a fourteen-cart unescorted convoy *en route* to Killarney was held up by armed men at Brennan's Glens, near Farranfore, and several tons of supplies were stolen. The army, in an attempt to shut the barn door after the proverbial horse had bolted, only managed to locate one or two bags of flour in a follow-up search. When the military provided an escort the convoys usually got through, habitually coming under heavy fire at several points *en route* and often at the cost of a couple of wounded men.

On Wednesday, 20 September a sixty-cart convoy was fired upon from three different points in Currans village, while in a second attack, at Ballybrack, Sergeant McSweeney, a driver (from Leeson Street Dublin) and Volunteer Dunphy, both Dublin Guards, were wounded. Around the same time an army driver named Magee died of wounds sustained in an ambush at Dysert near Castleisland a few days previously.[64]

At midnight on Sunday, 17 September, Patrick Power, a thirty-five-year-old Tralee man was walking along Rock Street when a shot rang out and killed him. The next day, a coroner's inquest returned an open verdict, which was another way of saying no one had a clue why he was killed or who might have killed him.[65] It is an illuminating insight into the jaded sense of 'conflict fatigue' that officialdom locked into in Kerry after two months of senseless killings. A few days after Power's death, Thomas Lyons, 'a thirty year old taxi driver, and a native of Muckross, Killarney in the employment of McCall of Camden Quay in Cork was driving some lady patients from the Mercy Hospital in Cork to their homes in Tralee. As he arrived at Ballycarthy Bridge, about two miles from Tralee, a shot rang out, resulting in a serious wound to the head. Fr McDonnell arranged to have the ladies conveyed by pony and trap to Tralee, and had Lyons' body taken by horse and cart to Tralee. Following the attack the car was driven away and has not been seen since.'[66]

In some respects this killing allows more speculation as to what might have happened than the open verdict surrounding Power's death. Since the start of the Civil War, Ballycarthy had been a favoured ambush point for republicans. At the time most chauffeurs and taxi drivers wore a livery which could easily be mistaken for a military uniform. Most probably the sniper identified the driver as a senior officer in the Free State army, and acted accordingly. His skill as a marksman is not in doubt. It is probable that the passengers were screened behind opaque glass and were thus invisible to the sniper. Had he chosen to spray the vehicle with gunfire no one would have survived the ambush.

Jeremiah Hannifin, a father of ten children, was seriously wounded near his residence at Knockreigh, Milltown on Saturday evening, 23 September when bullets passed through his chest and shoulders. A young boy named Robert Heffernan, who was saving hay with his father the same evening, heard shooting, and as he ran for home received flesh wounds in the neck. This has all the hallmarks of a local feud and a conflict devoid of any political context.[67]

On Tuesday, 19 September the Killorglin garrison outposts came under fire from republicans, in an engagement that lasted four hours. Even though they didn't know it at the time the republican barrage was a reconnaissance exercise aimed at evaluating the respective strengths of the three military strongpoints in the town in preparation for a much more ambitious assault the republicans were planning to launch on Killorglin the following week. Around the same time as the Killorglin ranging exercise on 19 September, a republican unit in east Kerry carried out a rifle and machine-gun attack on the barracks in Rathmore. The latter incident would be a routine action by the IRA and had no wider military objective. There were no injuries reported in either exchange of fire, but republicans also killed and maimed government troops in random attacks. Volunteer Chase, a Limerick man in the 1st Westerns, was on sentry duty at Tralee prison when he was hit in the arm by a rifle grenade. He lost a limb, but survived his injuries.[68]

A few days later Colonel Michael Hogan was driving two civilians and John Lyden, an army medic from Galway (who had missed the departure of the Dublin boat from Fenit), to Blennerville to enable them to make a later sailing. As they passed through Blennerville village, Hogan spotted what he believed was a group of anti-Treatyites. He parked his car on the bank of the canal, and as he had a pistol, he released several shots at the republicans, who returned fire. Hogan's car was peppered with bullet holes as a result of the fusillade, which also claimed Lyden's life.[69] Hogan's behaviour was reckless in the extreme. To challenge armed men when he had civilians in his party could have cost him not only his own life but also the lives of his passengers.

Government troops could also be subject to death and injury in routine weapons drill. On Saturday, 23 September, Captain Matthew McGrath (aged twenty) from Feakle in County Clare died in Listowel in what was described as an accidental shooting, though no further details were provided.[70] The next day, Sunday, 24 September Volunteer J. Looney from Ballybrack was shot dead in Killorglin while taking part in the lineout where troops coming off duty collectively removed the magazines from their rifles. The soldiers would then routinely 'clear the action', i.e. discharge a 'shot', secure in the knowledge that all the weapons were unloaded and contained no ammunition. Unfortunately, one bullet remained in the barrel of one of the rifles and the consequent shot killed Volunteer Looney, who had served in Kenmare until the 9 September reverse and was subsequently redeployed to Killorglin. He was tended to by local GP, Doctor C. Hannigan, who noted death was immediate.[71]

On Saturday night, 23 September the coastguard station at Fenit came under attack from a force that the garrison estimated at between 130 and 150 anti-Treatyites. This seems an incredible figure, as to get a force of this magnitude with sufficient weapons and ammunition to mount a sustained attack on a fixed position seems highly unlikely. Notwithstanding Hogan's sweeps, following the earlier setbacks in Tarbert (10 September), a force of this magnitude operating in darkness would be likely to inflict more casualties on itself than on the enemy. All of a sudden the assault was abandoned, and speculation was that the republicans had aborted the attack because they feared they would be encircled by government troops.[72] It seems the reverses in Kenmare and Tarbert had spooked many of the local garrisons, to the extent that many outposts were terrified by the prospect of an attack by republicans. In their state of mind, a 'mouse' could cast the shadow of an elephant.

The *Irish Times* (23 September) devoted a sizeable number of column inches to reporting Kerry's experience of the Civil War since government troops had arrived in the county in early August. The report was an accurate but hard-hitting assessment of the military situation in Kerry up to that point. Under the headline 'The Army's Task in Kerry', the report observed:

> Irregular strength of about two thousand rifles. The three local brigades contribute 1,000 to 1,200 which along with the support of adjoining forces can call upon 1,800 to 2,000 men. These figures are guesswork, as there is not sufficient information … In truth beyond the occupation of some important towns, where the National Army are pinned to their barracks … and cannot leave in less than Columns of one hundred men … Even in their barracks they are harassed by sniping, or are subject to even more aggressive attacks, while enemy Columns several hundred-strong move along the hills in full view and with complete impunity. Arms and supplies reach the Irregulars along the coast without challenge, while peaceful trading ships are attacked on the high sea and relieved of their cargoes, while on land every movement of goods needs armed protection to ensure it reaches its destination safely. On the other hand, Brigadier Daly, and Colonel/Commander Hogan have an able Staff, and possess several strategic advantages, but need to develop sea power, so that regular sea communication can be established. Troops numbers could be doubled, or tripled … a force of 8,000 men would bring the campaign in Kerry to a successful conclusion sooner. A wireless set should be provided for each post.

The *Irish Times* didn't pull its punches in an editorial line that was a grudging admission (though not stated) that the anti-Treatyites in Kerry were offering stiff resistance to the government and its army's attempts to pacify the county. Consisting of a force of between 1,000 and 1,200 men, the national army was grossly overstretched, even if judged by its strength 'on paper', which of course was drastically reduced by having scores of troops tied down in static positions such as barrack duties, guarding prisons, etc. All these factors reduced its ability to mount an effective offensive against the republicans, who, being a mobile force, had far fewer constraints on their manpower and could pick and choose when and where to engage the enemy.

General W. R. E. Murphy, the O/C over Kerry command (until his promotion in the army restructuring in December 1922), was constantly lobbying Mulcahy to commit an additional 250 troops to Kerry, which he estimated was a realistic figure allowing his troops to switch from a largely defensive posture to an offensive capability, and bringing the army's strength to over 1,500 troops. All the while small-scale – though incremental – captures of republican prisoners were whittling down the size of the anti-Treatyite volunteer pool, which was geared for a summer campaign, as once one entered October a colder and wetter climate made the republican 'war' out in the open countryside far more difficult to sustain.

The ink was hardly dry on the *Irish Times'* Kerry editorial when the republicans sent an envoy to Killorglin informing the population of an imminent attack on the main military outposts in the town, and for their own safety advised them to leave town. Most people heeded the advice. While the republicans (to their credit) were anxious to avoid civilian casualties, a totally or partially evacuated town made their task much easier; as 'linking' was a major factor in the Kenmare victory, it was decided to use similar tactics against the Killorglin garrison's strong-points. The fact that the Killorglin force was about half the size (60–70 men) of the contingent they had overwhelmed in Kenmare made the republicans confident of victory. Captain Dan Lehane (twenty-four), the commanding officer in Killorglin, put his men on 'stand to' in anticipation of an immediate attack, and established an additional outpost (three men) to protect the town's railway signalling equipment in anticipation the republicans would attempt to destroy it during the course of the assault. The defending garrison were on 'stand to' for three days, and so were on the verge of exhaustion when the republican attack began at 6 a.m. on Wednesday, 27 September 1922. During the night republican sappers had tunnelled down the entire length of Upper Bridge Street and placed a massive land mine on the upper floor of Dodd's, the house next door to what was Killorglin RIC barracks. A massive explosion shook the building and blew slates from the roof, the force of the blast literally throwing Lieutenant O'Callaghan and some of his men from their beds. They sustained minor injuries but it was the building that saved them, as it had only been constructed between 1895 and 1900 and was far more robust than most of the older housing stock in Killorglin. Republicans would make two additional attempts using land mines to destroy the building but only managed to demolish Dodd's house.

While republican artillery (i.e. land mines) was being used against the Upper Bridge Street outpost the Carnegie and Morris' hotels were subject to rifle and machine-gun fire. The fact that the Carnegie was a lone standing building and the hotel garrison was partially isolated and had a machine-gun post on the square tower of Killorglin Protestant church prevented the republicans from getting close enough to use land mines against both these outposts. The *Cork Examiner* did contain a report that republicans had succeeded in setting fire to the roof of the Carnegie. If the report was accurate, the garrison seem to have got the blaze under control.

During the course of lulls in the fighting the republicans would call on the defenders to surrender. The replies varied between 'never', 'up Clare' and 'up the 1st Westerns', indicating a strong sense of local pride in both their unit and county of origin, and a determination to resist that was lacking among the troops serving in the Kenmare garrison. Captain Dan Lehane, the O/C of the Killorglin garrison, seems to have been an inspiration to his men. On one occasion during a lull in shooting he stormed the building across the road from Morris' hotel, and although he sustained a head wound he and his men managed to take eight prisoners and neutralise the main republican threat to his headquarters. Later on in the day his luck ran out, however, and as he advanced, against the advice of his men, towards a republican position he was killed in a burst of Thompson sub-machine-gun fire near O'Shea's pub on Langford Street.

Dan Lehane was the third member of his family to suffer a violent death during the War of Independence/Civil War period. In the series of reprisals following the Rineen ambush when six RIC men were killed in County Clare in the summer of 1920, Dan Lehane's father, also named Dan (aged sixty), and his elder brother, Pat (aged twenty-two), known as 'Pake', were both shot by the security forces on their farm at Cregg, Lahinch on 20 September 1920. Pake Lehane's body was never recovered as following the shooting his killers burned his cottage to the ground, while Dan Lehane senior died of wounds on 26 September 1920, by a cruel twist of fate almost two years to the day before his son was to meet his death in Killorglin.

The republican headquarters were based in the Railway hotel, directly across the road from the railway signal box where the Free State forces had set up an outpost a few days earlier. The post came under sustained attack throughout the day, but held out against the odds; claims made by the garrison that they killed at least six anti-Treatyites while defending the post seem to be without substance. The defending garrison claimed that between six and ten anti-Treatyites lost their lives during the assault, including a leader named Clifford, an officer named Slattery, and Jeremiah Keating of Caherciveen. In fact only one republican, Patrick Murphy of Dooks, Glenbeigh, was killed in action. Their second fatality, Con Looney of Kenmare, was sniped at by Lieutenant Corry, O/C at the Carnegie, to avenge the part he was alleged to have played in the death of the Scarteen-O'Connor brothers in Kenmare. Corry was wounded himself while he fired the shot that killed Looney.

While convalescing in hospital Lieutenant Corry gave an interesting account of the Killorglin battle to *Iris an Arim*, the 'in house' army newsletter, in which he estimated between 300 and 500 anti-Treatyites were involved. The reason such a large concentration of men was available, he explained, was as a result of General Dalton's sweep of the flying columns in north Cork which saw contingents from Limerick, Tipperary and Cork head for Killorglin to fight alongside their Kerry counterparts. At least eight machine-guns were used in the attack and much of the ammunition stock taken at Kenmare. During the conflict

Frs McGrath and O'Donoghue and Dr Hannigan administered aid (both medical and spiritual) to all parties, both national army and anti-Treatyites alike.[73]

As dusk fell on Killorglin, fearing the republicans would sabotage the town's electricity generating powerhouse on Mill Road, a handful of troops crawled from their Upper Bridge Street base and set up a guard on the building. Random shooting continued throughout the night, but after eighteen hours of sustained and violent assault, attack and counter-attack the anti-Treatyites had not breached the garrison's defences. News of the town's difficulty had already reached military HQ in Tralee. The first reinforcements, a cycle patrol, were fired upon at 4.30 a.m. at Castlemaine in an engagement that lasted an hour, before proceeding to Killorglin. The patrol was only the vanguard of a much larger force under General W. R. E. Murphy and Colonel Michael Hogan which included the armoured car 'Danny Boy'. Given the intensity and the numbers involved in the fighting it is surprising that the casualty levels were so low: eleven wounded among the defending garrison and only fifteen on the republican side. Then again, the practice of 'linking' radically reduced the risk factor for the assault force. In the days that followed, two of the injured would die of their wounds: Jeremiah Keating of Caherciveen on the republican side and Volunteer Denis O'Connor, who was described as a 'local scout' for the national army. It appears that James Guerin was the only civilian casualty; he was seriously wounded when he was caught in crossfire early on Wednesday morning.

The garrison took eighteen republicans prisoner during the course of the fighting in Killorglin, 'including Galvin', it added menacingly, 'the man who killed Captain Burke'. This was referring to an incident that happened at Castlemaine a month earlier when Burke was shot dead at the head a column of 1st Westerns *en route* from Killorglin to Tralee. Under interrogation following his capture, in which John Galvin's arm was broken, he admitted that he had fired the shot that killed Burke, a close personal friend of Colonel Hogan, O/C the 1st Westerns.[74] As the column reached Ballyseedy, Galvin's captors took him aside, shot him several times and threw his body over a ditch. The official version of the event was that the army was attacked by republicans and John Galvin was killed in the ensuing firefight. The deaths of both Con Looney and John Galvin show the willingness of the 1st Westerns to engage in reprisal killings. In this regard it seems they had little to learn from the Dublin Guard whose core members came from Collins' Squad and had a culture of political assassination.

At 6 p.m. on Wednesday, 27 September, as battle still raged in Killorglin, a three-vehicle convoy of Dublin Guards (thirty men) was fired upon as they turned on a bend in a densely wooded part of Brennan's Glen, near Farranfore. Two men, Daniel Hannon from Belfast and John Martin from Dundalk, were killed and seven were wounded in the attack, which occurred so quickly the patrol were unable to return fire. When the military authorities released details of the attack, it included the information that an anti-Treaty prisoner, Bertie Murphy, who was in the custody of the patrol at the time, was also wounded, and later died of his injuries. On Friday, 29 September the county coroner, Dr William O'Sullivan, presided over an inquest into the death of Bertie Murphy that was unique not only in the fact that it took place at all but in the urgency the military authorities devoted to establishing the facts surrounding Murphy's death.

Julia Murphy, the boy's mother, giving evidence at the inquest, said Bertie (seventeen), one of three children, was her eldest son and she had last seen him alive on 27 September travelling on the back of an army lorry. Brigadier Paddy O'Daly, O/C the Dublin Guard, giving evidence, emphasised that the ultimate responsibility for her son's death lay at the hands of the anti-Treatyites. 'While sympathising with you, as I sincerely do,' O'Daly said, addressing Murphy's mother, 'I cannot help reminding others that two other men lost their lives in the attack which leaves three women bereaved ... two mothers and a wife ... thinking at present that their sons and husband are alive in Kerry.'[75]

Bertie Murphy was in military custody when the Brennan's Glen ambush occurred, having been arrested in the Brennan's Glen/Farranfore area earlier on 27 September. He was in one of the basement cells in the Great Southern hotel, Killarney, the Dublin Guard HQ at the time of the ambush. When news of the attack reached Killarney, it was assumed that Murphy, a native of the area where the attack occurred, would know who was involved. Following a brutal interrogation during which he revealed no information, Bertie Murphy was shot dead.

On Friday night, 29 September, republicans set fire to the lock house at the entrance to the Tralee canal, and blew up the lock gates. The next day a barge carrying fifty tons of maize was sunk near the entrance to ensure the waterway could no longer be used for either military or commercial traffic. In the process another vital lifeline in the county's transport infrastructure was taken out of use. A notice on board the sunken vessel warned of dire consequence for anybody who attempted to remove the craft from the canal. Around the same time as the canal post was destroyed, a group of off-duty soldiers from the Dublin Guard were talking outside the courthouse in Rathmore. The republicans opened fire with a Lewis gun, killing Sergeant Noonan and wounding four others. In a separate incident Captain John Young was wounded in an ambush on the Killarney–Rathmore road.[76] The week following the *Irish Times* feature on Kerry (23–30 September) had been an eventful one in a campaign – from the perspective of both sides – that was far from a successful conclusion. The *Freeman's Journal* of Tuesday, 26 September 1922 carried the news that Kerry was to become a separate military command under the stewardship of General Galvin, presumably Denny Galvin of Knocknagoshel. From August up until that point Kerry/west Limerick (mirroring the Dáil constituency, perhaps) was a single command area under *de jure* command of General W. R. E. Murphy, but to all intents and purposes controlled by Brigadier Paddy O'Daly, O/C Dublin Guard. According to John P. Duggan, in his *History of the Irish Army*, O'Daly's command changed on 4 October 1922.[77] There was considerable public disquiet (well founded as it happened) concerning that unit's conduct of the war, and placing a Kerryman in charge of the county created the illusion of responding to public opinion by removing O'Daly 'sideways', although in reality nothing changed as the ethos of the Squad still infused the officer corps of the Dublin Guard. Michael Collins, Richard Mulcahy and Paddy O'Daly – all IRB men – had been through 1916 and the War of Independence together and their bonds of loyalty went back a long way.

8

What We Have, We Hold

By the beginning of October neither of the belligerents were in the position they had expected to be when the war began in early August. At that point Collins had sent his two best units (both from the point of view of political reliability and military competence), the Dublin Guard and the 1st Westerns, to Kerry, anticipating having to face down and confront the republicans in a short, sharp campaign that would be over by early September. Collins' 12 August visit to Tralee (in the wake of successful troop landings at Cork city and Kenmare), organised to arrange peace talks with the republican leadership in Kerry, was abandoned when he learned of the death of Arthur Griffith and returned to Dublin. Even if the meeting had taken place, it is unlikely that it would have brought the war in Kerry to an end at that point. The Fenit, Tarbert and Kenmare landings had taken the republicans totally by surprise; but equally, Free State advances across the county took place in a military and political vacuum and were largely unchallenged militarily by the IRA, who consequently would not have seen them as victories. In many ways Free State troops were seen by the republicans as marooned crews who controlled a series of island outposts across the county, like an archipelago set in turbulent seas. The fact that the troops were 'outsiders' (from Dublin and Clare/Galway predominantly) was also a source of inspiration for the defenders. The death of Michael Collins – who was both admired and mourned by many republicans because of his role in the War of Independence – was seen as a major military and political setback for the Provisional Government within the republican leadership in Kerry, not least because his successors, W. T. Cosgrave, Richard Mulcahy and Kevin O'Higgins were regarded as lightweights who would 'cave in' if the republican offensive continued.

Once they recovered from the initial shock of the sea-borne landings, both Kerry No. 1 and No. 2 brigades fought a vigorous county-wide campaign during August and September that resulted in the death of thirty-five soldiers and about one hundred wounded. To put these casualty levels in context, the Kerry body count can be compared with the casualties suffered by the army since the war began in late June and, equally illuminating, how these figures compare with the numbers of crown forces killed in Kerry during 1920–21.

From the bombardment of the Four Courts (28 June) to 31 July 1922, Free State forces had fifty-nine troops killed and 160 wounded nationwide.[1] By mid–late September the casualties had increased to 185 killed and 674 wounded.[2] The Kerry figures, 35 killed and 100 wounded, in a single county, represent a high proportion of the national total. The corresponding death toll for the republicans in Kerry (that I can substantiate) for the same interval was nine, four of which were reprisal killings carried out by both the Dublin Guard and the 1st Westerns.

Comparing the army's death toll for August–September 1922 with the number of police killed by the IRA in Kerry during 1920–21 is interesting. During 1920 thirteen RIC men were killed in Kerry, while a further twenty-three policemen lost their lives up to the calling of the truce on 11 July 1921.[3] The Free State army death toll for the month of August 1922 was twenty-two, while thirteen died during September, which contradicts the popular view that Kerry republicans had no stomach for civil war. The death toll for the first two months of the Civil War indicates that the republicans waged a far bloodier campaign against the Provisional Government forces than that fought against the British over the period from 1920 to July 1921 during the War of Independence. If the IRA death toll during the first two months of the conflict is accurate, (nine killed, though I suspect it could be an underestimate) it would represent a lot lower death toll at the hands of the Free State (up to that point) than occurred in Kerry under the British occupation, when thirteen Volunteers were killed in 1920 with a further twenty-seven deaths between January and July 1921.[4]

The assault on Killorglin on 27 September 1922 represented the high-water mark for the republican offensive in Kerry in terms of the time taken to plan the attack, and the number of weapons and men available to attack the garrison on the south-western boundary of the Free State's 'safe' enclave in Kerry. Ironically, the defence of the town became an epic victory in Free State army mythology. An action where two anti-Treatyites were killed and fifteen wounded had within a week been transformed into a battle that inflicted fifty-one dead and ninety wounded on the force assaulting Killorglin.[5]

Had the Killorglin action been successful, representing as it did all the capital – both the weapons and propaganda – the republicans had won at Kenmare, a front line might have developed along the river Laune, extending across the Killarney lakes and into the mountainous areas of east Kerry, giving anti-

Treaty forces *de facto* control over the Iveragh peninsula, not unlike the thirteenth-century division of the county between the Anglo-Norman shire of Kerry and the mountainous Gaelic territory of Desmond. In north and central Kerry government troops were increasingly consolidating their control over territories that were marginally and irrevocably being lost to the republicans in the county.

Coincidentally, 27 September 1922 saw the defence and justice ministers, Richard Mulcahy and Kevin O'Higgins, introduce legislation before the Dáil, the Emergency Powers Bill, which was in effect an admission that, militarily, the government army was proving inadequate to deal with the resistance it faced in areas of the country – such as Kerry – where republicans had reverted to a guerrilla campaign akin to that waged against the British during the War of Independence. For Mulcahy, as defence minister, it was also an attempt (largely unsuccessful) to reassert central government control and prevent the commission of *ad hoc* executions and reprisal killings at local level. The legislation gave the government wide powers against a whole range of offences including possession of a weapon, ammunition and explosives, which were all designated as capital offences punishable by death. The Emergency Powers Act, carried by forty-eight votes to eighteen (the Labour Party opposed the terms of the bill vigorously), allowed a two-week amnesty, extending from 3–12 October, during which time individual republicans could hand over the offensive items proscribed by the legislation.[6]

The Executive Council, largely at Cosgrave's behest, persuaded the bishops to endorse the Emergency Powers legislation. In a pastoral letter issued on 10 October 1922, the Catholic hierarchy urged anti-Treatyites 'to take advantage of the Government's offer ... and make peace in our country'. The bishops determined it was a matter of divine law '... that the only legitimate authority was the Provisional Government. There is no other Government, and cannot be.' In specific terms, it deliberated that the warfare carried out by the anti-Treatyites was without moral sanction; therefore the killing of a national soldier in the course of his duty is murder before God. In conclusion the pastoral stated that any Irregular contravening the pastoral's moral guidance would not be absolved in confession, and would not be allowed to receive holy communion. In a high-risk conflict situation where a republican (as often as not, a devout Catholic in his 'world view') risked his life for his political beliefs and principles, to be refused the sacraments was literally a fate worse than death.

It is unclear how seriously the average IRA activist took the death threat implicit in the terms of the new act. In reality it would be nearly four months (20 January 1923) before the legal powers conferred by the 27 September act were used in Kerry. In the interim, however, individual officers carried out ad hoc/ reprisal killings in 'the heat of the moment', or on a whim, if one of their own unit was killed. Individual IRA men were especially at risk if they were captured after engaging in a holding action that enabled the remainder of their unit to escape. No fewer than nineteen republicans met their deaths in this manner throughout Kerry between October and December 1922.[7]

Regarding clerical criticism, as outlined in the 10 October pastoral, many republicans saw the 'panel' coalition TDs, which included pro- and anti-Treaty wings, to be endorsed by the electorate as the legitimate government of the country in the 16 June election. It was Collins, they argued, not the republicans, who repudiated the decision of the electorate. Furthermore, the Provisional Government started the war on 28 June when they opened artillery fire on the Four Courts garrison.

Over two hundred republicans were taken prisoner in Kerry during August and September. Some were incarcerated at the county jail in Moyderwell, others in the workhouse, but a large number were held at Ballymullen barracks, where the size of the compound and constant troop concentrations provided the most effective way of guarding the maximum number of prisoners while tying down the least number of troops. As the numbers in custody expanded, however, the greater was the danger of a mass breakout, possibly aided and abetted by a military assault on the barracks as a decoy, drawing troops away from the prison compounds, while a landmine could demolish the walls, enabling many prisoners to escape while their republican confederates provided covering fire. If the escape attempt failed it could result in a bloodbath. If it succeeded, as well as 'swelling the ranks' of the IRA, it would represent a major propaganda coup for the anti-Treaty cause, not only in Kerry but on a national scale.

The largest single concentration of prisoners to be captured in Kerry in a single week occurred in the week ending Saturday, 7 October, when no fewer than eighty-six republicans were captured across the county.[8] At a time when a full-strength company averaged between fifteen and twenty-five members (depending on the availability of rifles and ammunition) the loss of such a large number of men represented a serious setback to the republicans on a county-wide basis. It seems that it was details provided by individuals on the movement of local columns that facilitated such a large number of arrests.

The *Cork Examiner* observed: 'It is not to be wondered as the farmers, who are the heart and soul at the back of the Government, are sick and tired of enforced housing and feeding of the Irregulars for months past.'[9]

Significantly, the motivation for providing information rested on a combination of political opposition to the local columns and with a genuine sense of economic grievance for losses incurred at the hands of the republicans. Timing (early October) probably galvanised the farmers' determination not to be fobbed off at harvest time when their larders were well stocked, and fodder, grain and animal foodstuffs were plentiful for the forthcoming winter but could quickly vanish given a week or two feeding a large IRA column. Providing the authorities with details on the republicans was not a risk-free activity, however:

> On Saturday, 21 October, at 10 p.m. the family of Daniel Brosnan, of Cloghmoola, Obrennan, Ballymacelligott were saying the rosary when they smelled smoke coming from the hay shed. Brosnan went into the outhouse, which lay between the hayshed and the family dwelling house, where he stored his mowing machine, chaff cutter, pulper, cart and other farm implements. He brought the cart out onto the farm yard and returned to the house. There was a massive explosion (landmine) from the hayshed, which demolished the gable wall of the outhouse and destroyed its contents, but left the family home unscathed. Neighbours surmised that the only motive for the outrage was the owner's sympathy to the Irish Government and his hostility to the anti-Treatyites.[10]

The Ballymacelligott bombing, unique as it was, was probably intended as a deterrent – a warning to the general public as to what would happen if they assisted the civil and military powers in identifying the movements and location of republicans – rather than an attempt to kill or injure members of the

Brosnan family. Nevertheless, the circumspect response of the neighbours (as recorded in the *Cork Examiner*) indicates that the message was not lost on the wider public of the political consequences of crossing the hazily defined line between passive acceptance and active intervention in the conflict, even in the most marginal way.

While public opinion in many quarters in Kerry was tired of, and opposed to, a continuation of the conflict, republican commanders and many of the rank and file were largely impervious to civil, public, journalistic or ecclesiastical criticism. A volunteer force, many of whom were part-time (and unpaid) in what was in many respects a part-time and intermittent conflict, felt that they had fought hard and long during the summer campaign but hadn't really beaten or dislodged the government's armed forces' grip on the county. Even for those who were full-time volunteers, the prospect of living a hand-to-mouth existence, constantly on the move, living out under the elements or in caves or dugouts as the weather deteriorated and winter set in, was a demoralising prospect. When sleeping in barns or outhouses the republicans usually stored their arms in specific weapons dumps, the location of which would only have been known to the quartermaster or the company commander. Consequently if the column were surrounded and arrested their arms and ammunition would not be captured as in many respects it was easier to replace captured men than captured weapons. The downside of this was that an unarmed column was much more likely to surrender if surrounded by a heavily armed enemy force and, even when armed, a small force would in a daylight confrontation be limited by both its size and finite ammunition stocks *vis-à-vis* the government forces' resources. And each and every prisoner capture reduced the republicans' ability to wage large- (or even small-) scale engagements with the enemy. Of course as the more moderate members were taken out of the conflict the hard core who remained were more determined than ever to continue to the bitter end insofar as anyone on the anti-Treaty side knew in October 1922 exactly what that meant.

The influx of new prisoners provided the authorities with an opportunity as well as a problem. By early October it was becoming increasingly difficult to recruit labourers to carry out repairs on damaged roads and bridges. Even when provided with military escorts while travelling to and from the location and while carrying out the repairs on site, workers were afraid that booby traps left in and around the dismantled structures by republicans would result in the loss of a hand, an arm or a leg in an explosion. In an era when permanently disabled workers had no source of income, and little chance of earning a living, the IRA deterrent was very effective. The threat wasn't only off-putting to labourers. In late October, Tralee harbour commissioner announced there were no plans to remove the barge scuttled in the canal locks by the republicans almost a month earlier, as no contractor or salvage crew was willing to move the vessel.[11]

In a cynical move the military authorities decided to use republican prisoners to fill the vacuum caused by the acute labour shortage brought about by the IRA's own successful sabotage of both the transport infrastructure and the mechanisms used to repair the damages. The army still provided military escorts, but now it seemed the policy had the potential to neutralise the effectiveness of the republican tactic, if by continuing to implement that particular course of action they risked the lives of their own comrades.

Republican prisoners took the initiative to rectify the situation themselves on Saturday, 14 October when those in custody in Tralee jail went on hunger strike. The next day about a hundred women and girls made an uproarious protest outside the prison walls. Machine-gun fire from inside the prison directed over their heads failed to disperse the demonstrators, who only desisted from their protest when a clergyman informed them that the hunger strike had ended as the protest of the prisoners had been effective.[12]

On at least one occasion, as recorded by John Joe Sheehy, republican prisoners were used as a human shield. Early one morning, as Sheehy's column was preparing to open fire on one of the daily military convoys that travelled between Tralee and Killarney, an armoured car approached from the direction of Castlemaine. As the first army lorry approached, the republicans noticed that some of their own prisoners were dispersed among the soldiers. Sheehy noted that he had no alternative but to call off the attack.[13] Unfortunately, no date or time frame is given for this incident. It is probable, given the timing and location, it may have been early October and inspired by the precedent used in the Brennan's Glen incident surrounding the death of Bertie Murphy.

On Friday, 6 October Marshall's Bridge, spanning the river Maine, was blown up, complementing the earlier destruction of Currans railway bridge, for which the GS & WR estimated a replacement cost of £10,000.[14] In Spa village the same evening the house of Dowling, the chemist, was blown up because republicans expected it would be used as a military post.[15] Aghadoe House, Lord Headley's residence (unoccupied at the time), was burned on 19 October for the same reason (valued at £20,000 for compensation purposes), indicating that the republicans could see that the Provisional Government's army had no intention of leaving the county and intended to consolidate and deepen its foothold in north and central Kerry.

In Rathmore village, in an unusual – if not unprecedented – move, the Free State army set up a military outpost on the ground floor of the house of the Cox family who had fled Belfast in July to escape the sectarian pogroms visited on the nationalist population of that city. Over 12–14 October the house was barricaded front and back, its windows sandbagged and loopholed and ramparts erected around the door and ground floor windows, while the whole of the front was draped in a high netting to serve as protection against hand grenades. A seven-man garrison of the Dublin Guard under Sergeant Kavanagh was billeted in the house while normal family life was expected to continue upstairs.[16] According to Jeremiah Murphy similar troop deployment measures were used in Barraduff that autumn and winter, in a policy that – he claimed – was deliberately framed to use the civilian population of east Kerry as a screen to protect government troops and deter attacks in areas where the republican hinterland was almost impenetrable.[17]

Tralee was still among the most dangerous postings in Kerry. On Friday, 6 October at 8 p.m. two officers were having tea at the Grafton café on Lower Bridge Street when a man with a revolver opened fire on them through the widow. Most of his shots hit the pummelling.[18] Fortunately for the soldiers in question, the would-be assassin's inexperience, lack of nerve and the comparative darkness saved their lives and his shots only damaged the furniture. More professional assassins such as Collins' Squad (since late August no strangers to Tralee, or Kerry for that matter), even when stalking only one victim, always used two or three men to reinforce and protect each other and guarantee a 'hit'. The experience of James Healy at Ballonagh in August showed that people could sometimes survive even their attacks, provided it wasn't a single shot to the head.

It was just that, a single shot to the head, fired by a sniper on Friday night, 13 October, that took the life of Volunteer Timothy Goggin from Abbeydorney (aged twenty-two) while he was on sentry duty at a dugout in Fenit.[19] The following afternoon, Saturday, 14 October, Volunteer Gilligan from Limerick was shot in the stomach while chasing a prisoner at McCowen's Lane, Tralee. Taken to the county infirmary, he died of his wounds on Wednesday, 18 October.[20]

The road between Tralee and Fenit saw a massive increase in freight traffic, and armed hold-ups of cargoes they transported, since the canal was put out of use and blockaded by a sunken barge. A ton of flour being transported by horse and cart (to McCowen's) was commandeered by armed men, and in a separate hold-up a cargo of sugar (for Musgrave brothers) was looted.[21] It is impossible to say who carried out the robbery. It may have been republicans, who routinely took foodstuffs for their own needs, and often as not for distribution to safe houses by way of payment to their supporters for providing food and shelter. Just as likely it may have been freelance criminals, for whom an unescorted vehicle provided easy pickings.

On Friday, 6 October a military rations convoy was fired upon by republicans at Ballymacthomas, *en route* to Farranfore. Two members of the Dublin Guard were wounded in the course of the attack.[22] In late October, under instruction from

General W. R. Murphy, a curfew effective from the hours of 10.30 p.m. until 5.30 a.m. was imposed on Tralee urban area, including the districts of Ballybeggan, Oakpark, Cloughane and Rock Gates. It is unclear what incident triggered the introduction of curfew so late into the conflict.[23]

According to the *Cork Examiner*:

> On 10th October the farmers of Killarney acting in the interests of the general community pooled their available transport, formed into a procession of 150 [actually 125] miscellaneous farm carts and vans, and travelled 25 miles to Fenit. Here the carts loaded with foodstuffs and supplies and without rest returned to Killarney 30 hours later having covered 50 miles. The army provided a strong military escort which was ambushed at Ballyseedy and Ballymacthomas … a twenty minute engagement in which two soldiers from the Dublin Guard were wounded, but in return of fire, an expert estimated that they killed 4 and wounded a further 9 Irregulars. As the convoy approached Killarney, it came under attack in Dirrane, where fire was concentrated on the carters. A horse belonging to Denis Courtney of Larry's Cross was shot dead.[24]

It is highly unlikely the casualties that the military claim to have inflicted on the republicans during the ambush are accurate, and were broadcast primarily for propaganda purposes. The targeting of the civilian draft animals used in the convoy also represents a new departure in the republican tactics, if it was a deliberate policy. It is possible that the horse was killed unintentionally, as such a strategy could as easily lead to the death of a civilian driver, which would have huge negative consequences for the perception of the IRA and its campaign among both the wider farming community and the townspeople of Killarney.

In an additional editorial comment the *Cork Examiner* of 21 October noted:

The result of the blockade is being keenly felt already, and will be intensified should it last through the winter, the poor being the greatest sufferers … Farmers are also feeling the pinch, the price being reduced by 10 shillings per Cwt to cover porterage/cartage from Tralee Bacon Factory to Fenit for cross channel transport. People throughout Kerry are suffering similarly, Killarney deprived of its tourist traffic and the dislocation of its rail service is in a pitiful plight.

We are living in genteel starvation, we are hungry but are too proud to admit it, and even if we did there is no hope of relief. We expected that the government would come to our assistance sooner by protecting us and putting an end to the warfare waged against us by people who should devote themselves to helping us instead of starving us.

The anonymous contribution articulates the sense of despair no doubt shared by many in Kerry at the time. It is also very much a broadside directed against both belligerents; in short the message is, 'A plague on both your houses'.

The British refused to recognise the 1919–21 conflict as a war, assigning it the status of a 'police action', hence the RIC and paramilitary like the 'Black and Tans' and the 'Auxiliaries', rather than the British army, bore the brunt of the campaign against the IRA in Kerry as elsewhere. Any claims made in respect of damages to property or persons during that conflict were seen as criminal or malicious injuries, and compensation claims could be made through local government channels. The new state inherited this administrative device for its own war damages, although all the claims received by Kerry County Council were dealt with through central government, namely the Department of Local Government in Dublin. Up to the end of September Kerry County Council had received submissions of £400,000 in respect of damage to property and personal injury arising out of the conflict in the county since hostilities commenced on 3 August. The deadline for submissions in respect of the first two months of the war was extended to 11 October to allow people to submit their claims.

A total of £533,876–06s–03d was the tally for malicious damages (see Appendix 4 for an indication of the scale and nature of the claims).[25] This figure roughly broke down in a ratio of about six to one, with around £450,000 estimated in damages to property, and in excess of £80,000 for personal injury claims.

The destruction of two properties – Ardfert Abbey, the residence (uninhabited) of the Talbot-Crosbie family, and Derry-quinn House, the residence of Charles Warren near Kenmare (each valued at £100,000) – was responsible for almost half of the total damages incurred. Even though both properties were 'big houses', it was their suitability as potential military barracks rather than their association with the ascendancy that led to their destruction. Virtually all the bombings or burning of property were carried out by republicans, with probably the one exception being the 'medical hall', Hartnett's chemists in Kenmare, which was destroyed by the Free State army on the basis it was used as a bomb factory.[26]

In the summer of 1922 a life was valued at £8,000 for insurance purposes. Surprisingly the next of kin of two soldiers, Michael Purcell and Jack Lydon, both serving in the national army and from Tralee, submitted claims for compensation under the terms offered to civilians when the two men were killed while on duty in the town.[27] The sum of £533,876 only represented private claims. It did not include the destruction of roads and bridges and the cost of wages and materials involved in their repair, which was estimated at another £500,000.

Apart from the identifiable cost of damages to private and

public property, the value of the loss of normal trade and commerce due to the war is harder to quantify, though it had a negative impact on the local economy. The loss of tourist revenue in Killarney, for example; the non-payment of rates to Kerry County Council (estimated at £118,000); the loss of income by the railway companies and their employees due to the cessation of services; plus the impact the absence of fairs and markets as outlets for livestock and farm produce had on agricultural incomes, meant that virtually every section of the community in Kerry suffered and was poorer because of the war.[28]

While the republicans no longer mounted assaults on the scale of Kenmare, Tarbert and Killorglin after September, there was no let up in sniper attacks or rifle and machine-gun attacks on smaller outposts, or ambushes on convoys of military vehicles. It was noticeable, possibly because of the smaller numbers involved on the republican side, that more men were being killed, injured or captured in waging such attacks than in previous months. It is also possible that the Free State forces were getting better at detecting and anticipating anti-Treatyite methods. Nevertheless, the cumulative cost of a series of small-scale engagements in terms of killed and injured was high.

On Friday, 20 October an armoured car carrying general W. R. E. Murphy, O/C Kerry/Limerick military district, and a Crossley tender with fifteen men on board, left Limerick city bound for Tralee. At 8 p.m. the convoy stopped in Duagh village as some of the men dismounted to remove a farm cart that was obstructing the road. As they cleared the obstacle, republicans positioned in the nearby houses opened fire, killing Sergeant John Browne (aged twenty-eight) of Effin, County Limerick and wounding Jason Byrne.[29]

Rathmore barracks and the other military outposts in the town came under rifle and machine-gun fire from about 3 p.m. on Sunday, 15 October. During an exchange of fire that stretched over two hours the only casualty was Mrs Ryan, a national schoolteacher, who was wounded in the hand while attending a funeral at Novaldaly cemetery. The republicans abandoned the assault when a military aircraft arrived on the scene, although there are no details of the aircraft firing on the republicans.[30] The army had set up an air service earlier in the year, consisting of a number of de Havilland aircraft, flown by former RFC/RAF pilots. The planes were equipped with machine-guns and could carry bombs, but also had radio contact as reconnaissance was a significant part of their duties. The plane that over-flew Rathmore that particular Sunday operated out of an airfield in Fermoy in the Cork military area. It was a single-seat 'Martinside Scout' piloted by Lieutenant Fitzmaurice and was used to monitor Irregular columns in north Cork and east Kerry, districts that were still inaccessible 'no go' areas as far as the national army was concerned.

On 16–17 October senior republican military commanders met at Ballybacon near Tipperary town to discus the Emergency Powers Bill, and the bishop's pastoral of 10 October which condemned the anti-Treaty military campaign. At a meeting dominated by Liam Lynch's views and reflecting by and large the perspective of the Munster divisions, the council agreed to continue the war. In a separate but related meeting, held in Dublin on 25 October, a number of anti-Treaty TDs elected Éamon de Valera as president, giving him the power to nominate a twelve-member Council of State, in effect creating a government in exile in which Austin Stack was appointed

Minister for Finance. In reality the republican 'government' served only a propaganda purpose; its political representatives didn't control its own military wing.

On 20 October 1922 Patrick O'Connor of Causeway and Patrick Joseph O'Halloran of Ballyheige were both found in possession of a rifle and ammunition at the house of Pierce Godley of Ballyheige. A few days later, 27 October, Hugh O'Neill and Seamus O'Reilly, who had been taken prisoner following the republican assault on Killorglin less than a month earlier, were released from jail. At a military court held at Ballymullen barracks on 3 November, however, both O'Connor and O'Halloran were sentenced to five years in prison.[31] The contrast between the two incidents shows a lack of consistency in the authority's penal policy. Obviously the government were determined to show republicans in Kerry that the Act had teeth, and carried severe penalties for anyone found in breach of its provisions.

While many republican activists were willing to kill and were prepared to die in defence of the republican ideal and in challenging the Provisional Government's military presence in the county, for a substantial number of Kerry people the metaphysics of the war, or the life-or-death nature of the conflict, was a luxury they couldn't afford. In practical terms the disruption of road and rail transport as a result of the war made it more difficult to emigrate. The *Cork Examiner* reported the following incident to highlight the risks some people were willing to take to escape the poverty and lack of employment opportunities the newly independent state (whether it was a 'Free State' or a republic was increasingly irrelevant) offered many of its citizens as a birthright:

On Saturday afternoon, October 21st, a small fishing boat, with auxiliary motor power landed in Cobh, carrying 30 emigrants from Kerry. The craft had left Kerry the previous Monday (16 October) and during the voyage passengers endured great hardship and suffering. A small cabin, with two bunks, provided shelter for two women and four children; the remaining passengers, nearly all women, stayed on the deck for the duration of the voyage.[32]

On 21 October an army lorry came under fire from republicans at Lawlor's Cross, Rockfield, about two miles from Killarney. In the ensuing twenty-minute firefight, Corporal John Corcoran (thirty-three) from North Circular Road, Dublin was killed and two others from the Dublin Guard wounded.[33] On 23 October Sergeant James Marum (twenty-eight) of Blackrock, County Dublin was killed; no further details are provided on the location or circumstances surrounding his death.[34] On 25 October a military convoy was ambushed at Ballyrobert between Ardfert and Abbeydorney. Private Gilchrist, a machine-gunner from County Longford, was killed in the attack and a soldier named Kiely, from Limerick, was wounded. Both men were in the 1st Westerns.[35]

Republicans, however, didn't always emerge unscathed in confrontations with the enemy. On the same day as the Ballyrobert attack a Free State army cycle patrol came upon a party of republicans at Dungeel, about three miles from Killorglin, where they were removing the contents of a cargo boat transporting goods on the river Laune in the direction of Killarney. In the ensuing exchange of fire William O'Riordan from Glenbeigh was killed, and two other anti-Treatyites were wounded.[36] On the same day at Pallas, near Beaufort Bridge, Captain Michael Ahern of Glencar, Killorglin and two other men making their way towards Fossa were passing a dug-out, under surveillance by a Free State patrol, when the troops opened fire. Michael Ahern was killed; the two other men fled, one hiding in a briar patch, the second evading capture by taking refuge in a nearby house and hiding in a wardrobe.[37]

On Friday, 27 October Private Nagle, a native of Killarney serving with the 1st Westerns, was killed in an exchange of fire at Tonevane, near Castlegregory.[38] A republican, William Myles, was also killed in the attack. It seems Myles was captured earlier in the attack, and was shot as a reprisal following Nagle's death. Around the same time as the Tonevane incident, Free State troops surrounded a republican column operating in the Glen Farm at Ballyheige. Republican resistance was such that the army brought in an eighteen-pounder field gun from Tralee to capture the post.[39] John Lawlor (twenty-three) volunteered to stay and offer covering fire, enabling the entire republican garrison to evade capture. Largely as a result of his actions, in which he was badly wounded, the 1st Westerns executed him early on Tuesday, 31 October 1922.

'Early one morning in late October a large body, between five and six hundred men, with two armoured cars and about a dozen trucks, left Killarney and passed through Glenflesk and the Loo Valley. We were expecting such a move for some time, suspecting they intended to retake Kenmare. Some of our scouts engaged the column at Killagha, but they were too large to take on.' This is how Jeremiah Murphy recalls the opening salvo of the incident. Unfortunately he does not specify the exact date in October that the confrontation took place. He was part of a twenty-man unit too far away to hear the exchange of fire at Killagha, and by the time Murphy's column became aware of the Free State task force the column had already passed 'Robbers' Den', the most suitable ambush point on the road to Kenmare and the site of a successful ambush on 25 August that forced a relief column with similar objectives to abandon their mission.

Murphy's column opened fire at long range, and by his estimation wounded as many as ten men at the head of the government force. The republicans managed to position a Lewis gun on an outcrop of rock at a point where the road narrowed and there was a steep cliff on the other side of the road, thereby enabling a small unit to pin down a large force without the government troops having any way of knowing how large an adversary they faced. The ambush site was not far from the Headford railway line, and a group of republicans under the command of Jerry Kennedy decided to double back and try and encircle the rearguard of the Free State column. As they moved to carry out this objective, Kennedy noticed the outline of a large group of men on the brow of a hill about half a mile away, which he took to be a unit of government troops deployed to prevent the very action they were attempting. As a result he abandoned the plan. As it turned out the men he observed were members of the Kenmare battalion who has abandoned their posts in the town as a way of avoiding being surrounded and captured by the Free State force advancing on Kenmare.[40] Meanwhile the O/C of the government troops decided to follow the precedent of the 25 August ambush and abandoned the advance on Kenmare.

The reverse was a victory of sorts for the republicans, and significantly there was no press coverage of the encounter as evidently the army did not wish to divulge a setback and hand a propaganda coup to the republicans. On the other hand the lack of communication between the Barraduff and Kenmare battalions squandered an opportunity to capture large quantities of arms and ammunition.

As the conflict entered its fourth month Jeremiah Murphy and his comrades began to discuss where the course of the war was heading. The prospect of a winter campaign did not appeal to any of them; but neither did being captured and spending months in a Free State prison. Many rank and file republicans felt the struggle would last until Christmas, by which time the military and political wings on both sides would reach an agreement on ending the war. This suggests they knew as little about their own high command's position as they did about the Provisional Government's stance on the war.

In their own localities in Kerry most people who supported the campaign were tired of feeding and billeting large numbers of fighting men. Even within the local IRA units there was a degree of hostility to a neighbouring column that sought refuge in their back yard. Added to this, better military intelligence on the government side on safe houses meant many such refuges were no longer safe, and people on the run had far fewer places to run to that would not be checked in follow-up searches after an ambush. The practical difficulties these constraints placed on the republican campaign were double-edged. The advantage of having a large force was negated by the difficulty of feeding and billeting them in secrecy; but while smaller units were easier to conceal and provision, their size meant their effectiveness in challenging the larger patrols the government troops were now increasingly using, either in an attack or a defensive manoeuvre, was radically diminished.

While the Catholic Church publicly nailed its colours to the

Free State mast in the October pastoral, many republicans did not regard their decision to bear arms against the Provisional Government as being in conflict with their beliefs as practising Catholics. In the rural Irish calendar, All Saints and All Souls days (1 and 2 November) were particularly important devotions. Many of the Barraduff column wished to observe their religious duties, but knew the church would be under surveillance on those days. Instead they decided to attend mass on 2 November but as a precaution posted armed scouts. While at mass the republicans got word that the Free State troops were surrounding the village but they all managed to escape and avoid capture. Even the back altar and sacristy were checked, which suggests there was clerical collusion in the overall operation.

As the Free State patrol – a forty-man unit under Lieutenant Michael Lyons – returned to Killarney they were subject to harassment in the form of sniper fire from republican scouts positioned along the route. Returning fire at a point nearer to Killarney, government troops wounded Michael O'Sullivan of Cloghane, who was brought to a farmhouse at Knockanes by his fellow scout, Dan O'Connor. Destroying his rifle, O'Sullivan urged O'Connor to leave the area. On arrival at the farmhouse the troops dragged the wounded O'Sullivan from the cottage and shot him dead. It was similar to the reprisal killing carried out on John Lawlor a few days earlier. According to Jeremiah Murphy's account, Michael O'Sullivan's death was the Barraduff column's first death since the conflict began in August. Afterwards the republicans carried out reprisal actions of their own against those whom they suspected of assisting Free State intelligence-gathering efforts in the area.[41]

Michael O'Sullivan wasn't the only casualty of the conflict

in Kerry that day. Private John Caddigan was also killed on 2 November but little additional information is available on his death.[42] On the morning of Saturday 4 November the outpost guarding the drawbridge and lock gates at Blennerville came under fire from two republican snipers operating from the vantage point of nearby warehouses. All three soldiers at the dugout – members of the 1st Westerns – were wounded in the attack. A civilian arriving on the scene cycled to Tralee and Dr Walsh, the military surgeon, A. O'Halloran, chemist, and Fr O'Connor (St John's church) arrived to tend the wounded. Within an hour, Private Peter Conroy (Limerick) died as a result of abdominal injuries sustained in the shooting.[43] In a separate incident Private Thomas Gallagher, Dublin Guard, was killed at Ballineen on 4 November. Little additional information is available on his death.[44]

Since the start of the conflict in August all rail communication with Killorglin had ceased, and every delivery of supplies by road from Tralee ran the risk of being held up and having its goods confiscated by republicans *en route* to Killorglin. At the beginning of November a weekly sailing by a 'schooner of light draft' was established from Cork city, serving both Dingle harbour and the ferry pier at Ballykissane, about a mile from Killorglin.

The service was a great improvement for Killorglin, which had seen little republican activity since the attack on the town in late September. Killorglin's rural hinterland, however, was still firmly in republican hands. On Friday night, 3 November they blew up a bridge at Meanus to impede government troop movements on the back roads between Killorglin and Killarney.[45] The establishment of a maritime trade link to Killorglin was also seen (to a lesser degree) as a back door, an alternative way of getting much needed foodstuffs to Killarney without the risk of the convoy being held up, as was the norm on the Tralee–Killarney road. For republican units based in the foothills of Macgillycuddy's Reeks, procurement of food and shelter was a paramount concern. Purely for their own survival they were going to make use of any opportunity to obtain both. At Dunloe Cross on the night of Saturday/Sunday, 11/12 November armed men held up a food convoy travelling between Killorglin and Killarney and took eight loads.

Many households that provided lodgings for republicans in districts such as Derrynafena, Lisliebane (Glencar) and Dunloe, and many other areas, received generous quantities of stolen food (and probably the horse and cart that transported them) in recognition of their support of what they would have regarded as the republican resistance of a foreign government (i.e. Dublin) supported by Britain. At a more parochial level the anti-Treaty IRA were locals – Kerrymen, friends and neighbours that had 'stood up' to the British during the War of Independence – whereas the Free State forces stationed in Kerry, predominantly units drawn from the Dublin and Clare/Galway areas, were seen as outsiders; but worse than that, they were perceived as settling for far less than the ideals the IRA in Kerry had fought for between 1919 and 1921.

At the other end of the spectrum many Kerry people accepted the Treaty terms as a good deal for Ireland, and actively worked to popularise the Provisional Government's position and perspective on the ground in their localities. Killorglin was no exception in this regard, though it was not a risk-free activity to nail one's colours too firmly to the mast. Daniel

O'Donoghue, a shopkeeper from the Caragh Lake district of Killorglin, was kidnapped and the contents of his shop were looted in mid-November because he had recruited for the national army and got neighbours to repair broken bridges.[46] It was obviously meant as a deterrent to him and a warning to others.

On Sunday, 5 November Archdeacon Marshall, parish priest of Kenmare, left the text of the bishop's pastoral on republican violence on the pulpit, to be read by his curate. After first mass, a girl, a national schoolteacher in the town, seized the document and shredded it. Next morning on the way to school pupils pelted her with potatoes. That night their houses were raided and quantities of potatoes seized. The following Sunday (12 November) Archdeacon Marshall denounced the thefts. Later the same night three of the parish priests' fat bullocks were commandeered by the IRA.[47] It is interesting that a schoolteacher took such radical action, not least because she would have been employed by the parish priest, who was also the school manager, and was putting her job on the line for the sake of a political principle. The tit-for-tat reprisal actions prompted by No. 2 brigade commander, John Joe Rice, may seem petty minded and somewhat comical, but they contain a far more sinister tone in their subtext, namely a total disregard for freedom of speech for those who opposed their actions. Equally, the economic penalties republicans imposed on their opponents were disproportionate to the level of criticism offered by their political adversaries. The dispute was also personal. In late August John Joe Rice's mother wrote to the bishop of Kerry complaining about Fr Marshall's homily directed at her son, where he referred to the IRA as 'misguided youths and uneducated boys, led by officers infinitely worse ... her son,' she wrote, 'would stand a better test of character than the Priest, being a total abstainer from alcohol and tobacco. The Priest, on the other hand, was accustomed to drinking whiskey ... and knew all the brands of whiskey better than any barmaid. She could not be expected to listen to a man like that abuse her son or any IRA man.'[48]

Around the same time a group of armed men seized a vessel of 300 tons owned by the Spiller and Baker Line as it docked at Kenmare pier, and forced the crew to head for Sneem, where they unloaded and seized seventy tons of flour. The *Cork Examiner*, in an editorial comment, noted there was already a considerable shortage of food in the area, a situation further exacerbated by the fact that rural people had no means of marketing their butter, eggs and other produce, to the economic detriment of both town and county dwellers.

While the republican military campaign was largely directed against the national army, there were rare occasions when civilians were caught up in the crossfire. On one such occasion, Wednesday, 8 November, Jeremiah McKenna (thirty), an unmarried man, and his mother (sixty) fell victim to an ambush by anti-Treatyites on a patrol of cycle corps of the national army near Milltown village. 'The son, who was shot in the abdomen, died in the County Infirmary, Tralee, this morning (Sunday). His mother, who was shot in the head is still unconscious at the same Institution.'[49] Subsequent editions of the *Cork Examiner* provide no additional information on the McKennas, who lived near a wood on the Castlemaine side of Milltown.

In the midst of the Civil War private conflicts brought forth violent actions, which appear to have had their origins in disputes over land. Denis O'Sullivan (sixty-nine) was fired on by a shotgun as he entered his house at Bunygara, Listowel. He was shot in the back and was said to be perilously wounded in the attack, which occurred around 11/12 November.[50]

Later that same week, Thomas Geraghty, a steward at Arthur Blennerhassett's Ballyseedy demesne, was challenged at 10 a.m. by a man wielding a shotgun, who subsequently shot him in the chest. As he lay on the ground his assailant reloaded and fired at his head, but missed. The man then fled the scene.[51] Ostensibly, neither of these two murder attempts had anything to do with the Civil War, yet the sense of normality of the daily exchanges of fire between the two belligerents created a culture that – in deed, if not in fact – violence was an effective and an acceptable way of resolving conflicts. Added to this the knowledge that the likelihood of being punished for any wrongdoings by the civil power was extremely slim only encouraged unscrupulous people to take the law into their own hands. Few could argue that the Civil War didn't create a murderous environment in Kerry.

On Friday, 9 November at 9.15 p.m., while curfew was in operation in Caherciveen, Sergeant John O'Callaghan (originally from west Cork but serving with Free State forces in Kerry) and his girlfriend were walking down one of the laneways in Caherciveen. When they were about 400 yards from the sentry post the soldier on duty called on them to halt, a challenge he repeated three subsequent times. He then shot Sergeant O'Callaghan beneath the heart; O'Callaghan died of his injuries early on Saturday morning.[52] The military authorities in Caherciveen held an immediate inquest into the circumstances surrounding John O'Callaghan's death. The sentry (whose identity was not disclosed to the press) who fired the fatal shot was distraught at the consequences of his actions, and explained that he had been sniped at while on duty at the same location on a previous occasion. The seemingly irrational explanation the soldier provided for the shooting would now be identified as post-traumatic stress disorder by military psychiatrists, although such a medical condition would not have been recognised in the 1920s.

Since September the mainstay of the Free State military strategy in Kerry had been to concentrate forces in an area where republican activity was high and actively seek out the local units, surround and capture them and seize their arms and ammunition. On the other hand, the republicans' aim was to sabotage and disrupt both road and rail communications and, where the terrain and cover was suitable, harass and ambush smaller motorised or foot patrols. In reality this was a high-risk strategy for both sides; while the larger force and firepower favoured the government troops, the element of surprise and local knowledge gave the republicans an edge. Once an exchange was under way, however, even a simple mistake or miscalculation could easily alter the course of events and the hunter could become the quarry.

On Thursday, 9 November a detachment of Dublin Guard under the command of Captain Culhane and Lieutenant Michael Lyons was operating in the mountains between Rathmore and Headford when the anti-Treatyites opened fire on them. Realising they were being surrounded, Lyons flanked, forcing the republicans to retreat towards Culhane's column. Over a period of an hour a running gun battle took place across the hillside, during which time the republicans had to fight hard to avoid being encircled. The government force estimated five or six republicans were wounded during the exchange of fire. Lyons was promoted to captain in recognition of the role he played in averting what could have been a major reverse for the national army.[53]

On Monday, 13 November a patrol of 1st Westerns travelling between Castlemaine and Tralee was ambushed near Farmers' Bridge. Two soldiers were wounded in the initial exchange of fire, but the initiative changed in the army's favour when they captured three prisoners, including Staff Captain Peter O'Connell of Aunascaul (who was regarded as a significant figure, and would be sentenced to death in January 1923 for being in possession of a weapon in this incident), and seized a rifle, forty rounds of ammunition, three sticks of gelignite and three detonators. The claim was also made that several of the republicans who escaped had been wounded.[54] The next day, 14 November, in separate sweeps in Abbeydorney and the Castlemaine/Ballymacelliggott areas troops took twenty-five and twenty-three republicans prisoner, the equivalent of an entire column and a substantial setback for the republican cause in both areas.

Around the same time a sweep of the Dingle, Cloghane and Castlegregory districts unearthed two huts/dugouts containing over one hundred detonators, substantial quantities of ammunition and two tons of flour. The manoeuvre led to the capture of eleven prisoners, including two girls. In the Slieve Mish/Derrymore area (Paddy Cahill's old stomping ground) troops wounded two republicans and killed one, Michael Flynn from Tralee, during the course of the search. The following Sunday, 20 November, during Flynn's funeral, troops surrounded part of the cemetery and arrested fourteen men on the basis that they were all active republicans and the deceased's comrades in arms.[55]

Elsewhere in Kerry, sweeps produced comparatively small, but nonetheless significant, gains for the Free State side, especially when viewed both in their cumulative effect and their local impact. In Caherciveen, for example, on 18 November, Commandant Griffin took nine republicans prisoner and captured nine rifles, four revolvers, seventeen grenades, 500 rounds of ammunition, a quantity of explosives and three motorcycles. The loss of that number of men and materials must have been a major setback for the anti-Treaty force in Iveragh. In Glenbeigh a few days later the Dublin Guard took six republicans prisoner (named as Frank Griffin, Michael O'Connor, Jeremiah O'Sullivan, Thomas Cahill, Hugh O'Neill and Michael Hogan) and captured their rifles, ammunition and grenades. Three republicans were arrested at Ballyheige on 25 November; two were charged with a robbery of dog tax from Abbeydorney post office, while the third was charged with desertion from the Free State army in March.[56]

There was no coordinated republican campaign at this point, each local column being left to its own devices and initiatives. An anonymous phone call to Ballymullen barracks alerted the authorities that the railway line between Tralee and Castleisland was mined. The crew dispatched to inspect the line found nothing, but were subjected to hostile fire as they returned to Tralee; no injuries were reported. Around 21–22 November the road bridge at Derryquay between Tralee and Camp was blown up and a road bridge at Abbeydorney was destroyed but later repaired by civilians. On 27 November the railway bridge on the Tralee–Limerick line between Listowel and Lixnaw was destroyed in an explosion. The bridge was repaired, but it was decided to establish a permanent guard post at Lixnaw to protect the bridge from future attacks. The army also decided to carry out night patrols at random on the north Kerry rail network in the hope of capturing rail saboteurs red-handed.

On Saturday night, 25 November a patrol of 1st Westerns challenged a group of men interfering with the railway line at Ballynascare, near Abbeydorney. The republicans opened fire, wounding Private Edward Kavanagh before surrendering to the larger force arrayed against them. Among the five men arrested was Humphrey Murphy's brother, who because of the darkness was mistakenly identified as Humphrey Murphy. Both the *Freeman's Journal* and the *Cork Examiner* featured the capture of Humphrey Murphy in their 28 November 'War News' columns. Had the premature 'news' been accurate it would have been a major advance militarily as well as a massive publicity coup for Kerry command, not least because Murphy himself was an adept practitioner of the propaganda value of news. As recently as 18 November he had announced that from 20 November onwards all military/Red Cross ambulances operating in his command area would be regarded as armoured cars and fired upon, his point being that Free State authorities were using them to transport armed (able-bodied, not wounded) troops and ammunition, and as such in violation of the Geneva Convention for a non-combatant vehicle.

The Emergency Powers Act had been in operation for over a month by mid-November, but hadn't really brought about the sea change Mulcahy and O'Higgins had anticipated in the anti-Treaty side's attitude to, and activities against, the Provisional Government. Unless and until an IRA Volunteer was shot for possession of a weapon, the deterrent value of the law would be useless, O'Higgins argued. Erskine Childers was arrested in Glendalough, County Wicklow in mid-November and was charged with possession of a weapon, ironically a pistol given to him by Michael Collins during the War of Independence, in the event he might need it to shoot his way out of being captured by crown agents. Childers was a *bête noir* to many senior figures in both the political and military leadership of the Provisional Government. Once Childers was apprehended it was inevitable that he would be found guilty and executed, although it is inconceivable that such a killing would have received Collins' approval had he been alive.

In order to prepare the ground and mould public opinion for the execution of a national figure, and to bring home to rank and file republicans that the terms of the law applied to them just as much as it did to a high-profile figure such as Childers, O'Higgins sanctioned four executions to show that the government could control things in its own back yard, the national capital. Figures published in the *Freeman's Journal* in early November on street ambushes and attacks in Dublin since August provide interesting reading, not least when viewed in comparison with the casualty levels experienced in Kerry during the corresponding three-month period.

At Kilmainham jail on Friday, 17 November James Fisher, Peter Cassidy, Richard Twohig and John Gaffney met their death by firing squad in what were the first judicial killings of the war. It is worth pointing out that by this time there had already been between six and ten *de facto* summary executions in Kerry. In poor health, Childers was appealing the legality of his sentence, when on 24 November 1922 he was placed before a firing squad at Beggars Bush barracks, Dublin, the national army's headquarters, and shot dead.

Casualties in street ambushes – Dublin

Month	National Army	Anti-Treatyites	Civilians	Total No. attacks
	K/W	K/W	K/W	
August	1–2	0–4	1-18	32
September	2–6	0–1	1–11	28
October	0–4	0–1	0–14	19[57]

Casualties in the War in Kerry

Month	National Army	Anti-Treatyites	Civilians	Total No. Attacks
August	22–c.50	5–n.a.	1–5	n. a.
September	13–c.50	4–n.a.	2–2	n. a.
October	8–12	5–n.a.	0–0	n. a.[58]

During the War of Independence, Cumann na mBan, the republican women's association, aided the IRA's campaign in urban areas by helping to dispose of weapons (pistols or revolvers in particular) after an ambush, thereby preventing activists being apprehended with a 'smoking gun'. Given the central role being found in possession of arms or ammunition played in the public order legislation, Kerry command saw female activists as a loophole that needed to be closed off to secure more prosecutions. Thus in late November 1922 a room was set aside in the county jail, Moyderwell (now a Kerry County Council depot), to accommodate female republican prisoners. Among the earliest inmates of this new facility were Miss M. Breen, Miss N. Hurley, both of High Street, Killarney, Miss O'Connor, New Street, Killarney and Miss O'Leary of Kilgarvan.[59] A few days later they were joined by Miss Molly Hughes who was found in possession of arms and arrested in Castlemaine.[60] At most perhaps no more than two dozen women were incarcerated at Moyderwell, and most of them (along with hundreds of male prisoners) were transferred to prisons in Dublin in January and early February 1923 to alleviate serious overcrowding. In the general scheme of things prisoner comfort was not a consideration in either the male or female prisons. According to Billy Mullins, some had a more sinister purpose, recalling that during the winter of 1922–23 prisoners lit a fire in one of the cells at the prison only to find themselves at the receiving end of a massive explosion caused, he claimed, by someone placing dynamite in the chimney shaft.[61]

Between four and five in the afternoon on Saturday, 25 November the various army outposts in Rathmore came under sustained fire from Lewis and Thompson machine-guns as well as rifles. The Cox family home, which also doubled as a Dublin Guard outpost, also came under fire from republicans who were based in Mickeen's copse, a wooded area about 400 yards north of the house. Michael Cox later recalled the experience:

> One evening there was a great commotion in the house … Sergeant Kavanagh was lying on the floor below the level of the window sill. Meanwhile soldiers were running about the place and in a moment one or two shots rang out to be followed by a rapid fusillade. We were ordered to lie on a mattress on the floor, and keep our heads down … and from that position we became aware that a soldier manned every sandbagged loophole and the house was, in fact, under attack … The sound of bullets hitting the stonewalls outside, and the ping of ricochet was nothing compared to the ear splitting noise of rifle shots from inside the house. In total darkness it was not a pleasant experience … and in the very height of the firing everything was almost totally excluded by the smell of gunpowder.[62]

Amazingly, no casualties were sustained in any of the outposts in Rathmore, according to Captain O'Donnell, O/C of the local garrison. A local youth named Hickey, from the west of the village, had a lucky escape, only suffering a flesh wound when a bullet grazed his stomach during the attack. The next day, Sunday, 26 November, Volunteer Michael Casey was reported to have been shot dead in Rathmore, but O'Donnell's comments, printed in the *Cork Examiner* of 30 November makes no reference to this fatality.[63] If Michael Casey was killed, he was the fifth national soldier to die in Kerry during November (a few days earlier Private F. Mullen – Curragh Reserves – died of shotgun wounds he received in an ambush in Lixnaw), making that month's fatalities the lowest since the conflict began in August. In fact the losses for both October (eight killed) and November (five dead) were the same as the entire death toll for September, which was well below the comparatively high levels of twenty-two men killed in action during August. The decline in the number of fatalities combined with the widespread and relatively high numbers of prisoners taken into custody (well in excess of two hundred, including eight women) during these two months was objective proof (or so it seemed in government circles) that the tide was flowing very much in the Free State's favour across the board in Kerry.

As November progressed into December this trend continued. A joint sweep carried out by the Dublin Guard and 1st Westerns across Rathmore, Kilcummin and Barraduff districts in the week ending Friday, 1 December led to the capture of thirty-nine men (one of whom was wounded in the 'round up') and the seizure of substantial amounts of equipment. The same week fifteen men were arrested in the Currow/Scartaglen area and thirty-nine grenades and a quantity of explosives were recovered. In Spa four prisoners (named as Walsh, Few, Lane and Leary) were captured in a dugout where they were found in possession of two rifles, two Colt revolvers and one hundred rounds of ammunition. Even allowing for the 'spin' used in the press to announce these advances, they were evidently damaging the republicans' ability to wage an effective military resistance in large areas of the county.

Sometimes a patrol went out with a limited and more sinister agenda. On 30 November two Free State troops called to the house of Patrick Lynch at the family farm at Moyreisk, in the Ballinaskelligs/Caherciveen district. According to Dorothy Macardle, whose *Tragedies of Kerry* account of events is strongly biased in favour of the republican line, they asked him to identify himself and shot him dead.[64]

9

A Light at the End of the Tunnel?

On Friday, 1 December an ambulance was held up near Castle-island. Both crew members were unarmed, but the republicans took the soldiers' greatcoats and leggings.[1] This action was evidently carried out to bring home to the military authorities that Humphrey Murphy's warning of 18 November regarding ambulances as military vehicles wasn't an idle threat. One wonders what action would have been taken by the republicans had one or other of the crew been armed. The discovery would have been a great propaganda coup for the republicans, and a vindication of Murphy's allegations. Would they have been shot or even killed to set a precedent? Taking the crew's greatcoats, etc. was a practical measure, providing protection against the elements, but would also enable republicans to appear as government troops staffing a military checkpoint. On Sunday evening, 3 December, in a separate and (as far as I can determine) totally unrelated incident on the main street in Castleisland, William Brosnan, a twenty-six-year-old butcher was shot dead while walking along the street with a friend. An army foot patrol was on the street at the time, and the newspaper report assumed they carried out the shooting. No inquiry was carried out to determine the circumstances surrounding Brosnan's death.[2]

During the first week in December Sergeant A. Daly and

five civic guards arrived in Listowel to police the town. It was expected that District Magistrate O'Donoghue would introduce regular petty sessions at the courthouse very soon.[3] This represented a huge leap of faith on the part of the military authorities in Kerry, as it handed over responsibility for law and order (leastwise within a 'safe' area) to an unarmed police force in a county where what might be described as 'normal' civic society was far from universally agreed, never mind fully implemented, and in an area that was still highly militarised.

In late November and early December, for example, ordinary (reported) crime in Kerry involved large-scale looting in the Milltown/Castlemaine district. The army arrested several suspects at Callinafercy and burned their boats. A commercial traveller was robbed and had cash and cheques taken while on his rounds in Glenbeigh; while in Killarney, a carter transporting a consignment of boots from the railway station to a drapery shop in the town had his entire load taken.[4]

Politically motivated violence directed against the rail network, or aimed at intimidating prominent individuals who might be termed government activists, continued. In the former category, a train driver (unnamed) travelling on the Tralee–Fenit line suffered shrapnel injuries when a landmine exploded under the 'cow catcher' part of the locomotive he was driving. James O'Sullivan, a national teacher from Rockfield (near Killarney), had his coach house and stables burned, resulting in the loss of a pony, a trap, harnesses and the buildings in question. Its modern day equivalent would be the destruction of a car, major property damage and the cause of substantial financial hardship.[5]

During the course of a sweep in the Dunloe/Beaufort district, which in early December 1922 was still very much a republican enclave, Colonel James Dempsey of the Dublin Guard was wounded in the eye in an area known as the Devil's Punchbowl. While the wounded officer was being led to safety by two other soldiers, the party was challenged by John Kevins, a local republican officer, who recognised Dempsey. Realising the military were increasingly using Emergency Powers legislation against republicans, Kevins saw the value of having a high-ranking hostage in republican custody should the authorities in Ballymullen barracks decide to execute republican prisoners for firearms offences in Kerry. Dempsey could be used in negotiations for a prisoner exchange if the need arose at a future stage in the conflict. Kevins brought Dempsey to Nurse O'Sullivan in Beaufort to have first aid administered to his prisoner's wounds. She referred him on to Dr Conroy, who was sympathetic to the republican cause to the extent that he would administer medical assistance to republicans if they were wounded. As soon as Conroy saw the extent of Dempsey's injuries he told Kevins that such a wound could only be properly treated in a hospital, and persuaded Kevins that he (Conroy) should hand over Dempsey to the military authorities in Killarney.[6] Dempsey underwent a medical examination in Killarney and was transferred to the Mater hospital in Dublin, as the level of medical expertise available to treat military injuries in Kerry was rudimentary. During December, Dempsey was one of among thirty army wounded in Kerry who were sent to various hospitals in Dublin to have their wounds properly treated.[7]

Though of negligible value militarily, Kenmare, because it represented the government army's greatest military reversal in the war in Kerry, was a source of great embarrassment and trauma for many senior officers in Kerry, not least because of the brutal murder of the O'Connor brothers that occurred during the September attack. As the only town in Kerry still in republican hands in December, Kenmare represented a huge challenge, a psychological barrier, and a prize that once captured would shorten the war, not only because it would open a shorter supply route to Killarney, but also because its capture would deprive republicans of a sea port that facilitated the replenishment of food, supplies and ammunition. At least this was how the town was seen from Ballymullen barracks. Two previous attempts, in late August and late October, had been made to relieve the town, but both had to be abandoned *en route* in the face of clever use of topography by a comparatively small republican column that forced both relief columns to return ignominiously to Killarney. Under the cover of darkness over the night of 5/6 December three distinct (but coordinated) columns of government troops converged on Kenmare. One, the 1st Westerns under Michael Hogan, approached the town from the north (Killarney); the second, a Dublin Guard unit under Paddy O'Daly, landed on Dinish island; while the third column, commanded by Commandant Griffin, set out from Caherciveen, approaching the town via the Kenmare river. All three forces arrived in Kenmare at 1.15 a.m. on Wednesday, 6 December where they met with no resistance.[8] The date of the capture, 6 December, was highly symbolic as the very same day in the Dáil the Provisional Government would cease to exist and be replaced by the Irish Free State. The fact that the two senior commanders in Kerry – O'Daly and Hogan – personally led their own commands indicates that they were determined to take Kenmare on that day regardless of the resistance its garrison might offer to prevent the town's capture.

While the conflict in Kerry was in many respects an intensely local affair, it did not exist in a vacuum. The inauguration of the Free State parliament on 6 December 1922 not only represented the first anniversary of the signing of the Treaty, but it also brought home to the general public that militarily the anti-Treaty campaign had not succeeded in the overthrow of the Provisional Government. Six months into the conflict, however, many on the anti-Treaty side did not concede defeat. Liam Lynch, as the military leader of the republicans, announced in early December that if the policy of executing prisoners continued, any member of Dáil Éireann who had signed what he termed the 'murder bill' (Lynch's shorthand for the Emergency Powers Act) would be regarded as a legitimate target for assassination.

On 7 December members of the Dublin brigade shot Seán Hales, a government TD from Cork, and Pádraig Ó Máille, the leas ceann comhairle (deputy speaker of the Dáil) near Leinster House, killing Hales and seriously wounding Ó Máille. The government response, seemingly initiated by Richard Mulcahy, defence minister, was draconian. On 8 December four senior republican prisoners who had been in state custody since the seizure of the Four Courts in June – Rory O'Connor, Liam Mellows, Joe McKelvey and Dick Barrett – were executed by firing squad. Like the background to the Childers execution the event featured poignant twists. Kevin O'Higgins, justice minister, who agreed to the executions with great reluctance, had to issue the death warrants, including the one for Rory O'Connor who had been the best man at his wedding.

The eighth of December was a Church holiday, and traditionally one of the most important pre-Christmas shopping days in Kerry. A grand bazaar was held at the skating rink in Tralee that evening. There were about five hundred people attending the event, including many women and children, when a five-man uniformed military patrol arrived at the hall.

Three of the soldiers – Lieutenant Joseph Parsons, Thomas Knowles and Seán Walsh – were military police corps; they drew their revolvers and fired warning shots in the air, while the other two soldiers stood guard at the entrance to the building. Not surprisingly the gunfire caused a panic and a near stampede in the hall, with several people attempting and being allowed to leave the building. William Harrington (aged twenty-three), described as an only son and a builder's labourer who spoke with a slight stammer, challenged Parsons about his patrol's actions in the hall, comparing their behaviour to that of the Black and Tans.[9] According to Parsons, Harrington then grabbed his free arm and attempted to wrench the revolver from his right hand. In the ensuing struggle the weapon was discharged, fatally wounding Harrington, who died at the scene.

Because of the very public nature of the circumstances surrounding William Harrington's death, the military authorities were anxious to have – and to be seen to have – an enquiry into the sequence of events that led to the death of an unarmed civilian. The investigation carried out by Superintendent Hennigan, civic guards, Tralee stretched on into late January 1923 (it was adjourned due to the death of one of the witnesses, Eugene Collins, a grocer from Bridge Street, Tralee, who died in a house fire on 30 December along with his daughter, Lily). When it did offer a verdict, it produced an inconclusive result. Witnesses Michael O'Driscoll, Caherina, Tralee and Ellen Breen of Rae Street, Tralee both said that Parsons fired the shot. John Coughlan, one of the military attending the search, gave evidence that Parsons did not shoot Harrington.[10] The presiding judge suggested that the next of kin submit a malicious injuries claim for the loss of their son.

In mid-December the staunchly pro-government *Freeman's Journal* produced an upbeat editorial, commenting on the changed nature of the war in Kerry. It observed:

> Six months ago nobody could stir with any degree of safety outside Tralee … and within the town snipers were very active. National army posts were continually sniped at, and troops travelling from Tralee to Spa/Fenit (on one side) and to and from Tralee, Killarney, Farranfore, Killorglin … in fact anywhere in the county, considered it lucky that they were not shot up at least twice during the journey. Looting was common. Traders were afraid to make any road journey owing to numerous hold ups and seizures of goods. Across the entire area of Kerry three months ago rail travel was impossible due to wholesale destruction of bridges, the dragging up of rails, the burning of signal cabins and stations. People were in many cases actually starving. As a matter of fact it is common knowledge that there was a split in the Irregular Camp because of the tactic of ambushing food convoys. As a result there was a marked slackening of convoy attacks. The success of army sweeps in the intervening months has done much to limit Irregular activity in the county.[11]

Around the same time as the *Freeman's Journal* penned its feature article on Kerry, the commander of the Limerick/Kerry military district, General W. R. E. Murphy, in an official communiqué to Richard Mulcahy, the defence minister, conveyed the impression that the war was virtually over – if not necessarily won – in Kerry. He wrote: 'The Irregular organisation here is well nigh broken up. The capture of Kenmare will dispose of their last rallying ground … We are still 250 men short of the 1,000 I budgeted for. With these we could put posts in Barraduff, Beaufort, Glenbeigh and in Kilgarvan. Then you can mark off Kerry as finished. In fact it nearly is now.'[12] At the start of the second week in December additional troops arrived in Killarney, to be billeted at the Glebe hotel.[13] Some of the new arrivals were sent to Beaufort, where an outpost was established so as to enable government troops to make inroads into the hitherto impregnable republican heartland of Macgillycuddy's Reeks.

Following the capture of Kenmare fourteen prisoners were taken, among them Humphrey Healy of Kilgarvan, who was identified as having played a prominent role in the September assault on the town. The army also reported that substantial quantities of looted material were recovered. A sweep of the Bandon/Castlegregory area on Saturday, 9 December led to the capture of ten prisoners, two of whom (Spillane and Murphy) were identified as deserters from the Free State army, who presumably were among the fifty or so soldiers who joined the republican side after the fall of Listowel the previous June. Captain Roche and Lieutenant Kennelly, who made the arrests, estimated their sweep had radically reduced the effectiveness of Paddy Cahill's column.[14]

Republicans, however, were still able to mount large-scale ambushes on government troops. On Friday, 15 December a unit of the Dublin Guard travelling between Barraduff and Rathmore was attacked by an anti-Treaty force of about seventy men in an exchange of fire that lasted between three and four hours. The government force sustained no injuries in this attack. As republican fire petered out the column moved on from the Bower only to fall victim to a second attack a little further along the road, which lasted about an hour, and left three soldiers wounded, one of whom, Private Matthew Ferguson of Virginia, County Cavan, died of his injuries on Sunday, 17 December.[15]

According to the official – i.e. army – version of events they inflicted heavy casualties on the anti-Treatyites during the course of the Bower attack. Interestingly, Jeremiah Murphy, who was active in the Barraduff column at this time, barely mentions the ambush in his memoir, *When Youth was Mine*: '… a small force of IRA were unsuccessful … when they attacked the patrol at the Bower.'[16] Even then all he noted was that Canon Carmody, parish priest of Rathmore, gathered a large crowd of sympathisers to remove trees the republicans had felled to impede Free State army troop movements in the area. As they worked, the IRA fired shots above their heads, dispersing the crowd. Later on three or four of the canon's fat bullocks were taken as a reprisal and used to feed the local republican column. An army patrol arrived to seize the cattle of Jeremiah Reen, a republican sympathiser, bringing them to Killarney, where they were never heard from again.

The Barraduff column had been in action in the Macroom/Ballymackeera/Millstreet area in tandem with the west Cork brigade, where the levels of republican activity had increased considerably since Tom Barry returned to his old stomping ground following an escape from Gormanston camp in September 1922. Barry's unit had acquired two armoured cars in raids in Bandon and in Macroom. Jeremiah Murphy and many in the Barraduff battalion hoped that the west Cork brigade might repay the Kerrymen by lending its support and one of their armoured cars on an attack on the Rathmore garrison. This did not happen because the Free State authorities in both counties had invested huge resources in recapturing the vehicles, not least because one of them, the 'Slievenamon', was in the convoy that had accompanied Michael Collins to Béal na mBláth.

Private Ferguson appears to have been only the second fatality Free State forces sustained in Kerry that month. Earlier in December Volunteer John Martin was killed, but I have not been able to unearth any information on the circumstances surrounding his death.[17] In Dingle two days later, 19 December, Private Mullhall of the Dublin Guard was also killed, but again, details of the circumstances surrounding his death are hard to come by.[18]

At a meeting of Tralee Rural District Council held on 16 December, when nine councillors were in attendance, Councillors Maurice Keane and D. Long proposed the motion, 'The actions of the Irish government – on executions – exceeds the worst tyranny of the British government', and called upon the Kerry TDs to resign in protest.[19] The blanket criticism was by no means unanimous, as in early January the seven other councillors present at the meeting would visit military headquarters at Ballymullen to repudiate the wording of the statement issued on their behalf. Republican TDs did not attend the Dáil in any case, so any appeals to government TDs to repudiate a measure (the execution of O'Connor, Mellows, *et al.*) that was intended to prevent further assassinations of pro-Treaty parliamentarians by republicans was unlikely to garner much support among the very people it was aimed to protect.

Since early December the military court sitting at Ballymullen barracks, presided over by General W. R. E. Murphy, had been deliberating on the charges of possession of arms and ammunition – a capital offence – brought against four republicans. Legal counsel included Joseph McCarthy, BL, D. P. Kenny and Dr O'Connell. Present in the dock were Matthew Moroney, Boherbee, Tralee; Cornelius Casey, Bridge Street,

Tralee; Dermot O'Connor, Moyderwell, Tralee; and Thomas Devane of Dingle, County Kerry, who had been arrested near Knockane in late November.

The death sentences were announced by General Murphy on Wednesday, 20 December but a stay of execution was granted post-21 December. Immediately posters were put up in and around Tralee announcing an indefinite stay of execution would apply if: 1. Irregular ambushes or attacks on national troops ceased; 2. interference with railway and road communications stopped; and 3. interference with private property came to an end.[20] It appears peace feelers were being sent out by Free State sources to the republican leadership around this time (according to Jeremiah Murphy), possibly a variation of the meeting held at Ballymacelligott in the autumn (mentioned by Ryle Dwyer), attended by Paddy Daly and David Neligan (on the government side) and Tom McEllistrim and John Joe Rice (on the republican side). Thus, the stay of execution may have been a genuine attempt to offer an olive branch to the enemy and avoid further antagonising republican opinion in Kerry.

This incident seems to be the only occasion such a policy was used during the Civil War. According to an interview given much later in his life, Con Casey's wife indicated the sole reason that the four men's lives were spared was a counter poster campaign organised by Humphrey Murphy, O/C Kerry No. 1 brigade, in which posters were put up around Tralee announcing that republicans would execute eight government supporters in Kerry (eight individuals were identified) if the sentences announced on 20 December were carried out.[21]

On Thursday night, 21 December the house of Thomas Blennerhassett, Cullenagh, Beaufort, was entered by anti-Treatyites. Blennerhassett's family and his brother's family took refuge upstairs. Armed men piled furniture near the door and poured paraffin oil on it and set it alight. The Blennerhassetts left the building. The house was subsequently destroyed by fire.[22] This was an ownership dispute that predated the Civil War and owed its origins to the Land War agitation of the 1880s. In reality the arson attack owed more to local loyalties than to any politico-sectarian fault lines. A few days before the Cullenagh attack, on Sunday, 17 December, members of the newly established army garrison in Beaufort village came under fire from republicans while marching in a Church parade. Two soldiers were wounded in the exchange of fire, in which they claimed to have inflicted injuries on their assailants.[23] Evidently the Free State presence was causing problems for the republicans as it made further inroads into what was up until that point a safe haven.

The arrival of a party of civic guards in Killarney around Christmas eve, where they took up temporary residence at the Glebe hotel, was further proof that the military authorities in Kerry saw the introduction of an unarmed police force as a yardstick of the return of a normal civil society to another pacified area of Kerry.[24] It was a brave – though probably still a premature – bow to optimism rather than to realism.

On Saturday, 23 December, Daniel J. Browne, solicitor, a close associate of Austin Stack, was arrested at the railway station in Tralee. It was probably a case of guilt by association, as there is no evidence that Austin Stack had (either through an intermediary or otherwise) any involvement in directing either the IRA's campaign militarily or politically in Kerry during the Civil War period. Of course it is quite possible that the Free

State military authorities believed he had a leading role, with Daniel Browne serving as a proxy commander. Around the same time as Browne's arrest two anti-Treatyites, one named Healy (from Limerick), the other Gleeson (from Sixmilebridge, County Clare) were captured. One of the prisoners was wearing the uniform of Dr Lynch, who had been captured by the anti-Treatyites some time previously.[25] The report doesn't say where in Kerry the arrest took place. One can imagine that both prisoners would have been at the receiving end of a fairly brutal interrogation.

While attending midnight mass at Curragheen church on Christmas eve, no fewer than twenty-two republicans were arrested by the military, seven of them captured while hiding under the altar, in an operation facilitated by the local parish priest. The security situation in Tralee generally was regarded so positively that Christmas that no curfew was enforced over the festive season. On St Stephen's day, Tuesday, 26 December James Mangan, a nineteen-year-old from Mangerton View, Killarney was walking with two friends, Hugh O'Sullivan and James O'Connell, through Fair Hill/Spa in the direction of the heavily wooded Kilbrean area when they heard a shot from far off followed by two calls. At the next shot Mangan fell and his friends dived for cover and did not move for ten minutes. Two men approached them, one carrying a gun, and told them to put up their hands. He said he saw the three men, called on them to stop, thinking them to be a plainclothes (undercover military) patrol. He brought Mangan's body back to the house, washed it and said a rosary. An inquest presided over by Doctor W. O'Sullivan and Inspector Ryan, civic guard, returned a verdict of wilful murder against a person or persons unknown.[26]

On Friday, 29 December republicans opened fire on an army foot patrol returning to their barracks in Castlegregory. Two soldiers, Private John Talty of Lisadeen, County Clare and Private Henry McLoughlin of Buncrana, County Donegal, were killed in the attack and another two were wounded. The republicans also burned a portion of the station.[27] The two soldiers were the last recorded fatalities of the Civil War in Kerry during 1922 and Privates Talty and McLoughlin represented the fifty-third and fifty-fourth soldiers to be killed in action – or die of wounds – in confrontations with the enemy in the six months since 30 June, when twenty-year-old Edward Sheehy was killed in Listowel.

It is much more difficult to ascertain the number of republicans killed during 1922. At one end of the spectrum, *The Last Post* compiled by republicans in the mid-1930s, noted ten Kerry volunteers were killed in action during the latter part of 1922. Dorothy Macardle gave the number of republicans killed in Kerry that year as seventy-nine, which seems an exaggerated figure, and is probably a more accurate tally of IRA dead in the county for the entire conflict. My own research suggests at least twenty (including two who died of wounds sustained in Limerick during July 1922) whose names I have included in Appendix 2; though I would concede this could be an underestimate.

The Castlegregory ambush brought consequences that made it seem inevitable that the sword of Damocles that had hung over the four prisoners on stay of execution in Tralee jail since 21 December would finally fall. The whole 'hostages to fortune' aspect of Kerry command's execution policy seems to have captured the imagination of a large section of the British tabloid press. As soon as news of the 29 December killings became known across channel, sources such as the *International News Service*, the *Daily Herald*, the *Evening Standard* (London), the *Evening Chronicle* (Manchester) and the *Evening Express* (Liverpool) all reported that the four prisoners in custody in Tralee were executed in reprisal for the Castlegregory attack.[28]

The army publicity office at Portobello barracks (Dublin), in response to numerous requests from both Irish journalists and concerned members of the public to clarify the situation in Tralee, issued a statement that they had received no information from Ballymullen barracks confirming that the death sentences had been carried out. A *Cork Examiner* journalist put the question to W. T. Cosgrave, chairman of the Executive Council: 'Would the Kerry prisoners be executed?'

Cosgrave's reply was terse: 'I very much regret it. I'm afraid they will be.'[29]

As it turned out the four death sentences were commuted to ten years' penal servitude, and in January 1923 the prisoners were transferred from Tralee jail to Mountjoy prison to serve their terms of incarceration. It is unclear how the wider republican movement in Kerry saw the withdrawal of the death sentences. Most probably the gesture was perceived as a sign of weakness, and probably emboldened the more radical republican column commanders to contemplate more audacious actions in the future.

In early January 1923 General W. R. E. Murphy was transferred from Kerry command to assume responsibility for 'operations and organisation' in the army at national level, a post he would retain until the cessation of hostilities in May 1923 when he left the army for an administrative post in the garda síochána, the state's new police force. Brigadier Paddy O'Daly,

O/C Dublin Guard, was appointed GOC Kerry command, a promotion approved by Defence Minister Richard Mulcahy and Murphy himself; a decision Murphy would have made differently, he admitted, with the benefit of hindsight, given subsequent events in Kerry during the spring of 1923.

During early January local arrests in various parts of the county reinforced the view that militarily the republican force was crumbling, and that the conflict in Kerry was heading towards a speedy finish. In the fortnight up to 14 January eight prisoners had been arrested in Killorglin, nine in Castleisland, five in Muckross, seven in Aglish and fourteen in Faha, according to military sources. On Saturday, 6 January Pat Raymond (parish court registrar) and James Barrett, both described as 'close associates' of Humphrey Murphy, were among three republican activists arrested in Tralee. Unusually, seven women, among them sisters Ethel Hartnett, Sheila Hartnett (aged seventeen), Paulina Ryan, Hannah Lyons, Hannah O'Connell, Nora Healy, Miss Randall were part of a consignment of ten prisoners transported from Kenmare to Tralee by boat.[30]

On one occasion, on Wednesday, 10 January republicans attempted to rescue eighteen of their colleagues while they were being marched under armed escort between Beaufort and Killarney. According to Commandant Leonard, leader of the prison escort, the attack/rescue attempt occurred in the gap of Dunloe and resulted in the wounding of four prisoners. It is not clear if the prisoners were shot 'while trying to escape' to use the oldest cliché in the military lexicon, or were inadvertently injured by their would-be rescuers.[31]

On Monday, 8 January the Great Southern and Western Railway, in tandem with Kerry command, carried an announcement in the *Cork Examiner* that from Monday, 15 January 1923, after an absence of six months, a full rail service – including postal, telegraphic, freight and passenger facilities – would be available throughout Kerry. It was even speculated that the 'new' network would facilitate the holding of the January fair in Killarney. Combined army and GS & WR repair crews worked frantically that week to complete the rebuilding of the wooden railway bridge at Ardagh, Currans, which was the lynchpin of the entire network in the county. Currans railway bridge was ready for use by Wednesday, 10 January. In many respect the state of the county rail system was a barometer for the way the conflict was going in Kerry at any given moment, and a yardstick that both Free State and republicans could agree on as an indication of success or failure of their campaigns in the county.

Overnight on 10/11 January the newly reconstructed railway bridge at Currans was burned by republicans, severing in one fell swoop the rail link between Tralee and Killarney (Kerry's principal market towns) and, via Farranfore, spur lines to Killorglin, Caherciveen and Castleisland. The next day the GS & WR announced that the services of the linesmen working between Gortatlea and Killarney would be dispensed with following the destruction of the railway bridge. The old horse and cart convoy, which was both slow and expensive to operate and a procedure everyone had hoped was a thing of the past, was reintroduced. On Tuesday morning, 16 January a 100-cart convoy (with a transport cost of £3–15s–00d a ton) travelled from Tralee to Killarney under military escort.[32] If there was an improvement, it was only the circumstance that the troops guarding the convoy did not come under fire *en route*.

On Sunday, 14 January the Ballymacelligott battalion launched a concerted campaign against road and rail infrastructure in its immediate area. The rail and road bridges at Ballymacthomas were destroyed. Both the railway stations at Gortatlea and Molahiffe were burned down. Ballycarthy House, Tralee (unoccupied) was destroyed by fire in anticipation that it was being earmarked for use as a military outpost. Fr Trant, parish priest of Ballymacelligott, vociferous in his condemnation of the arson attacks on the local railway stations because of the hardship their loss inflicted on the local population, had his hayshed burned by republicans, resulting in the destruction of thirty-five tons of hay and three tons of turnips.[33] Elsewhere in Kerry smaller-scale acts of sabotage, though nonetheless debilitating in their immediate locality, were carried out: on 14 January the railway station at Kilgarvan and signal huts at Headford and Kilgarvan were burned down on the Killarney–Kenmare branch line. At the opposite end of the county, T. Allen, stationmaster of the Listowel–Ballybunion railway (Lartigue) was arrested by armed men on Saturday night, 20 January, and forced to open the station. He was held prisoner while the waiting room and goods store were sprinkled with paraffin and set alight. Some hours later on the same night the stationhouse at Lisellton was burned to the ground.[34] Evidently, the selective and comprehensive destruction of not necessarily large – but key – chunks of the Kerry rail network in a period of ten days (10–20 January) was intended to bring home to both the military authorities and the wider population that the war in Kerry was far from over.

On 16 January troops searching in the Ardfert and Ballyheige area discovered three unoccupied dugouts. They arrested one local man, Eugene Fitzgerald, who they believed was a republican and would know the location of the men and arms dumps they were hoping to capture. According to Dorothy Macardle, Fitzgerald was shot because he refused to divulge this information to his captors.[35]

On Wednesday, 17 January Colonel Jim McGuinness decided to use a joint ground patrol in tandem with a reconnaissance plane to check out reports of a concentration of republicans in the Brennan's Glen area, near Farranfore. At the time both Tralee and Killarney race courses were used as makeshift runways for a Bristol/De Haviland aircraft, which also operated out of Fermoy in County Cork. It was late evening when the plane flew over Brennan's Glen, a heavily wooded area and ideal ambush country. As the plane circled above the trees the republicans on the ground opened fire with a Lewis gun. The pilot, Lieutenant Delamere, brought the aircraft down to about 300 feet, allowing his gunner, Lieutenant Flanagan, to drop a bomb, which he claimed wounded as many as half a dozen anti-Treatyites and caused many of the others on the ground to scatter. A motorised column of Dublin Guard was approaching Brennan's Glen at this point, but light was fading rapidly and all the republicans fled under cover of darkness and evaded capture.[36]

Operations carried out under the cover of darkness were extremely risky at the best of times. An army patrol left Listowel at 3 or 4 a.m. on Sunday, 14 January expecting to apprehend a party of anti-Treatyites at a dance in Rathea. Troops took up positions around the house and as a man emerged he was challenged and called upon to stop and identify himself. There was no response and a volley of shots was fired, killing the man, who it emerged was Private Patrick McCarthy (aged twenty-three), a member of the patrol, from Ballinaclogher, Lixnaw. He was buried the next day.[37] Around the same time as the Brennan's Glen ambush a republican sniper opened fire on a Red Cross ambulance near Rathmore, seriously wounding the driver.[38] It was the third attack of its kind in east Kerry, and an indication that Humphrey Murphy's policy was now being implemented with far more lethal force than the first reported incident of its kind in early December, when the crew was stopped but not harmed.

On Thursday morning, 18 January at about 1 a.m. Thomas Prendeville, a farmer from Kilcushan, Castleisland, a married man with four children, was taken into custody along with a friend, named Daniel Daly, by Lieutenant Larkin and questioned at the military post at Hartnett's hotel, Castleisland. While in military custody, Prendeville was shot dead by Lieutenant Larkin, the senior officer at the outpost. The military authorities held an inquest into the circumstances surrounding Prendeville's death in late January. Paymaster Thomas O'Loughlin, a fellow soldier and a friend of Larkin, told Dr O'Connor, the district coroner, his recollection of the sequence of events prior to, and surrounding Thomas Prendeville's death in custody. Terence J. Liston acted for the national army, J. M. Murphy was legal counsel for Lieutenant Larkin, while Thomas O'Neill, Castleisland, represented the interests of the next of kin.

'I went to Castleisland on 17/1/23 to pay the men,' O'Loughlin recalled. 'I met Lieutenant Larkin, and spent the evening in Hussey's public house. We both left the public house at 1 a.m., and proceeded to the Hospital Barracks at the opposite end of the town. Passing Kelleher's public house we saw two individuals leave the house ... questioned them, asking them where they were going. "Home," Prendeville said. He was a Republican and he came in to blow up the Barracks.'

In reply to the coroner, the witness said he took the remark as a joke.

'Both men were strongly under the influence of drink, and we brought them to Hartnett's Post. Lieutenant Larkin took one of the men, Daly, into the Guard Room, while the witness remained outside with Prendeville. Larkin, who had a parabellum revolver, took Prendeville into the guard room, and asked him had he seen any Republicans? Prendeville replied, he'd seen none for three years, but said he knew where arms and ammunition were hidden, but ... would not tell him. Larkin, who had a parabellum, hit Prendeville several times with an open hand. Prendeville ducked, Larkin overbalanced and fell over against him. At the same time three shots rang out and every man in the guard room ran out, except the witness and lieutenant Larkin. There were about five other men in the guard room at the time that the shots went off. Prendeville fell to the ground and the witness grabbed Larkin's revolver.

'It was Lieutenant Larkin who fired the shots. When the witness grabbed the revolver, fearing any further firing would occur, Lieutenant Larkin told him it was all right and the witness did not interfere further.

'Larkin lifted Prendeville onto a bed and whispered an Act of Contrition and sent for a priest and a doctor. Prendeville died about a quarter of an hour later. Larkin wired the authorities as to what happened an hour later.'

In reply to the coroner, the witness said he was with Lieutenant Larkin from three in the afternoon until 1 a.m. Lieutenant

Larkin had drink taken – seven or eight glasses of port and three or four glasses of whiskey, but he was fit for duty. O'Loughlin said he believed the shot went off automatically. O'Loughlin said he came from west Clare, Larkin from east Clare.

Sergeant John Treacy, 1st Westerns, gave a very different account of events to that outlined in O'Loughlin's testimony. He recalled (he) '… saw Larkin challenge Prendeville with a revolver and said, "You must tell me where the irregulars are, and their rifles and ammunition." He had Prendeville standing up against the wall, and Lieutenant Larkin was standing two yards in front of him. While in that position he fired two shots at Prendeville, who fell to the ground. O'Loughlin then attempted to take the revolver. It was not the first time that people were put on their knees in situations like these and threatened.'

In reply to the coroner, Treacy said he 'did not see Larkin strike Prendeville, nor did he see Larkin lurching.' Volunteer Daniel Meaney corroborated Treacy's evidence, adding, 'Larkin was under the influence of drink and was not in a fit condition to be in possession of a loaded weapon, but as he was the senior officer nobody would dare take the revolver from him.'

The jury agreed that the shots were fired by Lieutenant Larkin, adding that the state should compensate the deceased widow.[39]

During the War of Independence many railway workers assisted in the struggle for independence against the British. Their level of involvement varied; generally crews refused to transport military materials, i.e. troops carrying arms and ammunition. Many drivers also participated in Collins' intelligence network, in particular the 'fast track' system, where important messages were sent from Collins' HQ in Dublin to the provinces and vice versa. And of course some rail workers were active in the IRA. With the drift towards Civil War, some of those sympathetic to the republican side did what they could to assist the military struggle against the Provisional/Free State Government. Thus, the IRA in north Kerry received information of a troop train scheduled to travel from Limerick to Listowel on Thursday, 18 January, going from there to Tralee late on Thursday evening. Tom Driscoll of the Kilmoyley column decided the embankment leading to Liscahane Bridge, near Ardfert, would be a good location to both derail and ambush the troop transport. A section of the track was removed. The military train did not arrive in Listowel on schedule, and after allowing time for a delayed arrival, the GS & WR rescheduled the time slot and gave the go-ahead for a freight train to travel from Listowel to Tralee around seven in the evening. Once the IRA unit became aware of the change, it was too late to replace the track, so they changed the signals to red and began firing shots at the train as it approached Liscahane Bridge. It seems this tactic was so familiar and so commonplace as a ruse by republicans before hijacking or robbing a train that in the darkness the driver, Patrick O'Riordan, ignored the challenge.

At about 7.30 p.m. the locomotive pulling twenty-six wagons and with a crew of three on board reached Liscahane, was derailed, jackknifed, and tumbled down the side of the steep embankment. The driver, Patrick O'Riordan (aged fifty) from Tralee, and his fireman, Daniel Crowley (aged thirty-six) from Lower Glanmire Road, Cork, were pinned beneath the locomotive, whose boiler had ruptured; both men received horrendous injuries and were literally crushed and scalded to death. The train guard, Jack Galvin, survived the crash.[40]

The Liscahane rail tragedy raises interesting questions about the republican mindset, and the tactics they were willing to use in their war against the Free State 'occupation' in Kerry. Had the original troop train arrived on schedule another GS & WR crew would have suffered a similar fate to O'Riordan and Crowley, but set against possibly dozens of military casualties their lives would have been seen as expendable by the republicans. Presumably the derailment was only the first part of the planned action, whereby the Kilmoyley column would have opened fire on the survivors as a prelude to capturing the arms and ammunition carried on board the train. All things considered, the attack was intended to be the Civil War equivalent of the Headford ambush.

Public opinion both in Kerry and Ireland generally was appalled by the death of the two railwaymen, and the republican action was condemned by both the National Union of Railwaymen and the Railway Clerks Association. The incident, which came at the height of what might be described as a republican blitz on the Kerry rail network, was perceived as a deliberate attack on civilians doing a day's work (rather than a mistake) in what had become a high risk occupation.

It had equally tragic consequences for four republican prisoners who had played no part in the atrocity. At 8 a.m. on Saturday, 20 January 1923 at Ballymullen barracks, Tralee, James Daly of Knock, Killarney, John Clifford of Mountlake, Caherciveen, Michael Brosnan of Rathenny, Tralee and James Hanlon of Causeway, Tralee were shot by firing squad, ostensibly for being found in possession of arms and ammunition.[41] In reality their lives were taken in a reprisal for the damage the republicans had inflicted on the Kerry rail network over a fortnight, culminating in the death of two railwaymen at Lis-cahane Bridge.

A month earlier, on 20 December, the then O/C, Kerry command, General W. R. E. Murphy, had passed a death sentence on, but granted a stay of execution for, four other prisoners, who by the time the derailment occurred had had their life sentences commuted to ten years in prison. In the interim period Murphy's optimistic view that the republicans in Kerry were virtually defeated was very much contradicted by events and proved to be a good deal premature.

The executions also represented a shift in military culture and demonstrated the differences an individual commander could bring to the management of the conflict. Murphy, a native of County Wexford, served at the highest level in the British army (divisional commander) in both the western and Italian fronts during the First World War, a conflict where the treatment of prisoners was strictly prescribed by the terms of the Geneva Convention. Like Emmet Dalton, who also served in the Great War, Murphy was uncomfortable with both *de facto* killing carried out in the 'field' and the pseudo-legalistic type of execution introduced following the Emergency Powers Act in October 1922.

Brigadier Paddy O'Daly, Murphy's successor, came from a very different military background, that of covert operations and counter-insurgency, most of which he acquired while involved in the shadowy amoral world of political assassination, personified by the Squad. It was a method of warfare typified by the maxim 'an eye for an eye, and a shoot for a shoot'. It was brutal, certainly, but had been a lethally effective instrument for Collins in destroying the network of police and military intelligence in Dublin during the War of Independence. What had been successful on the streets of Dublin would, if persisted with, bring similar results on the lanes of Kerry, and on the lines of republicans. In reference to the Kerry campaign, O'Daly himself is reputed to have said: 'Nobody told me to bring kid gloves to Kerry. So, I didn't bring them.'[42]

During January fierce pressure was being exerted on local area commanders by their political masters in Dublin to bring the war to a speedy conclusion. A regional execution policy was an integral part of this strategy, especially in districts such as Kerry where republicans showed no inclination to wind down the conflict. The Kerry executions should not be viewed in isolation, however. During January 1923, for instance, no fewer than twenty-one republican prisoners were executed by firing squad in a single week:

20 January: four shot in Tralee, two in Limerick, and five in Athlone.
22 January: three shot in Dundalk.
23 January: three shot in Waterford.
26 January: two shot in Birr.
27 January: two shot in Portlaoise.[43]

On Tuesday, 23 January at 8 a.m. a column commanded by Tom McEllistrim and John Joe Sheehy launched an attack on the military garrison at Castlemaine (manned by about sixty troops) which was carried out primarily to test the effectiveness of a trench mortar the republicans were developing for future use in attacks against heavily fortified military outposts. Castlemaine was chosen because of its relative isolation, and elaborate measures were carried out to prevent news of the attack leaking out (especially to Tralee) so that reinforcements would not arrive, forcing the artillery crew to abandon the tests.

The republicans set up a roadblock at a point on Tralee mountains that was about equidistant from Castlemaine and Tralee, and offered commanding views of both the Lee and Maine river valleys. People travelling in both directions were detained, some being held for up to four hours, especially those heading towards Tralee, to prevent details of the operation reaching Ballymullen barracks. Those who were under protective custody claimed they were well treated by the republicans.[44]

Jeremiah Murphy of Barraduff was assigned to the road block detail and provided useful information on the exercise from a republican perspective. The tests carried out on the mortar weren't that successful; only one of the shots secured a 'direct hit', several rounds went off trajectory, missing their targets, and a large number of the shells failed to explode. These failures are not just down to the 'home made' nature of the republican weapon or its ammunition; during the First World War the mass artillery barrages that preceded an infantry attack saw a huge proportion of the shells fail to detonate due to impacting on soft or boggy ground; the wet lands of northern France and the marshy fields around Castlemaine were both testing terrain. From their mountain-top viewpoint, republican scouts using binoculars could see the army reconnaissance plane on the runway at Tralee racecourse. So it is probable that the military authorities in Tralee (through radio contact, perhaps) knew what was going on at Castlemaine. For some reason, either due to mechanical faults or adverse weather conditions, the craft did not manage to get airborne on that occasion, to the great regret of Pats Healy, one of Jeremiah Murphy's column members, who had been a machine-gunner in the British army during the First World War and was hoping to bring down the plane if it approached their position on a reconnaissance flight.[45] Once the mortar testing part of the exercise was carried out, the republicans continued with a conventional assault on the various outposts at Castlemaine. Stretching out over a period of two hours, until reinforcements arrived from Killorglin, forcing the republicans to abandon the attack, the assault force burned a large part of the railway station and blew up the road bridge over the river Maine, thereby severing road contact between Tralee and Killorglin. One member of the Castlemaine garrison, Volunteer Ferguson, was killed in the attack, during which the defending garrison claimed to have killed four republicans.[46] The exposed nature of the location, according to Jeremiah Murphy's account, deterred any such direct attack, and the republicans suffered no casualties.[47]

At 7.30 p.m. on Tuesday, 23 January Daniel Daly (aged twenty-five), an engine driver with the GS & WR, a married man with five children and a native of Killorglin, and his fireman, Daniel Lynch (aged sixty) from Cork, were challenged by two men in trench coats as they were finishing work and leaving the precincts of Tralee railway station.

'Are you Daly?' one of the men enquired.

'Are you Lynch?' the other man asked.

Daly and Lynch confirmed their respective identities, whereupon the two men drew revolvers and shot Daly in the heart, hitting Lynch in the arms.[48] Daniel Daly died of his injuries. The blatant and cold-blooded nature of the shooting in an area so close to an army post (set up to protect the railway) was seen as a major escalation in the republican campaign against rail workers, coming so soon after the deaths at Liscahane Bridge. Like most observers, Lieutenant Niall Harrington was appalled by both the deaths of the two railwaymen killed at Liscahane and the assassination of Daly at Tralee railway station, which at the time everyone in Kerry assumed was carried out by the IRA.

Within a few days the military authorities held an inquest into the circumstances surrounding the double shooting. Brigadier Paddy O'Daly, the state's principal witness, caused consternation when he revealed the killing had been carried out by members of the national army. This was an epiphany for Harrington, who realised he had seen two men in trench coats leave the workhouse where he was billeted (later St Catherine's hospital, now the headquarters of Kerry County Council) and saw them as they returned from the operation.

Four men were arrested between midnight and 1 a.m. on Thursday, 18 January and documents were found implicating Daniel Daly in several acts about to be carried out against the public good, including:

1. Helping to dismantle a railway engine
2. Assisting in the kidnapping of a Free State army officer
3. Assisting an attack on the military post at Tralee railway station.

To pre-empt his action and prevent these things from happening, Paddy O'Daly explained, the military authorities felt they had no option other than to kill Daniel Daly.[49] The act itself was not that unusual; local executions had been carried out in Kerry as far back as late August 1922 when Seán Moriarty was killed. What was unprecedented, however, was that this was one of few occasions, if not the sole occasion, that the GOC/Kerry command publicly admitted that such a policy existed. It is probable that the same objectives could have been achieved by arresting Daniel Daly. But the death sentence was probably carried out as a warning to railway employees who colluded with or provided information to assist the republicans in their campaign against the Kerry railway network.

On Thursday, 25 January 1923 a group of unarmed soldiers travelling from their barracks to Caherciveen town came under rifle and machine-gun fire, resulting in the death of Private Patrick Roche and the wounding of another soldier.[50] Later on the same day an army cycle patrol came under fire while in the Waterville area. They suffered no casualties but claimed to have wounded a number of republicans. According to Dorothy Macardle, Dan Foley, Kerry No. 3 brigade, was killed on 25 January 1923.[51] It was probably during this exchange of fire.

On Saturday, 27 January the army reconnaissance aircraft noticed a column of about a dozen men on Derrymore mountain and radioed back their location to their HQ in Ballymullen barracks. A large ground force was subsequently sent out, surrounding the men, who had taken refuge in a hut. They opened fire on the building and the occupants soon raised a white flag and surrendered *en masse*, giving up their arms and ammunition. Among those arrested was Paddy Cahill, the column commander and a republican TD for Kerry. The report made much of the propaganda value of the use of aircraft in the capture, more so than it did of the capture of a senior republican such as Cahill.[52]

On Sunday, 28 January a patrol of 1st Westerns under Captain Patrick Coye came under fire from republicans near Feale's Bridge, Kilmaniheen in Brosna. Captain Coye was killed and three other soldiers were wounded. A republican,

Denis O'Connor of Kilmaniheen, was also killed in the engagement.[53] Captain Coye was the third serviceman to be killed in action that month, representing the lowest government military casualty levels since hostilities began the previous August. Even the number of men wounded (four) during January was low, due partly to a change in emphasis and a shift in the republican strategy towards focusing on the destruction of property.

On Sunday, 28 January a summer residence near the golf course in Dooks owned by Senator Dr O'Sullivan of Killarney was burned by republicans. Prior to setting the building on fire valuable furniture was looted. On Tuesday, 30 January, shortly before the 10.30 p.m. curfew, a group of armed men entered Tralee gasworks and held up the night shift. Using sledgehammers they smashed the two gas engines and the retort that connected them to the pumps. The town was in darkness, with hundreds of users of gas cookers, bakeries, and the factories which used gas to power and operate their machinery suffering serious shortages of power.[54] The destruction of the gasworks' domestic converter had no military significance whatsoever, and only added to the levels of discomfort and deprivation the republicans' actions imposed on the lives of the ordinary citizens of Tralee. The *Freeman's Journal* questioned the degree of vigilance and effectiveness of the military curfew that could not prevent a major act of sabotage.

To alleviate the serious overcrowding in Kerry prisons and reduce the problem they posed from both a security and manpower perspective, it was decided to transport 220 Kerry prisoners to Mountjoy jail in Dublin.[55] The prisoners travelling on board the steamer, the *Mayfield*, experienced a dread-

ful passage, spending most of the time in standing positions
and with virtually no sanitary facilities. Rough seas further
worsened the situation, dragging the voyage between Fenit
and Dún Laoghaire over three torturous days. The decision to
transfer the prisoners appears to have been prescient, as in late
January the authorities in Tralee jail (Ballymullen) reported the
discovery of two tunnels; one had its source at the prisoners'
cookhouse, and the other was discovered in the prison hospital. Both escape routes were very nearly completed when discovered by the authorities.[56]

Since the departure of the remaining British army units following the implementation of the Irish Free State (6 December), the government was able to deploy troops from the capital to areas of the country such as Kerry, where republican
resistance wasn't totally defeated. Additionally, troops already
stationed in the county had six months' 'hands on' experience
in Kerry, a better idea of the county's topography and a much
better intelligence network.

The columns that remained in the field, in peripheral areas
in mountainous districts of south and east Kerry in particular,
led a hand-to-mouth existence, funding themselves by petty
theft. In the first week in February, for example, post office
robberies took place in Kilcummin, Killarney, Headford and
Ballybunion. Jeremiah Murphy, writing on the conditions that
prevailed for east Kerry column during February 1923, provides useful insights into the anti-Treaty forces' predicament
at this time:

> The village of Barraduff was under consideration for attack, but
> the scattered location of the garrison presented certain problems
> that were not easily solved. The troops lived in the homes of the

people and in the case of attack a great many lives of innocent neutrals would be endangered. A lot of small sniping incidents occurred from day to day but these had little or no effect on the course of events. A patrol was usually too large to attack without help from neighbouring battalions and these were so hard pressed themselves that defensive rather than offensive action was found advisable ... We used many deceptive tactics to keep the enemy off balance and prevent him from learning our location, our strength and our attitude ... and rarely moved around the open country in daytime except in large numbers to keep up appearances and boost our image.

For this reason the enemy rarely went out from his posts except in large patrols which were easy to spot and avoid. He knew our situation was critical and engaged in reprisals to terrorise our supporters, such as arresting relatives of some of our men. We began to be referred to as 'Diehards' by the enemy and in the press, but the loyalties which bound us together were far stronger than those which tried to rend us apart. The hard core of our organisation were resolute men who had become hardened by the gains and defeats of guerrilla warfare and were not easily intimidated. True, their nerves and physical endurance could not last indefinitely and some became ill from stomach and lung ailments.

On Saturday, 4 February a 'gander' party was planned for a prospective bride at Moynihan's house near the base of the Paps mountains at Shrone, in Rathmore. Jeremiah Murphy described what happened:

We were billeted around the neighbourhood and many of the fellows decided to attend, even though it was possible the place might be raided. Some of us decided to give the place a wide berth and take no chances, even though sentries were to be placed on all roads. Jerry Reen was returning from a sentry post with Michael McSweeney and when close to the party they were called on to halt and put their 'hands up'. At first they thought it was a joke and asked who was there, but were answered with a volley. As they turned to run for cover, McSweeney was hit and fell. Reen ran towards a fence and lay down for a few seconds. Our men had been completely surprised from the rear ... Some of the Rathmore garrison, aided by local intelligence eluded the sentries and surrounded the house and captured those inside it. There was no chance of resistance as the place was thronged with innocent people. Five men – Con Moynihan, John Reen, Pat Nagle, Pat Duggan and John Crowley – were taken prisoner, brought to Rathmore and then to Cork. As some of the men were captured with arms their chances of survival were small … Michael McSweeney's body was given to his father and members of our section dug his grave in Kilquane cemetery. Later in the day he was buried with military honours as three of us held back a patrol from Barraduff which made an attempt to attend the funeral.[57]

The placing of sentries as a precautionary measure was based on bitter experience as on numerous previous occasions the Free State authorities had used republican funerals to trawl the attendance in expectation of rounding up a large number of the local column as they paid their respects to their fallen comrade. All in all, the Shrone incident shows that even in safe republican areas such as east Kerry both the government's military presence and security measures had done much to constrain the republican campaign.

While republican activists like Jeremiah Murphy could criticise the cynicism of the government in billeting troops in among civilians – and within civilian homes – Patrick Cox of Rathmore, whose family shared their house with a section of Dublin Guard, had fond memories of the house NCO, Sergeant Kavanagh, who seems to have been seen as a benign uncle figure by all the Cox children. On another occasion, Cox recalls an incident in Rathmore when a young man in the village, who was known to be mentally retarded, while travelling on horseback ignored a command to halt at a military checkpoint and jumped over the roadblock. As the horse and rider ambled away from the roadblock the officer on duty drew his revolver and shot the horse, who threw his rider violently on to the ground.[58] The majority of local people were appalled at the arrogance and insensitivity of the officer's action as all the military stationed in Rathmore knew the person who ignored the military checkpoint had diminished responsibility. An incident such as this could easily turn an entire community against the military, whom the government and the press were eager to portray as the people's army.

Tralee Urban District Council passed a resolution, at its January meeting, that given the improved security situation in respect of Irregular attacks in the county, the army (Kerry command) should relax the death sentences imposed and reprieve the five men sentenced to death and awaiting execution in Kerry.[59] One of the five, Peter O'Connell of Anascaul, was sentenced on 6 January in respect of possession of firearms the previous November, but the other four men must have formed a supplementary list drawn up after the 20 January executions. In a typical response Brigadier Paddy O'Daly justified both his own command's conduct and the national government's position on the war (including the executions policy) and transferred the blame by explaining the draconian measures in operation as a legitimate response by an elected government to an atrocity campaign initiated by the anti-Treatyites: 'While innocent railway men are killed, the administration of a freely elected government is interfered with, and people like Emmet McGarry and Seán Hales are killed, there will be no end to this policy.'[60]

On Sunday, 11 February republican gunmen called to the home of Thomas O'Higgins (father of Kevin O'Higgins, the home affairs minister) at Woodlands in Stradbally, County Laois and shot him dead in front of his wife and seventeen-year-old daughter. The murder was carried out in reprisal for Kevin O'Higgins' role in initiating and overseeing the government's policy of executing republicans found in possession of firearms. Kevin O'Higgins wasn't the only senior government minister to be personally affected by the republican strategy to target family members of those in power in the Provisional Government/Free State administration. Patrick Cosgrave, W. T. Cosgrave's uncle, was shot dead by republicans in Burke's pub in James' Street, Dublin; Eoin MacNeill's son, Brian, was killed in Sligo while serving as an officer with the national army in the opening weeks of the Civil War; while in early December a series of arson attacks by republicans on the homes of government deputies in the wake of the O'Connor/Mellows executions resulted in the death of Emmet McGarry, the ten-year-old son of Deputy Seán McGarry, TD.

In Kerry, Killarney Urban District Council passed a resolution at their February meeting expressing their regret at the death and offering their condolences to the family of Thomas O'Higgins. There was no corresponding motion from Tralee UDC, which suggests the Killarney authority was more pro-government than its Tralee equivalent. For Brigadier Paddy O'Daly, O/C Kerry command, the O'Higgins killing would only have reinforced his resolve to make no unilateral concessions to the republican side, or those like Tralee UDC advocating a more conciliatory approach on their behalf.

On Monday, 6 February 1923 two trains arrived at Killarney. The first, arriving at 9.30 a.m., carried thirty passengers, twelve goods wagons, mail and parcels. The outgoing service departed a quarter of an hour later. The second train arrived at 2.30 p.m. and left at 3 p.m. Both trains, whose arrival was made much of from a propaganda point of view by the staunchly pro-government *Freeman's Journal* newspaper, seem to have come from Mallow, and thus represented one of the first occasions that Kerry had been connected to the national network since the outbreak of hostilities the previous August.

More telling from a practical point of view to the actual state of Kerry railways was the admission that plans to hold the February fair at Killarney on Sunday, 5 February had to be abandoned due to a lack of rolling stock available to transport livestock to Killarney from other parts of the county. By the middle of the month republican saboteurs had again targeted Ardagh railway bridge at Currans, using explosives and also setting fire to the timbers over the night of 14/15 February to put the bridge beyond use. Telephone and telegraph lines were also cut and some of the poles were burned to further hinder rail communications.

The pendulum seems to have swung back in the government's favour by the end of the month as the 28 February edition of the *Cork Examiner* noted that on Tuesday, 27 February a full train service – including mails – resumed between Tralee and Killarney, while on the same day a train arrived at Killorglin station, the first rail connection into the town since 3 August 1922.

Liam Deasy, one of the senior republican commanders in Munster, was arrested in mid-January. While in custody he was persuaded by W. T. Cosgrave to issue a statement calling on all republicans still in the field to agree terms for an unconditional surrender in return for an amnesty. Essentially, Deasy's 9 February statement was an acceptance of the peace proposals the Provisional Government had offered republicans the previous

October prior to the passing of the Emergency Powers Act. Four months and scores of deaths later, many republicans still active in Munster or those incarcerated in Free State prisons and holding centres began to articulate their own misgivings about continuing the war once they saw a republican of Deasy's stature question the value of Liam Lynch's strategy – 'not an inch/no surrender' until the securing of a republican military victory. A statement signed by 600 republican prisoners in Limerick jail in February noted: 'It [the war] has gone far enough and ought to stop now.' Around the same time the *Freeman's Journal* reported anti-Treaty IRA columns had surrendered in Newmarket and Kanturk (County Cork) and at Knockmore, Clashmore and Ardmore (County Waterford).

It was inevitable that a section of republican opinion in Kerry would both echo and find much merit in Liam Deasy's arguments. Seventy republican prisoners in Tralee jail petitioned the prison authorities that they would sign a pledge not to bear arms against the government if they were released from prison. They also requested temporary parole so that they could persuade their comrades in arms to accept the offer.[61]

On Thursday, 22 February Michael Pierce and sixteen members of his column formally surrendered to Brigadier General Paddy O'Daly, handing over rifles and ammunition and signing a pledge that they would not bear arms against the government. They were then allowed to return home. The formality of the surrender 'ceremony', evidence of a degree of magnanimity on the government's military representatives' side, was further reflected in a letter of thanks W. T. Cosgrave wrote to Pierce:[62]

I appreciate most heartily the very honourable action of yourself and your men, taken, to use Deasy's words, 'for the future of Ireland'. A few weeks will demonstrate very clearly the regrettable actions of the last few months can be forgotten ... And every man in Ireland can work in friendliness and without violence – along his own particular path – to make Ireland (and its resources) a great and happy country.

While the momentum to bring the conflict to an end received a boost with Liam Deasy's plea to republicans still engaged in armed resistance to the elected government to abandon their campaign, a substantial minority of activists continued to challenge, albeit at a much reduced level, army foot and motorised patrols. At the other end of the spectrum, government troops still stalked (in covert operations) individual republicans. On Monday, 13 February 1923 troops under Captain Wilson raided a number of houses in the Curraghane area hoping to capture Michael Sinnott and James O'Connor, who at that time were living in a dugout hidden beneath the hayshed in Lyons' farm on Currane Sands. Unable to find their quarry the military arrested three local men named Clifford, Drummond and Greer, taking them to Ballymullen barracks for questioning. According to Dorothy Macardle, Greer – under interrogation – gave away O'Connor and Sinnott's whereabouts. Later that night a group of soldiers returned to the Lyons' farmhouse, searched the hayshed, and shot Sinnott and O'Connor (aged eighteen and nineteen) dead. It is unclear what action precipitated their executions.

The 17 February edition of the *Freeman's Journal* carried a brief report on the death of a soldier shot in Kerry which provides interesting insights into the quality of medical care given to wounded troops in Kerry and the communications network that liaised between the military authorities and the next of kin of soldiers who were killed or injured in the conflict. 'Death of Private Thomas Moran, Kimmage, at Saint Brecan's hospital, Dublin. He was wounded in the thigh by a shotgun in an ambush in Kerry. He had spent three weeks in hospital in Tralee, where the wounds turned septic. The mother of the deceased, Mrs Kathleen Moran, was appalled as she was only told of her son's injury when he arrived in Dublin.' Private Moran was the first fatality sustained by government forces in Kerry during February. A few days later, Lieutenant Thomas Slattery of Carrignafeela, Ballymacelligott, serving in the 1st Westerns, died of wounds received in an ambush.[63]

On Wednesday night, 21 February a column of Dublin Guard travelling between Tralee and Castlemaine were fired on by Thompson sub machine-gun. Two soldiers, John Mahony and Charles Toner, were wounded. A few days later a Red Cross ambulance carrying wounded soldiers from Killarney to Tralee was ambushed at Ballyseedy coming under rifle and machine-gun fire. No injuries were reported. Around the same time another Red Cross ambulance travelling to Killarney carrying the remains of Lieutenant Ahern, who was killed in action in Drimoleague, County Cork, was fired upon between Rathmore and Barraduff. There were no injuries. On Sunday, 18 February an army patrol under Lieutenant Conroy, searching in the Ballyferriter area, exchanged fire with republicans. Two prisoners were taken; one, Thomas O'Dowd, was wounded. According to the military communiqué the second prisoner, Thomas O'Sullivan, was shot dead as he attempted to seize Lieutenant Conroy's revolver.[64]

In a sense the republican attacks almost appear like a token response, carried out for no real military advantage other than to be seen to be still offering resistance to the Free State 'army of occupation'. More often than not the republicans emerged weakened from each engagement as their assault force was too small to be effective, and if one or two men were wounded usually surrendered themselves and their weapons. Most of the republicans still active in Kerry saw the Liam Deasy/Michael Pierce position as a practical and 'honourable' way to end hostilities, hoping there would be a general amnesty if and when the conflict ended. In the same week that the Pierce column surrendered, eight republicans were captured at Keelties, Milltown. At a dugout in Glenabally Wood, Kilflynn, Commandant George O'Shea, John Shanahan, Jeremiah Twomey and Stephen Fuller were taken prisoner, while during a raid on the home of Tadhg Coffey at Barleymount, troops captured Coffey and Jeremiah O'Donoghue as they sat cleaning their rifles.

From a propaganda point of view the formal surrender of the Kilmoyley column (thirteen men and their commander, Tom O'Driscoll) to Colonel David Neligan, director of military intelligence, Kerry command, on Wednesday, 28 February was given much media coverage.[65] Significantly, this was the unit responsible for the Liscahane Bridge derailment in mid-January in which two GS & WR employees were killed in an operation that was intended to derail a troop train. Had the original operation gone according to plan it would have inflicted scores of casualties among those on board. Interestingly, this was not referred to, suggesting a willingness to let bygones be bygones, and evidence of a high degree of magnanimity on the government side in their desire to bring the war to an end in Kerry.

According to a report in the *Cork Examiner*, sourced in Killarney, a corresponding willingness existed among republicans. 'One bright feature is that peace is without doubt being desired by the vast majority of Irregulars ... and that being so it is hoped that some means will be found to bring about a peace so ardently longed for by the entire civilian population.'[66]

On Saturday, 24 February 1923 a prisoner named Conway from Caherina, Tralee was shot and wounded while trying to escape from the prison at Tralee workhouse. Around the same weekend, but in a totally unrelated incident, twenty-year-old Joseph O'Sullivan of Steeple View, Tralee, was taken by two men dressed in civilian clothes and shot and wounded. O'Sullivan claimed that he was 'neutral' IRA. As the first incident took place in military custody some form of inquiry would be forthcoming. The second shooting was possibly carried out by anti-Treaty IRA as a punishment, or was perhaps the work of off-duty military from Ballymullen barracks whom O'Sullivan must have convinced of his innocence or that his 'crime' was not severe enough to merit a death sentence, as they usually shot to kill. Neutral IRA were anti-Treaty ideologically but did not offer armed resistance to the Provisional/Free State Government.

10

THE BITTER END

On Thursday, 1 March at 9 p.m. four masked men arrived at Ballyard House, the home of the county solicitor, Liston, with the intention of burning the house. Thomas Galvin, Liston's father-in-law, opened the front door and was confronted by three men carrying rifles and one holding a revolver. He told them he would phone Ballymullen barracks if they didn't leave.[1] Surprisingly, Galvin's threat to phone for military assistance was sufficient to convince the republicans to leave the area.

On Monday, 5 March 1923 at 7 a.m. the military authorities, having learned of a large concentration of republicans in a number of farmhouses around Gurrane Hill outside Caherciveen, carried out a series of actions aimed at encircling and capturing the entire force. One column proceeded towards Foilmore and took up positions between Carrignatrost and Dereenamona. The second group covered the area between Dereenamona and Knockenadean Cross, while a third column advanced from Waterville and went along the eastern side of the mountain. The first column came under Lewis and Thompson machine-gun fire from the republicans, who scattered following the initial exchange of fire. The second column under Lieutenant Timothy O'Shea opened fire on the building and O'Shea (a native of Caherciveen) was killed instantly as he took a bullet in the forehead as he led the advance. This engagement lasted half an hour, during which time the government troops claimed to have killed one Irregular, wounded another and taken seven prisoner. As this stage of the operation, as it was coming to a close, Sergeant Jeremiah Quane (Ardfert) was killed.

By 10 a.m. the republicans were successfully retreating in a rearguard action heading towards the Glenbeigh/Glencar area where they expected to join up with reinforcements. At this point troops under Lieutenant Golden advanced towards Tournahilla and attempted to assault a republican strong-point. Volunteer William Healy (Valentia) lost his life at this juncture and two other soldiers, Sergeant Dennehy (Valentia) and Volunteer Fennessy (Caherciveen) were wounded. According to the army the Red Cross ambulance was fired upon on each occasion they tried to rescue the wounded, as were Frs Behan and Curtayne while tending them. A small group of five troops, including a Lewis gun team under Sergeant Hedigan, got cut off from the main force and were surrounded by republicans and attacked throughout the day until relieved by an armoured car around 7.30 p.m. when the assault force withdrew. The claim by the army that they faced a republican force of 400 men is highly improbable; likewise the claim they killed five and wounded two anti-Treatyites is probably an over-estimate. The republicans taken prisoner were identified as Daly, Patrick O'Connor, Michael Griffin, O/C, John Ryan, brigade staff, Daniel O'Connor, quarter master, and a medical orderly named Brady.[2]

According to Dorothy Macardle the republican force at Gurrane consisted of no more than thirty-six men and their only fatality was Dan Clifford.[3] During follow-up operations on Tuesday, 6 March Seán T. O'Sullivan was killed near Gleesk. All things considered the republicans did well to extricate themselves from an encirclement by a much larger and better equipped force.

The tripmine explosion at Bairinarig wood in Knockna-goshel on Tuesday, 6 March 1923 and the series of atrocities carried out by government troop in retaliation for the deaths in that explosion have come to define the extremes of experience of the Civil War in Kerry. The 6 March atrocity grew out of a quarrel between neighbours, where a combination of personal animosity, local rivalry and the desire for revenge crossed over from the civilian sphere into the military arena. Pat O'Connor, a farmer from Glansaroon, Castleisland, got involved in a row with two local IRA men, Patrick Buckley and John Daly. A few days later a number of republican 'safe houses' in the area were searched by Free State troops. No arrests were made, but it was assumed the raid occurred as the result of a tip-off by O'Connor. Pat O'Connor was kidnapped by the IRA, held captive for three days and was fined £100 as punishment for informing; he refused to pay the fine. On 16 December 1922 the IRA broke into the O'Connor family home, ransacked it, and stole £36–05s–00d, seizing ten cows in lieu of the balance due on the fine.[4] Furious at the way his father had been treated by the republicans, Pat O'Connor's son, Paddy, went to military HQ in Castleisland to lodge a complaint. While there he was persuaded to enlist in the army. As a lieutenant, Pat O'Connor's local knowledge proved invaluable to the Hartnett's hotel bar-racks, leading to the arrest of many local activists, among them Patrick Buckley and John Daly, whose capture on 4 February 1923 must have brought a great degree of personal satisfaction for O'Connor given the family circumstances leading to him enlisting in the first place.

Humphrey Murphy, O/C Kerry No. 1 brigade and a native of Currow, viewed the issue very much from a local perspective and saw Lieutenant Paddy O'Connor as both an upstart and a thorn in his side and was determined to teach him a lesson. Attempts to deliver an explosive device to O'Connor in Castle-island barracks proved impractical. As an alternative strategy the republicans forged a letter in handwriting similar to that of someone they guessed was one of O'Connor's regular infor-mants telling him of the location of a republican arms dump and dugout at Bairinarig wood in Knocknagoshel.

At 2 a.m. on Tuesday, 6 February Lieutenant Paddy O'Con-nor led a party of eight men to Knocknagoshel to check out the tip-off. As the search party removed a pile of loose stones they discovered a large boulder and were working on moving this when they triggered the mine. The explosion blew Lieu-tenant Paddy O'Connor and four other men to pieces; a sixth man had his legs so badly mangled they had to be amputated. Among the dead were Privates Michael Galvin, Killarney and Laurence O'Connor, Causeway, County Kerry and Captains Michael Dunne and Edward Stapleton of the Dublin brigade, both friends of Brigadier Paddy O'Daly, O/C Kerry com-mand.

The loss of five men was the largest death toll the Free State army had suffered in a single day in Kerry since 2 August 1922, when ten soldiers were killed during operations surrounding the capture of Tralee. In the press statement giving the details of the Knocknagoshel explosion, Kerry command announced that in future any obstacles that troops might encounter would be removed by anti-Treaty prisoners. On the face of it this seemed a cautionary warning to deter republicans from using similar tactics in the future. When the reality concealed in the message was unravelled the statement appeared far more sinister.

On Wednesday, 7 March an army patrol travelling from Tralee to Killorglin discovered a pile of rubble blocking the road at Ballyseedy wood. Returning to Ballymullen barracks, nine republican prisoners were selected and brought to the site by lorry. As the prisoners began to clear the roadblock their movement triggered the landmine concealed in the debris. In the ensuing explosion eight prisoners were killed and three soldiers, Captain Ned Breslin, Lieutenant Joseph Murtagh and Sergeant Ennis, were injured. That was the official (military) version of what happened at Ballyseedy.

The reality was very different. Unwilling to wait until republicans set up another booby trap bomb, and eager to avenge the deaths at Knocknagoshel, those of Dunne and Stapleton in particular, engineers from the Dublin brigade at Ballymullen barracks constructed their own landmine and transported it to Ballyseedy, long a popular ambush point for republicans. The nine men, who had individually undergone a torturous interrogation as to who carried out the Knocknagoshel attack, were tied together at wrist level and had their shoelaces intertwined to prevent anyone from running away. Ironically, the prisoners thought the official version of their death was going to be 'shot while trying to escape', as no one had suspected they were going to be blown to pieces in an explosion. The military authorities identified the Ballyseedy dead as John Daly, Woodview, Castleisland; Patrick Buckley, Scartaglin; James Walsh, Lisdoigue, Tralee; Pat Hartnett, Listowel; Stephen Fuller,

George O'Shea, Tim Twomey, all of Lixnaw; and T. O'Connor, West Terrace, Liverpool. One prisoner was missing.[5]

Evidently John Daly and Patrick Buckley were selected because they had been associated in the quarrel with the O'Connors of Glansaroon when it was little more than an apolitical row between neighbours. According to T. Ryle Dwyer the other prisoners were selected by Colonel David Neligan and Ned Breslin on the basis that none of the men had relatives in the clergy whose scepticism of the official version would give them status and credibility in demanding an inquiry into the atrocity.[6]

The devastating effect of the explosion would have made *post mortem* identification of the victims' remains almost impossible. Though listed among the dead, Stephen Fuller was actually the missing prisoner; John O'Connell was the eighth victim. Stephen Fuller had his back to the explosion and, though badly burned on the back and arms, was thrown hundred of yards away by the force of the blast and so would not have been found by soldiers searching for the victims' remains. Once he recovered from the shock of what had happened he went to the nearest house, Currans at Hanlon's Cross. Contact was eventually made with Johnny O'Connor and Johnny Duggan of Farmers' Bridge, who brought him to a dugout where he received medical attention from Dr Shanahan of Farranfore.[7]

It was assumed that the missing prisoner had disintegrated in the blast and so those soldiers (many fortified by alcohol) given the unenviable task of collecting severed limbs, dismembered or decapitated bodies over a radius of several hundred yards haphazardly put the remains of eight men into nine coffins and transported them back to Ballymullen barracks from where at a later date their remains could be returned to their loved ones and next of kin for burial. When the relatives of the Ballyseedy dead called to the gates of Ballymullen barracks to collect the remains in advance of funeral and burial arrangements, their first instinct was to open the coffin to have one last look at their loved ones. They were appalled by what they saw as the contents proved, if evidence was needed, that the men had been through a charnel house. The families' response to the denouement was described as a 'frenzy'.[8] The collective response was possibly a mental breakdown verging on temporary insanity, with conflicting emotions hovering between inconsolable grief and incontrollable anger. The families took the bodies from the coffins the army had provided and smashed the coffins to pieces, putting their relatives into coffins they had brought themselves. The onlooking soldiers at the barrack gate were appalled by this behaviour, and soon found themselves at the receiving end of the crowd's hatred as they were pelted with stones by the angry relatives, friends and neighbours who had come to Ballymullen to attend the removals.

On the same day as the Ballyseedy explosion, Wednesday, 7 March 1923, in a separate but related incident members of the Dublin brigade based at the Great Southern hotel in Killarney brought five prisoners to Countess Bridge, an isolated location between Killarney and Killcummin, to clear another road obstruction. If the Ballyseedy mine represented retribution for members of Kerry No. 1 brigade, Countess Bridge was intended to inflict a corresponding punishment on members of Kerry No. 2 brigade. Tadhg Coffey, one of the five prisoners brought to the site (but who managed to escape the fate his captors had intended for him), recalls that while in custody in Killarney he and the other prisoners were often taunted by the prison chaplain, a Franciscan named Fr Fidelis, who asked: 'How much nearer to the republic we were now than when we started? We had the country destroyed; our leaders had cleared off to America and left us fools to fight for them.'[9]

When Coffey and the other four prisoners arrived at the bridge they found a large mound of stones blocking the route. As the prisoners began to remove the blockade the soldiers surrounding and guarding them lobbed hand grenades towards the men and sprayed them with machine-gun fire. In the confusion, noise and din of the gunfire and explosions Tadhg Coffey made a run for it and succeeded in reaching a friend's house in Kilcummin. A press release issued by Kerry command on 9 March identified the four Irregular prisoners who lost their lives while removing a barricade at Countess Bridge on 7 March as Jeremiah O'Donoghue, New Street, Killarney; Timothy Murphy, Kilbrean, Kilcummin; Stephen Buckley, Tiernaboul, Killarney; and Daniel O'Donoghue of Lacks, Kilcummin.[10]

While the twelve Kerrymen who were murdered by Free State forces on 7 March 1923 were transformed into martyrs in republican folk memory, and within a year would be eulogised by Dorothy Macardle in *Tragedies of Kerry*, the death of eighteen-year-old Private Christopher Green of 12 Railway Avenue, Inchicore, Dublin, who was shot dead by republicans while on sentry duty at Barraduff on the same day, would hardly register a mention, even though his death would be as keenly felt by his family as all of those who died at the hands of his colleagues in the Dublin Guard that day.[11]

Private Green was one of nine national army servicemen (six of them natives of Kerry) to die in Kerry in a three-day period. As well as those killed in action during March four more soldiers met their deaths in the county due to accidents with weapons. At the beginning of March, Lieutenant John Ryan of Loughrea, County Galway, a first cousin of Colonel Michael Hogan, O/C 1st Westerns and Patrick Hogan, Minister for Agriculture, shot himself dead in Brosna while cleaning his revolver.[12] On Monday, 13 March Lieutenant Alfred Glynn from Gort, County Galway and Captain Michael Cleary of Whitegate, County Clare, both of the 1st Westerns, were experimenting throwing hand grenades into the river Feale near Listowel. There was a premature explosion which killed Glynn instantly, and seriously wounded Cleary, who died in hospital the next day.[13] Late on Sunday afternoon, 25 March, Volunteer Hayes, a native of Killarney, was killed at Newtown Sandes when he was accidentally shot by one of the other soldiers in his unit.[14]

At 8 p.m. on Friday, 9 March Captain Wilson was escorting prisoners from Killorglin to Tralee when the escort was fired upon at Ballyseedy. A prisoner named Lawlor from Killorglin was shot dead.[15] The prisoner identified as Lawlor was James Taylor from Glencar, a staunchly republican heartland about fifteen miles from Killorglin, and while it is conceivable that the official version of what happened is true, given the location – Ballyseedy – it is more likely that Taylor (whose brother, Joseph, was killed in the 'Black and Tan' war in 1921) made an adverse comment about the 'murders' the Free Staters had perpetrated in the same area a few days previously. There was still a lot of anger among the officer corps in the Dublin Guard about the Dunne and Stapleton deaths in particular, and consequently it took little to provoke a knee-jerk reaction. James Taylor (incidentally, republicans record his death as 8 March) probably met his death in this manner rather than being killed during an IRA ambush on the convoy.

There was similar murderous intent behind the death of Frank Grady at the Mountain Stage near Glenbeigh on Sunday, 11 March. A group of ten prisoners, which included the men arrested in Caherciveen on 5 March, was being escorted from the holding centre at Bahagh's workhouse, Caherciveen to Killarney. At Mountain Stage the military patrol escorting the prisoners handed them over to troops commanded by Captain 'Tiny' Lyons of the Dublin Guard, who was responsible for bringing them safely to Killarney. According to Dorothy Macardle, there were about 150 onlookers watching as Captain Lyons checked the identity of each prisoner. In late February the road bridge on the Caragh river between Killorglin and Glenbeigh had been blown up by republicans allegedly acting on Frank Grady's orders. The disruption caused to traffic by damaging the bridge was minimal as it was only a few hundred yards downstream from a railway bridge that had been out of use since the previous August when train services between Farranfore and Valentia were suspended. Lyons challenged Grady, complimenting him on his 'handiwork', promptly drew his revolver and shot him dead.[16]

The summary execution of a prisoner on the whim of an individual officer was an all-too-common event in Kerry during March 1923. What was so unusual about the Mountain Stage killing was that it took place in public and in the presence of so many witnesses. On the same day that Frank Grady was killed, 11 March 1923, Tim Keating of Ballinaskelligs 'died of wounds', although *The Last Post*, a memorial roll of honour recording the republican Civil War dead published in the mid-

1930s (by which time Cumann na nGaedheal had left office) cites his death as 15 March. Most probably Keating had been wounded on 5 March during the 'Gurrane encirclement'.

In general killings took place in isolated areas. In fact during March undercover units (two or three soldiers carrying revolvers and in plain clothes) operating out of Killarney and Killorglin ventured deep into places that a few weeks previously were 'no go' areas and stalked and targeted individual republicans. On 15 March John Kevins was challenged by armed men in Carrinahone, Beaufort and asked to identify himself. He was shot dead. Two days later, on 17 March, an Irregular identified as James Donovan and described as a former RIC man died of wounds sustained near Macgillycuddy's Reeks, while on 20 March 1923 Jeremiah Casey was killed at Dunloe, Beaufort.[17] This was the Squad of old operating in a wilderness area, perhaps light years away from their familiar Dublin streets and alleyways but with the same determination and ruthlessness that had struck fear into hardened British intelligence agents in 1920–21.

On Monday, 12 March five or six officers under the command of a divisional officer of the Dublin Guard arrived at Bahagh's workhouse, Caherciveen, which housed about twenty republican prisoners. It seems they had hoped to collect the prisoners who had been arrested at Gurrane on 5 March but fortunately for them they were in the party that had left for Killarney on the previous morning. The divisional officer ordered the duty sergeant to open the door to the guard room and hand over five prisoners. The sergeant refused, referring them to his commanding officer, Lieutenant McCarthy, as the only person who could authorise such a release. At this point the senior officer drew his revolver, threatening to shoot the sergeant unless he handed over the keys.

Disgusted and outraged by what was subsequently done to the prisoners, Lieutenant McCarthy went public on what had happened and resigned his commission from the national army. He said he would serve the Free State as a soldier and fight the anti-Treatyites, but he would not be a party to murder. He described the perpetrators of the killings as a 'murder gang' intent on prolonging the war.[18] Meanwhile, the five prisoners, Michael Courtney, Eugene Dwyer, John Sugrue, Daniel O'Shea and Willie Riordan, all members of Kerry No. 3 brigade, IRA, who were told they were being transported to Tralee, were taken a short distance away from the workhouse where a landmine had been laid. Conscious that two men (Stephen Fuller and Tadhg Coffey) had survived and escaped from the two previous explosions, the men supervising the Caherciveen operation refined their methods and shot all five prisoners in the legs before placing them on the booby trapped barricade and detonating the charges. Three of the bodies were unrecognisable following the explosion, but some of the next of kin who saw their two relatives' remains in the church confirmed that the bodies contained bullet wounds.[19]

By the time of the Caherciveen atrocity, 12 March 1923, both Stephen Fuller's and Tadhg Coffey's stories and experiences were common currency throughout Kerry and were being used by Liam Lynch's propaganda department to discredit the government's conduct of the war.

At 8 a.m. on Wednesday, 14 March 1923 four prisoners who had been captured near Mucknish Pass, Gweedore, County Donegal in early November 1922 were shot by firing squad at

Drumboe army barracks, Stranlohar, County Donegal. Apart from Seán Larkin, who came from Derry, the other prisoners were all from Kerry: Daniel Enright and Timothy O'Sullivan, both from Listowel, and Charles Daly from Knockaneacouree, Firies, Killarney. Aged twenty-six, Charles Daly was a cousin of Charles O'Sullivan, bishop of Kerry, and a distant relative of Cearbhall Ó Dálaigh, a future president of Ireland. Joe Sweeney, the Free State O/C at Dromboe barracks who presided over the executions as Provost Marshall, had been a close friend of Daly when they were both students together. 'At that time,' Sweeney recalled, 'you had the barbarous system where the provost marshal had to deliver a *coup de grâce* by firing a pistol shot through the heart. I had to do it.'[20]

The events of 5 to 12 March shone a limelight on Kerry. Over a series of three features (19, 21 and 22 March) the *Freeman's Journal* focused on the changing face of the war in Kerry, but also looked at the conflict's impact on the wider social and economic fabric in the county. The newspaper's insight is worth quoting in some detail:

> Kerry today and last October are two vastly different places. Changes are to be seen everywhere, not least in improved economic conditions consequent on the re-opening of the railways and the running of trains … I went to Tralee by train, leaving from Dublin at 7.30 this morning and arriving shortly after four o'clock. In August last I made the trip from Limerick on the Armoured Car, the Ex Mutineer, which had been in the possession of Irregulars at the Four Courts.
>
> When I left Kerry in the middle of October the Irregular claim – while National troops held the towns they held the country – there was much truth in their boast. Railway trains were so unsafe even the eight miles between Fenit and Tralee was not guaranteed. Returning to Dublin last October I made the sea trip from Fenit to Limerick, as military parties invariably prefer the

sea route. Now arriving in Tralee there is increased business ...
with much rolling stock and bustle on the platforms in contrast
to the silence and desertion of the last few months. The town is
still agitated over the tragic happenings of weeks before, when
the death toll in the county was thirty three, the greatest since
fighting began in any area outside of Dublin. Of these nine are
National troops, four officers, five men.

There is little fight left in Kerry. What little there is is con-
fined to mountainous areas – Kenmare/Caherciveen in the south,
and the range between Barraduff and Rathmore in the east. North
Kerry is completely clear. Killarney is so quiet officers and men
ride horses around the lake district. Trouble has long since ceased
in Tralee, while Killorglin, Farranfore, Castleisland and Dingle
are thoroughly cleared out.

Turning its focus from the politico-military sphere to the economic arena, transport and local government received the most
attention:

It cost £1 a ton to cart supplies from Fenit to Tralee. With the
railway line open the cost is 15 shillings a ton. In the case of coal,
some months ago it sold at £5 a ton, now it sells at £3–10s–00d.
When the canal and railway were blocked 500 carts each carrying
a ton of supplies went in a single procession and brought considerable employment. In August 1922 there were 895 men unemployed in Tralee, in March 1923 there were 532, and, at the port
500 men at a time were engaged in driving.

In Killarney the March fair, the first livestock sale held since
August 1922, was seen as a hopeful sign, for both town and
county alike. According to the *Freeman's Journal* report: 'Unemployment rates of 95% in the tourism, shops, lace making
and the building trades. The Register of unemployed in the
town is 400 men and 100 women, with the boot and mineral
water factories the mainstay of paid employment in Killarney.'

Kerry County Council was £180,877 in debt, had outstanding (uncollected) rateable income of £163,685, and had not

paid its officials since the end of December 1922. The estimated cost of bridge repair alone was £130,000, notwithstanding the fact that the military had repaired fifteen bridges sufficiently for light traffic. Its average maintenance costs in a given year were £20 per mile for 2,300 miles of road (mainly filling potholes on unpaved roads) with steamrolling costs of £900 per mile on 500 miles of main road.

Unfortunately the report did not divulge the financial impact of the conflict, or to be more precise, the republicans' campaign of destruction, on the Great Southern and Western Railway Company's rail network in Kerry. The report also made reference to the figure of over two thousand defaulters on land annuity payments at the spring session at Tralee court of the Land Commission. Two-thirds of the cases had been quashed and the remainder had been settled. Admittedly the lack of livestock fairs and regular markets for the sale of their agricultural produce meant strained circumstances for most farmers (both big and small) throughout Kerry. If belt tightening was unavoidable it was a certainty that most farmers would default on both agricultural rates (Kerry County Council) and land annuities (payable to the British government) rather than eat into their seed grain or see their families go hungry.

During the course of its report on the various levels of military alertness in Kerry the *Freeman's Journal* referred to Killarney as being '… so quiet that officers and men ride horses around the lake district conveying an almost tourist image of the posting'. The officer corps would certainly have had more time to play golf. Brigadier O'Daly was president of the army golfing society, and during their sojourn in Killarney the army presented two trophies, the military cup (men's competition) and the guards cup (ladies) to Killarney Golf Club.[21] While improving one's handicap on the golf course was one of the unexpected bonuses of the improved security situation, if the package of measures Brigadier Paddy O'Daly announced on 20 March to combat excessive drinking among the troops stationed in Killarney is anything to go by, it would suggest poor morale was the norm for many of the soldiers stationed in the town. Among the restrictions introduced were:

A: Intoxicating liquor is not to be sold to soldiers between the hours of 7 a.m. and 10 p.m.
B: All Sunday sales are prohibited.
C: Sale of intoxicating liquor to soldiers of the national army carrying arms is prohibited.
D: Traders shall not permit soldiers under the influence of drink to enter or remain on their premises.

The penalties the ordinance imposed on vintners who chose to ignore the new laws were equally draconian. An initial fine of £50 would be levied on the publican for the first offence. A second breach would involve closure of the premises for a fourteen-day period. Any further breach would result in permanent closure.[22] The alcohol abuse could be a symptom of war weariness or combat fatigue, and frustration at being engaged in a conflict that should have ended months earlier but was being prolonged by an enemy that was still unwilling to countenance defeat. Increasingly this sense of anger was directed at individual republicans by a trigger-happy military.

On 24 March 1923 the IRA executive held its first meeting since October 1922, when the issue was: should hostilities continue in the wake of the Emergency Powers Act? The March meeting's agenda was identical: should the IRA continue the war? Éamon de Valera, though not an IRA Army

Council member, attended the meeting in his capacity as the republicans' principal political figure and president of the first Dáil; de Valera favoured a cessation of hostilities, a stance supported by Austin Stack. Even Tom Barry, the most able and experienced IRA leader still active in the Cork area, admitted the war was lost in Munster. Humphrey Murphy and John Joe Rice, O/Cs of Kerry No. 1 and No. 2 brigades, IRA also attended the meeting, but it is unclear how they voted – in the wake of the severe losses both their commands had suffered during March. Liam Lynch, the IRA chief of staff, who favoured carrying on the campaign, postponed a decision in expectation of better results for the republicans with the arrival of better spring weather.

During a round-up of republicans in east Kerry on Saturday, 24 March in which ten prisoners were captured, a blacksmith named Daniel Murphy from Knocknagoshel was shot dead.[23] On Sunday night, 25 March troops escorting prisoners from Dingle to Tralee were fired upon *en route*, resulting in the death of an anti-Treaty prisoner named Bob McCarthy.[24] On 27 March an exchange of fire between an army patrol and three republicans in the Currow area resulted in the death of James Walsh.[25] The proximity of both Currow and Knocknagoshel to the location of the 6 March landmine was sufficient motive in some soldiers' eyes for a summary execution of any anti-Treatyites captured in that area. The death of Jack Fleming of Tralee on 29 March was the last killing of a period of time that would enter republican folklore in Kerry as the 'terror month'.[26]

On the same day, Thursday, 29 March, troops returning from Sneem to Kenmare were ambushed. Sergeant George Copeland was killed and three other soldiers were wounded in an exchange of fire in which the Free State sources claimed they killed one and wounded another of their assailants.[27] Perhaps the luckiest soldier that month was Volunteer Greer who was stationed in Fenit. On Thursday, 22 March he entered O'Sullivan's public house alone, whereupon two men named Clifford entered the pub and beat him up. He succeeded in escaping, but was fired upon and wounded, and managed to reach the safety of his barracks.[28]

The 'terror month' is in many ways how both republicans and the wider folk memory in Kerry regard the terrible events of March 1923. During that month twenty-nine republicans were killed (not including the three Kerrymen shot by firing squad in Donegal), quantitatively the same number as the entire republican war dead for the six-month period from the beginning of August 1922 – the arrival of Free State forces in the county – to the end of January 1923. Qualitatively, it is the manner in which most of the deaths were inflicted (rather than the number of people killed) that shocks. It is possible that only three of the republican deaths could be described as 'killed in action/died of wounds' – all related to the Gurrane (Caherciveen) encirclement of 5 March, where those engaged in the conflict had a fifty–fifty chance of survival. Seventeen died from landmines deliberately detonated to kill unarmed prisoners, in which, miraculously, two men lived to tell the tale. Nine others were killed in summary executions, either a planned reprisal or shooting carried out in the heat of the moment.

It is often forgotten that six of the ten Free State soldiers who were killed in the county during March 1923 were also from Kerry. Perhaps the single most unfortunate development in the war in Kerry that March was the introduction of the landmine into the military arsenal, and the willingness of both belligerents to use it with lethal effect.

Over the weekend of 31 March/1 April the body of Michael O'Shea, Keel, was found about three miles west of Killorglin on the Glenbeigh road. Several bullet wounds were on the face and chest, and around his neck was a card with an IRA inscription. No traces of blood were found, suggesting the killing took place elsewhere and the body was dumped on the road. A railway linesman was kidnapped in Caragh around the same time.[29] The report doesn't clarify whether O'Shea was a civilian or one of the IRA's own members who had informed on the organisation. The GS & WR linesman kidnapped was Cornelius Hanafin, who was subsequently courtmartialled by the IRA and was sentenced to be shot at dawn on Friday, 6 April.

The Free State army's intelligence network seems to have been well primed at this point as a large force of troops converged on a cluster of houses in Derrynafeana, near Coose Lake, Glencar at the foothills of Carrantuohill under the cover of darkness, without being seen by republican sentries. Two republicans, identified as O'Brien of Derrynagan and O'Sullivan of Coolroe surrendered and were taken prisoner, possibly on the outer defence cordon.[30] At this point sentence had already been passed on Cornelius Hanafin; he had even dug his own grave in preparation for execution. As the Free State army burst into the valley, Hanafin was either rescued or escaped or was released by his captors whose priority now was to save their own lives rather than to take his. A vengeful guard on the republican side might have fired a single parting shot into the prisoner's head for spite, to deprive the Free State of the propaganda value of a successful rescue. To have done so would probably have guaranteed his executioner a similar fate.

During the course of a firefight which was principally a holding action to enable as many of the republican column billeted in the Derrynafeana safe houses to evade capture, George Nagle of Ballygamboon, Castlemaine and Conway O'Connor of Killorglin were wounded as they successfully resisted the Free State advance, allowing the majority of the IRA garrison to evade capture by fleeing higher into Macgillycuddy's Reeks. Nagle, wounded in the leg, went into Molly O'Brien's farmhouse for a drink of water and was taken prisoner there. O'Connor, wounded in the shoulder, was also taken away for questioning. Neither man was ever heard from again other than via the shots heard when they were killed. Their bodies were later brought back to the cluster of houses in Derrynafeana on the back of a cart. The army announced that three other anti-Treatyites were killed in and around Derrynafeana and a further four were killed in follow-up operations.[31] Apart from Nagle and O'Connor the names of no other republican fatalities were identified. Most probably the actual death toll that day was two rather than the nine claimed in the tally quoted for the press release.

According to Niall Harrington, George Nagle had participated in the attack on the military post at Dan Lyons' pub in Spa village in August 1922, where Sergeant Jack Lydon, Dublin Guard (a Tralee man) was killed.[32] It is probable that one of the Dublin Guard involved in the exercise (possibly even a Squad member) executed Nagle as a reprisal killing. O'Connor may have been killed simply because his actions delayed the Free State advance long enough to allow the majority of the republican garrison to escape. Effectively, the Derrynafeana battle was the last major action between the republican and Free State forces during the Civil War in Kerry.

Even before the Derrynafeana firefight there were signs in early April that conditions were beginning to improve. The Tralee branch of the Kerry Farmers' Union passed a motion calling on the government to abandon the executions policy.[33] This was probably a response to the 14 March executions in Donegal where three of the four republicans killed on that day were Kerrymen. Given that the executions were carried out as a reprisal for the death of a Free State soldier killed in an ambush a few days earlier in Donegal, the number of deaths was seen as disproportionate. The Tralee Farmers' motion received no formal response from either a national source or any spokesman in Kerry command.

Kerry command did announce in early April that the curfew that applied to Tralee urban area was no longer in force. A much greater degree of civilian and police control rather than a military presence (i.e. replacing the army by the civic guards) was also on the cards. On 5–6 April 1923 a large force of civic guards arrived in Listowel, from where they were to take up duty in local stations at Ballybunion, Ballyheige, Tarbert and Newtownsandes.[34]

In a very small column the *Cork Examiner* of Tuesday, 3 April observed: 'In recent days hundreds of young men and women have left west Kerry bound for America. It is the largest number experienced in the area for many years.' It is significant that as the new state began to consolidate its presence in Kerry a large proportion of its citizens saw little by way of employment opportunities or an economic future in an independent Ireland. They were voting with their feet as a matter of pure survival; the distinction between Free State and republic would seem rather academic, and certainly not the matter of life or death it had become for the political and military 'elites' on the ground in Kerry during the previous nine months of internecine conflict.

On 6 April the result of the inquest into the circumstances surrounding the death of John Conway was made known. Conway, a civilian prisoner from Caherina, Tralee, died on 24 February 1923 while under military custody in Tralee workhouse, which at the time served as both a prison and an army barracks. The report found 'Captain Patrick Byrne guilty of wilful murder', and added that 'there was no justification for the act'.

Brigadier Paddy Daly, O/C Kerry command, felt it necessary to outline Byrne's personal circumstances: 'Last October Byrne was attacked by Irregulars near Newcastle West, County Limerick during which he was horse whipped and badly beaten. His mind became unhinged and he became increasingly depressed and suicidal. Examined by Dr Griffin, Medical Superintendent, of Killarney Mental Hospital, he was assessed of being capable of carrying out light duties and was assigned such duties.'[35] Once O'Daly's evidence ended the court ruled its jurisdiction could not decide on Byrne's sanity at the time of the incident.

The fact that John Conway was a civilian prisoner – and not a republican – was crucial in terms of passing a guilty verdict. Presumably something Conway did caused a 'flashback' in Byrne's mind where he felt himself in the same life-threatening circumstances he had been in the previous October, only now he had a pistol with which to defend himself. In many ways the case is uncannily similar to the circumstances in Caherciveen the previous November where a sentry shot a fellow soldier dead (Sergeant O'Callaghan) thinking he was a republican sniper who had tried to kill him on a previous occasion when he was on duty at the same checkpoint and had returned to make another attempt to kill him.

The next day, Saturday 7 April, another tribunal of inquiry was held by the military authorities in Tralee. Presided over by Brigadier Paddy Daly and Colonel Jim McGuinness, Kerry command, and Bob Price from military headquarters, Portobello barracks, Dublin, the investigation purported to be an even-handed evaluation of the circumstances surrounding the deaths of seventeen republican prisoners (under military supervision) who were killed while removing landmines at Ballyseedy, Countess Bridge (on 7 March) and Bahagh's workhouse, Caherciveen (on 12 March). The review of the circumstances surrounding the deaths was a sham and a political charade perpetrated by the organisation that had carried out the atrocities in the first place. Apart from John Conway's death, when – for once – an open and honest verdict was given, every military enquiry from Bertie Murphy's death onward (in late September 1922) was a cynical opportunity to publicly discredit the republican version of events and exonerate the national army's behaviour.

Lieutenant Niall Harrington, a conscientious junior officer with the Dublin Guard, was suspicious of the 7 April verdict and began to collect information on the three atrocities with a view to compiling an open and honest report which he was going to send to the justice minister, Kevin O'Higgins, whom he knew was unhappy with Richard Mulcahy's handling of the defence portfolio and who might be willing to publish the facts of the case irrespective of their political consequences for the government. In many ways Niall Harrington's journey in Kerry assumes a curious parallel to that of Charles Marlow, the fictional character in Joseph Conrad's *Heart of Darkness* set in the nineteenth-century Belgian Congo. Harrington first met Brigadier Paddy O'Daly, O/C of the Dublin Guard, on board the *Lady Wicklow* on 2 August 1922 while travelling with the expeditionary force to Fenit. The sense of awe and almost reverence Harrington showed in meeting the man who directed the Squad's operations against British intelligence during the War of Independence was palpable even seven decades later in Harrington's memoir *Kerry Landing*, focusing on the early days of the Civil War in Kerry.

The shooting dead of Daniel Daly, a GS & WR engine driver at Tralee railway station on 23 January 1923 by Dublin Guard officers in plain clothes was an epiphany for Harrington, who, like most people in Kerry at the time, believed the act was carried out by republicans as a follow-up to the Liscahane derailment, when two railwaymen were killed in a republican attack. Like most in the county, Harrington was shocked when Brigadier Paddy O'Daly, only recently appointed O/C Kerry command, admitted in a public statement that members of his forces were responsible for the Daly killing.

The brutality of the Knocknagoshel trap mine and the horrendous deaths it inflicted on five members of the Dublin Guard, while appalling, was an act of war. The decision to inflict a similar fate on unarmed prisoners who had surrendered and had in effect withdrawn from the conflict was an entirely different matter and violated both the Geneva and Hague Conventions on the treatment of prisoners that most European governments had ratified governing the conduct of war. While neither the nascent Irish government nor its armed forces had ratified the terms of these conventions, and thus might be legally absolved from complying with the standards of behaviour they established, it would not excuse them of the morality of ensuring humane treatment of non-combatant prisoners. It is worth pointing out, however, that from the very first day of the war in Kerry, 2 August 1922, republicans had violated the terms of the Geneva Convention when they opened fire on Red Cross medics while they tended to wounded on Rock/Pembroke Street in Tralee, and continued machine-gunning even when a large Red Cross flag was unfurled and waved vigorously. From December 1922 onwards republicans routinely fired on Red Cross ambulances, which they regarded as military vehicles.

Niall Harrington's investigation concluded that all the deaths that occurred during the removal of three road blockages during early March were premeditated reprisals. He also knew that when his findings were made public (within military circles) his life would be in danger once his colleagues in the Dublin Guard figured out that he had penned the report. Consequently he put in for a transfer out of Kerry once he began his investigation. When army headquarters replied to his request, they informed him he was being transferred to Tralee. Fearing the worst, he took up accommodation at Benners hotel in Tralee and spent the night sitting in an armchair with two loaded revolvers at the ready, determined not to go down without a fight.[36] As it turned out nothing happened; his transfer to Tralee was as a result of an administrative error at military HQ. Nevertheless Harrington's response gives an indication of his sense of the depth of malaise that existed in military circles in Kerry at that point.

Harrington's report only concerned itself with establishing the facts of what happened in Kerry in early March 1923. He did not have to address why such a sequence of events occurred. Conrad's *Heart of Darkness* addresses the core philosophical and moral questions of an agency charged with bringing civilisation to a remote part of Africa (in this case the Belgian Congo), descending to the levels of brutality and savagery it was purporting to eradicate in the first place, and choosing to apportion blame to the native people and the primeval conditions it encountered in Africa. The parallel between the situation in Kerry in early March and Conrad's complex scenario in *Heart of Darkness* is apt. The military skills honed by the Squad during the War of Independence, displayed to lethal effect during the executions of fourteen intelligence agents in Dublin in November 1920 (Bloody Sunday), were part of the legacy the Squad members brought to their conduct of the Civil War in Kerry.

When defence minister Richard Mulcahy was questioned in the Dáil by the Labour leader, Thomas Johnston on 17 April 1923 concerning the value of any internal inquiry carried out by the army into the conduct of its own members in Kerry and whether such an investigation could ever be even-handed and impartial, Mulcahy's response was to stress the difficult conditions his troops encountered in Kerry and emphasise that the officer corps in Kerry command were men of the highest levels of integrity and standards of behaviour. Mulcahy observed:

> The troops in Kerry have had to fight against every ugly form of warfare which the Irregulars could think of. They have [had]

69 killed and 157 wounded, and their record there is such that it is inconceivable that they would be guilty of anything like the charges made against them in the Irregulars' statement ... On the other hand, the Irregulars in Kerry have stooped to outrage of every kind. Of the 69 of our men killed in that area, 17 lost their lives guarding food convoys to feed the people in outlying districts. The Knocknagoshel incident is typical of their methods of warfare.

As far as the Kerry officers were concerned, very few who know them, and very few, I think, of the civil population in Kerry will question their desire for discipline ... I have the fullest confidence that the honour of the army is as deeply rooted in them as it is in any of us here at Headquarters or in any member of the Government.[37]

Mulcahy's willingness to protect the reputation of the Dublin Guard was the result of a huge debt of gratitude that he (as defence minister) and others owed to the men of that unit. In a sense, the entire Provisional Government owed its survival to the willingness of people like Paddy O'Daly to place their lives on the line both in Dublin and Limerick in the early days of the conflict. The fact that the war continued in Kerry for so long was a contributory factor to the level of bitterness the government's troops stationed in the county showed towards their republican adversaries.

Contrary to Mulcahy's opinion, the Knocknagoshel incident was not typical of republican methods of warfare. In many ways it was a once-off incident that came, along with the reprisals it provoked, to define the Civil War experience in Kerry. Loyalty to his troops serving in Kerry was only part of Mulcahy's motivation in taking the line he did; political expediency was equally important. The Free State government as represented by the Cumann na nGaedheal party had to face the electorate again in August and public opinion (not only in Kerry) would be outraged if the truth of what happened in Kerry became known.

The electoral contest was at that point months away, but the government's policy of introducing local police units into towns and villages across north Kerry received a major setback on Saturday, 7 April when a body of armed anti-Treatyites visited a house occupied by civic guards in Ballyheige, removed them to another house in the village and burned the house they had occupied.[38] Investigation at local level would indicate that the eviction and barrack burning was carried out by members of Timothy 'Aeroplane' Lyons' column (nine men), one of the last republican units still militarily active in the county and challenging the government's writ in north Kerry.

On 10 April 1923 while on the run in the Knockmealdown mountains near Newcastle, County Tipperary, Liam Lynch, the chief of staff of the republican forces, was wounded in an exchange of fire with government troops and died of his wounds about 10 p.m. that night. He was twenty-nine. With his passing went the major obstacle on the republican side to a peaceful end to the conflict. Even up to the time of his death, Lynch, who seriously overestimated the republican military ability to continue the war, believed that victory was still in his grasp. If the republicans could obtain 'mountain artillery' (from sources in America and Germany), he believed these weapons would give the anti-Treaty forces that extra ingredient which would enable them to secure victory over their Free State adversaries. While Liam Lynch didn't have the power of veto over decision-making within the republican military executive, such was his prestige within the IRA that many members of the executive deferred to his point of view, thereby making the Lynch position the dominant one. Following Lynch's death there was a vacuum within the IRA's inner circle both on the question of Lynch's successor and what military strategy the republicans should follow in the war. Many of the executive were still on the run. Austin Stack was captured in Tipperary on 14 April, a few miles from where Liam Lynch was killed. On searching Stack his captors found a letter recommending to the executive members that the IRA abandon its campaign and dump arms. According to T. Ryle Dwyer the discovery of the letter probably saved Stack's life.

In Kerry, as in Tipperary, Free State army units continued to seek out and confront republicans still offering military resistance to the government forces present in their localities. At 6.30 a.m. on Friday, 13 April a patrol left Listowel for the townland of Tierneragh where a group of republicans were believed to be sheltering in a hay barn. The *Cork Examiner* of 14 April 1923 initially reported that the soldiers challenged the three men – John Linnane, a draper's clerk from Listowel, Richard Bunyan and John Mulcahy from Church Street, Listowel – to surrender, and then threw bombs into the barn. In a subsequent report the paper issued a correction, stating the patrol had opened fire with rifles, killing Linnane and wounding Bunyan.[39] In Dorothy Macardle's version of the incident the three men (she identifies the third as John Mullaney), who were sheltering in a dugout, agreed to give themselves up but the army opened fire regardless.

The next day, Saturday, 14 April, an army patrol left Ballyheige for Causeway to check a report that Timothy Lyons' column were sheltering in the area. Lyons, a native of Kilflynn, earned his nickname, Aeroplane, by a reputation for being able to appear out of nowhere, launch an ambush and escape against all the odds. Lyons' men were deemed responsible for the attack in Ballyheige a week earlier, on the civic guards' barracks. As the soldiers dispatched to apprehend the Lyons column were approaching Causeway, Lyons' men opened fire from several different vantage points, giving the impression they were a much larger force than the army patrol expected, though in fact there were only nine men in all. The two sides exchanged fire for several hours, during which time the republicans took one soldier prisoner and held their adversaries at bay until darkness fell. The Free State forces kept the houses under surveillance overnight and were joined by reinforcements early next morning. As both sides resumed fire that Sunday morning the republicans allowed their prisoner go free and decided to abandon their safe houses and go to ground elsewhere. To the chagrin of those sure of capturing the entire column, Lyons' Houdini-like ability to evade capture had come up trumps yet again.

Three of the column headed inland. But Lyons, Tom McGrath, Patrick O'Shea, Jim McEnery, Edward Greaney and Reginald Hathaway to took refuge at Dumfort cave, a seafront cave at the base of a cliff at Clashmealcon on the Shannon estuary between Kilmore and Kerry head. A long ridge running out along a narrow horseshoe-shaped creek led down to the cave entrance at sea level which was concealed behind several large boulders, making it invisible to the casual viewer but enabling anyone in the cave to have a commanding view of the steep pathway leading to the sandy seashore which was exposed at low tide. In their follow-up enquiries as to the whereabouts of their quarry on Sunday morning soldiers called to the home of Jim McGrath (whose brother Tom they knew was involved with the Lyons column) and brought him to Ballymullen barracks for questioning. During the course of his interrogation McGrath inadvertently mentioned that they might have gone to Dumfort cave, reckoning the likelihood of their being there was extremely slim. The soldiers asked if he would take them there and he agreed to do so, expecting the cave to be empty.

Early on Monday morning, 16 April 1923 a group of soldiers accompanied Jim McGrath to Clashmealcon. Entering the cave McGrath was stunned to discover that his brother, Tom, Timothy Lyons and four others had in fact taken refuge there. According to Dorothy Macardle's version of the siege of Clashmealcon his brother and the other men reassured him they did not consider him to blame for their predicament. As for the soldiers waiting outside, Macardle records: 'A soldier tried to follow him shouting "come out". A bullet fired from the cave killed him instantly, and he fell onto the flat rocks below. One more tried and was shot and fell into the sea. No soldier would go down after that.'[40]

Free State army sources identified the first soldier killed at Clashmealcon as Volunteer O'Neill, a nineteen-year-old Dublin Guardsman from Nile Street, Dublin. Attempts and requests to allow Red Cross stretcher bearers to retrieve his body before the incoming tide washed it out to sea were both thwarted and refused by the republicans.[41] It is difficult to establish the precise chronology as to when the second soldier wounded during the siege, Lieutenant H. D. E. Pierson, from South Circular Road, Limerick (described as a TCD engineering graduate) serving with the corps of engineers, was shot and wounded in the head. From information released after the event it seems to have occurred much later than O'Neill's death. The level of resistance they encountered at the cave led the soldiers to believe that they had inadvertently discovered a major republican command post. Speculation in Ballymullen barracks surmised that both Humphrey Murphy and Éamon de Valera were based there, according to Dorothy Macardle.[42]

The army set fire to sacks of turf and hay soaked in paraffin in an attempt to smoke out the occupants, but a sea breeze rendered this strategy useless. Two landmines were detonated near the cave entrance but had little practical effect. Lights were brought to bear on the area immediately near the cave as darkness fell. Nevertheless, over the night of 16/17 April Tom McGrath and Patrick O'Shea left the cave and attempted to scale the 100-foot cliff. During the course of the climb both men lost their footing and fell to their deaths; their bodies were recovered from the sea a few days later. Around midday on Wednesday, 18 April Timothy Lyons called out from the cave that he would give himself up, but asked the military to let the others go free. No terms were accepted. A rope was thrown down, but as Lyons was being hauled up the rope snapped, and as he fell troops opened fire, killing him instantly. His body was washed out to sea.

The Lyons family told a fairly macabre tale of an incident that supposedly happened at the time of his death. There was an old clock in the family home at Kilflynn that was out of order for fifteen years. It was without a pendulum or a minute hand, and the hour hand was pointing at twelve. At the exact time that Lyons was killed, the old clock struck the hour, and Lyons' parents, unaware of their son's fate, concluded that he was done for, and knelt down and prayed for him.[43]

The other three men and Jim McGrath (who was subsequently released) gave themselves up and were taken to Bally-mullen barracks along with the mortally wounded Lieutenant Pierson, who died of his wounds in hospital later that day. His death would have fatal consequences for the three prisoners. The announcement from Kerry command that James McEnery, Lixnaw, Edward Greaney of Ballyduff and Reginald Hathaway of Slough in England, who initially gave his name as Walter Stephens (he served in the East Lancs. regiment of the British army during the War of Independence in Kerry, deserted and joined the IRA and went anti-Treaty in the Civil War) were to face a firing squad was greeted with disbelief across a wide spectrum of opinion in Kerry, not least because three of the men involved in the siege had already lost their lives.

The military went into considerable detail to justify their actions. Primarily, the refusal to allow Red Cross medics to retrieve O'Neill's body and render medical assistance to the wounded Lieutenant Pierson was cited as the principal reason for their decision. Greaney and McEnery, both members of Michael Pierce's unit and in prison when Pierce's column surrendered in mid-February, had been released from custody because of their association with Pierce. They had also signed the pledge that they would not take up arms against the government in the future. Similar terms were given to Reginald Hathaway who was in jail when Tom O'Driscoll's column gave themselves up later that month. According to the military authorities, all three men were involved in the civic guard eviction and station burning at Ballyheige. In their defence, the three men said that they had been forced by Humphrey Murphy (under a threat of death) to join Lyons' unit following their release from prison. They also stated that Timothy Lyons had fired the shots that killed O'Neill and Pierson. Their pleas for clemency fell on deaf ears and their execution was set for Wednesday, 25 April 1923.

Eight members of Kerry County Council with republican sympathies – J. O'Sullivan, T. McEllistrim, J. Riordan, T. Lyne, F. H. Crowley, Miss A. Broderick, M. Murphy and D. Hegarty – resigned in protest once the sentences were announced, demanding prisoner of war status be given to the three men, thereby removing the execution order. James McEnery's brother, Tom, a priest serving in a parish in England, returned to Kerry to see his brother, but the military refused to allow him to visit Ballymullen barracks. The executions were carried out early on the morning of 25 April.[44]

Nationally, the week between the men's arrest (Wednesday, 18 April) and their execution (Wednesday, 25 April) was a momentous one for the republican campaign. On 20 April Frank Aiken was elected as chief of staff of the IRA. Aiken's political and military perspective was close to de Valera's position on the continuation of the war, and far more conciliatory than Liam Lynch's position. The IRA executive met in Tipperary over 26–27 April and approved the de Valera–Aiken line to bring hostilities to an end with a view to a negotiated settlement. National newspapers on 28 April contained the information that a ceasefire would come into effect from noon on Monday, 30 April 1923.

On either 25 or 26 April two civic guards accompanied by Lieutenant Michael Behan and Lieutenant Gaffney travelled from Castleisland to Currow to resolve a property dispute. They settled the dispute and as they were driving back to Castleisland they got out of their car to remove a fallen tree and came under fire from republicans. The two army officers were only armed with revolvers but retreated about a mile along the road, with the republicans in hot pursuit. Michael Behan was shot dead, Gaffney evaded capture and the two guards were stripped of their uniforms.[45] It is impossible to say if the attack was carried out as a reprisal for the execution of the three Clashmealcon prisoners. Lieutenant Michael Behan would be the last Free State soldier to be killed in action in Kerry during the Civil War, and the seventy-second fatality (fifteen officers and fifty-seven other ranks) in the county since Edward Sheehy's death in Listowel on 30 June 1922.

Under the cover of darkness the railway station and the stationmaster's house at Loo Bridge were burned down on 28/29 April.[46] The arson attack must have made people in Kerry wonder if the news they'd read in the newspapers earlier that day, Saturday, 28 April, concerning a ceasefire the following Monday would be implemented in Kerry. Later that same weekend Albina Broderick, a sixty-year-old republican and a member of Kerry County Council was cycling between Westview and her home in Sneem when she was challenged by a Free State army patrol who intended to place her under arrest.[47] She refused to co-operate and the troops opened fire, wounding Miss Broderick (who was known by the Irish version of her name, Gobnaid Ní Bhrúdair) in the legs. She was taken to Tralee initially but was later transferred to the North Dublin Union (workhouse) prison in Dublin.

11

RECONSTRUCTION

In early May column commanders in areas where republicans were still active confirmed to their rank and file that reports in the national press on a ceasefire effective from noon, 30 April were authentic, and not a ruse by newspapers with a pronounced government bias and an inbuilt hostility to the republican cause.

In Barraduff in east Kerry, Jeremiah Murphy noted: 'Our Captain, Jimmy Daly assembled our company ... and told us the order was official ... We assembled for the last time ... and disbanded with little thought that we would ever be together again. Thus ended, officially the resistance against the implementation of the Treaty which formed the Irish Free State. Many fine men had been killed, much property damaged, but worst of all the people had been divided down the middle. The North was lost, while the South fought between themselves. Everybody was disappointed, but at least there was an uneasy peace.'[1]

Murphy's comments – a mixture of fatalism and war weariness combined with a sense of relief that the conflict was finally over – were a sincere response to a unilateral declaration by the IRA, as articulated by Frank Aiken, that left a myriad issues related to the war unresolved. W. T. Cosgrave publicly stated that he would not meet with de Valera, as to do so would be formal recognition that an 'insurrectionist movement' was on a par with a democratically elected government. De Valera contacted Senators Jameson and Douglas, two unionist members of the Free State Senate, to act as intermediaries to facilitate a dialogue. They brought back a set of proposals from Cosgrave: 1. Republicans should sign a document acknowledging the Free State as the legitimate national government, and 2. They must surrender their arms to the government. These proposals formed no basis for a discussion as far as republicans were concerned.

On 13–14 May 1923 the republican government and the IRA met and agreed that republican TDs would take their seats in the Dáil if they did not have to take the oath of allegiance, thereby linking their military struggle for the republic to a legitimate constitutional issue. Without a pledge to give up weapons, the government refused to release republican prisoners. The talks had run out of steam. On 24 May de Valera and Aiken ordered the IRA to dump arms; they were calling an end to hostilities but were not conceding defeat.

The war placed a huge financial burden on the new state. A total of £10,664,500, a quarter of the national budget (£42,278,406) for the year ending 31 March 1923, was devoted to military spending. Over half that amount, £5,547,000 (£3,571,000 on soldiers' wages, £1,976,000 on dependants), went to pay an army that had swollen to 55,000 men and 3,000 officers. The exchequer had to provide for another army, the 12,000 republican prisoners in state custody. Property damages claims stood at £10,385,000 with an additional £500,000 in personal injuries claims. W. T. Cosgrave calculated the war cost the state the equivalent of £5–10s–00d for every man, woman and child in the country.[2]

Kerry must have contributed a significant proportion of the national total given the fact that the war continued in the county for so long and had already run up a tally of £538,000 for the two and a half months from August to mid-October 1922. The sustained campaign focused on the railways during early January 1923 (which also claimed two lives) meant that the Great Southern and Western Railway Company bore the brunt of the IRA's campaign against the government, bringing a private transport operator to the verge of bankruptcy in Kerry, if not nationally. Thus, once peace was secured a full restoration of the Kerry rail network was an immediate priority for the government as a practical way of bringing home to the ordinary citizen in Kerry that the government was in control. While the GS & WR was under siege from without by republicans during the nine-month conflict, Kerry County Council, the second most seriously affected organisation to be thrown off course by the war, was under siege both from without and within. The destruction of roads and bridges in the county, while debilitating, was overshadowed by a concerted campaign by farmers not to pay rates, which was as damaging to the local authority financially as the republicans' actions were to the county's transport infrastructure. Both realms needed immediate attention.

On Sunday, 29 April at 3 p.m. an armoured train arrived at Kenmare station. A large number of townspeople visited the railway station to see it, as it was nine months since trains had run to Kenmare.[3] There was more than an element of news management in the timing of this visit, as the previous night republicans burned the station building and the stationmaster's house at Loo Bridge, on the Headford Junction line, midway between Killarney and Kenmare. The *Cork Examiner* of 4 May contained the news that the Listowel–Ballybunion railway line had reopened following the restoration of rolling stock and the stations at Lisselton and Ballybunion, which had been burned by republicans a few months previously. In their haste to get the railway back into service, the railway maintenance and repair corps may have substituted speed for safety considerations. While carrying out repairs at Loo Bridge the armoured train collided with another train, crushing Volunteer Thomas Fitzgerald to death.[4]

A branch of the army with a budget of £1 million (10 per cent of total military spending), the railway maintenance and repair corps, under the control of General Russell, did Trojan work to counter the effects of the republican campaign to undermine the national rail network.[5] Visiting Kerry in mid-May to review progress since the ceasefire, Russell announced that 'broken bridges and other damages of a different nature have been repaired and precautionary measures have been taken to avert further damage. The Mallow–Killarney service will resume next Monday. Simultaneously Headford–Kenmare and Farranfore–Caherciveen/Valentia will resume. P. Tooher, Manager, Tralee–Dingle railway says the line will re open on Tuesday.'[6] The precautionary measures Russell alluded to were small army units based at key railway installations. The railway station at Ballybrack, near Farranfore, came under rifle and machine-gun fire from republicans at 12.45 a.m. on Monday, 21 May. The nine-man garrison repelled the attack, taking two prisoners, John McCarthy, found in possession of a . 45 revolver, and Frank Mulcahy, who was unarmed.[7] It seems strange that after almost a three-week lull in republican activities this attack should occur out of the blue.

Even though the government had announced there would be no mass release of republican prisoners until the IRA handed weapons over, Free State army patrols continued to search for both individual prisoners and arms and ammunition dumps. The policy on prisoners was under consideration. In May an intelligence officer visiting Kerry prisons noted:

> I must say I was surprised at the type of Irregular that I found. They are quite different from any other prisoners that I have seen and are mainly farmers' sons. I firmly believe that when things become normal that most could be released and they would give no further trouble. They are mostly men who have been led astray and really did not know what they were doing. They simply followed certain leaders who led them astray. This is the explanation for the tough fight they put up in Kerry. They are mostly men who thought they were fighting as in the old days and who were poisoned by Irregular propaganda. Now that they are beginning to see the light they are quite friendly towards our troops and I believe most will one day join either the army or the civic guard.[8]

Troops searching for arms dumps in Kilgarvan, Kenmare in late May discovered a bomb factory. The résumé of the contents found gives the impression that republican engineering units operated what was in effect quiet a sophisticated assembly line: 'Lathes, two gas generators, an electric fan bellows, short drilling gear, punching machines, iron and wooden moulds and thousands of bomb springs, necks and casings.'[9] Most probably this was the principal workshop for the entire Kerry No. 2 brigade area.

Efforts to remove the remnants of the war were only part of the recovery programme. There was also a priority to restore normal legal and judicial mechanisms for resolving disputes. On Wednesday, 16 May District Justice Johnson opened court sittings in both Caherciveen and Kenmare, where no courts had been held for over two years.[10] In early June over thirty people were arrested in Tannavalla, Lacks, Listowel in connection with land seizures.[11]

At the beginning of May Alderman Patrick Monaghan, lord mayor of Drogheda and a prominent member of Cumann na nGaedheal, was appointed commissioner for Kerry County Council with the onerous responsibility of recommending practical measures to restore local government in the county.[12] The cumulative effects of both the War of Independence and the Civil War hostilities on the county's road network combined with very effective non-payment of rates campaigns stretching back to 1920/21 meant that the local authority was virtually bankrupt and would depend in both the short and long term on central government help. It would cost a minimum of £50,600 just to repair the major bridges; he was satisfied that the army could maintain the minor ones sufficiently for tourist traffic during the summer months. As the war was coming to an end he suggested the soldiers stationed in the county be deployed in restoring the road network until sufficient national funding could be provided. There was only one steamroller and one stonebreaking machine in the entire county for road maintenance purposes, he explained. Monaghan's proposals also involved increasing the rates on both land and buildings in the six unions across the county as well as increasing some of the rents the local authority charged its own employees when a cottage was provided.[13]

In late May and early June two totally unrelated incidents involving members of the army, from the micro level of a local barrack to the top echelons of Kerry command, indicate that the military were still a law unto themselves in the county. On Tuesday, 29 May Joseph O'Leary, an IRA prisoner, was killed in military custody in Castleisland. On Saturday, 2 June between 1 and 2 a.m. three masked and armed men knocked on the door of Randall McCarthy's home at Inchlough, Kenmare. His daughter, Flossie, called out 'Who's there?' and got the response, 'Military'. Flossie and Jessie McCarthy promptly answered the door. The two ladies were covered about the face and head by a heavy class of motor oil.[14] John M. Regan identifies the three men as Major-General Paddy O'Daly and Captains Ed Flood and Jim Clark.[15] The incident, which became known in government circles as the 'Kenmare case', took on far more significance than an assault – however distressing – on the McCarthy ladies, according to Regan, because the three men implicated in the case had also been involved in the Ballyseedy atrocity carried out in early March 1923. At that point Richard Mulcahy, defence minister, publicly exonerated Kerry command of any responsibility for the deaths of republican prisoners killed in the March landmine explosions. At that juncture, Kevin O'Higgins tried – unsuccessfully, it seems – to exert central government control and public accountability over military affairs in Kerry. On this occasion the war was at an end and O'Higgins hoped he could use the 'Kenmare case' as a means of courtmartialling the three officers involved in both the June and March events. Both O'Higgins and Mulcahy dug in their heels at cabinet level – on 27 June the entire Army Council, including Mulcahy, threatened to resign if a prosecution went ahead. The approach of a general election in August made the assault case a sensitive one, not least because Dr McCarthy was a Cumann na nGaedheal supporter and was not really interested in the machinations at cabinet level between two rival ministers. His prime concern was for the civil powers to legally redress the assault done to his two daughters. Later in the autumn, by which time the elections were over, it was recommended that the McCarthys take a case for civil damages.

Apart from the single incident at Ballybrack in late May the IRA ceasefire had held resolutely throughout Kerry and no soldier had been killed or wounded by maverick republican attacks. Accidents with weapons still occurred, however. Volunteer Stephen McCabe, a Dubliner serving with the salvage corps – a widower and father of three children – was shot dead at Killorglin barracks while mounting guard in one of the town's three outposts.[16]

Even though the government had stated there would be no release of republican prisoners in advance of a weapons handover, in the three months since April over 800 had been released, 352 in April, 277 in May and a further 206 up to 27 June 1923.[17] It is not known how many – if any – Kerry prisoners were among those released.

The *Cork Examiner* devoted much attention, including a photograph, to publicising the arrival of the first American tourists in Killarney in mid-July, in what was reported as a vote of confidence in the town's tourist industry.[18] The weekend following the tourist visit, Fionán Lynch, Minister for Fisheries and Cumann na nGaedheal TD for Kerry, led a high-powered political delegation including President W. T. Cosgrave, Ernest Blythe and Desmond Fitzgerald, TD to Kerry to see how things were progressing in his native county since the cessation of hostilities and allow them to meet local activists in anticipation of the forthcoming Dáil elections.[19] Thursday, 2 August 1923 marked the first anniversary of the Free State army landings in Kerry. Church parades were held in Tralee, Killarney, Castleisland, Kenmare and Caherciveen. Colonel Stan Bishop and Colonel James McGuinness reviewed the Tralee parade, which involved a march of over three hundred troops.[20]

The third Dáil was dissolved on 9 August 1923 and the election date for the new parliament was set for the 27 August. The new assembly, which would reconvene on 19 September, would see Kerry county represented as a single entity, a seven-seat constituency in a Dáil whose membership was increased from 128 to 153 TDs. Thomas Dennehy, Tralee UDC and Professor John Marcus O'Sullivan, NUI Dublin and a nephew of the bishop of Kerry, joined the sitting government TDs, James Crowley and Fionán Lynch, on the Cumann na nGaedheal ticket. Lynch and O'Sullivan focused their campaign on south Kerry. Campaigning in Killorglin they were called to explain why republican prisoners still hadn't been released. Lynch stated he would not favour any release until arms were given up.[21] The reception the two candidates received in Caherciveen the following day was even more theatrical, where prior to their meeting a number of girls holding black flags and carrying dummy coffins paraded around the town cheering and shouting. When they were asked to move on by stewards, blows were exchanged and some of the Cumann na nGaedheal supporters and security staff were hit by flagstaffs. Scuffles ensued for ten minutes.[22] Reports on republican election meetings hardly feature in any newspapers, largely because most of their candidates – including Austin Stack, TD and Paddy Cahill, TD – were in jail and many of their election workers, IRA men acting in a civilian or political capacity, were also under arrest. No doubt Cumann na nGaedheal electioneering strategists took this element of the prisoners' role into account when deciding to defer making any decisions on prisoner releases, an action that also reduced the chance of widespread electoral violence. The campaign wasn't totally devoid of reminders of the recent conflict, however. In Lixnaw on Sunday, 26 August the convoy conveying Treaty candidates James Crowley and Fionán Lynch to a meeting in Listowel was attacked by a hostile crowd; shots were fired, seriously injuring a young man named Thomas Costelloe.[23]

Cumann na nGaedheal and the republican candidates did not have the field to themselves, however. The Labour party put forward two candidates, Cormac Walsh, president of the INTO, and Patrick Casey, a member of Tralee UDC, while the Kerry Farmers' Union selected Denis Brosnan and John O'Neill. A number of independents also contested the election, among them Tom O'Donnell, the former Irish Parliamentary Party MP who had represented the West Kerry constituency at Westminster between 1900 and 1918.

The election results for Kerry constituency represented a huge reservoir of political support for the anti-Treaty wing of Sinn Féin in the county, where a first-preference vote of 24,732 (45 per cent) saw the republicans win four seats in the new Dáil. The Cumann na nGaedheal party, by contrast, secured 17,808 first-preference votes (32.45 per cent), winning the remaining three seats representing Kerry in Leinster House. The republican vote was all the more remarkable in that none of their candidates could canvass their electorate (they were either in jail or in hiding), and most of their electoral workers were similarly incapacitated. Not only that – people cast their vote for their representatives in full knowledge that none of the republican TDs they had elected to the Dáil would take either the oath of allegiance (a prerequisite for entry) or their seats in the national parliament. The large support base evidenced for the republicans represents a protest vote against the Free State as much as a gesture of solidarity with the campaign waged against the government by the IRA during the Civil War in the county, which would have made life difficult for everybody irrespective of their political viewpoint.

ELECTION RESULTS, KERRY CONSTITUENCY
27 August 1923[24]

Total electorate: 90, 156 Total vote: 56, 451 Spoiled votes: 1, 691
Quota: 6, 856

Candidate	Party/affiliation	1st pref vote	Result
Stack, Austin	Republican	10,333	Elected
Lynch, Fionán	CnG	8,982	Elected
McEllistrim, Thomas	Republican	7,277	Elected
O'Donoghue, Thomas	Republican	4,414	Elected
Crowley, James	CnG	3,759	Elected
O'Sullivan, John M.	CnG	3,759	Elected
Brosnan, Denis	Farmers' Union	3,182	
Cahill, Paddy J.	Republican	2,708	Elected
Casey, Parick	Labour	2,329	
Walsh, Cormac	Labour	1,974	
O'Neill, John	Farmers' Union	1,674	
O'Donnell, Tom	Independent	1,640	
Dennehy, Thomas	CnG	1,303	
McSweeney	Independent	1,124	
Gleeson	Independent	382	

While electoral or economic-based parties such as Labour or the Farmers' Union secured 7 or 8 per cent respectively of the total vote, and independents a further 5 per cent, the two parties based on the Treaty/Civil War issue secured almost 78 per cent of all the votes cast in the county, making it the paramount political issue for eight out of ten voters in Kerry.

The election of John Marcus O'Sullivan, a National University of Ireland professor and nephew of Charles O'Sullivan, bishop of Kerry, as a Cumann na nGaedheal TD for Kerry in August 1923 provides a useful prism for the way the Civil War could divide families. Dr O'Sullivan was also a cousin of Charlie Daly of Knockane, Firies, who was among a party of four republicans (three of them Kerrymen) executed in Donegal in March 1923.

The first-preference vote secured by anti-Treaty candidates nationally, and the number of TDs returned in August 1923 on a republican ticket was phenomenal. They represented the political manifestation of the republican armed forces who had waged war against the Provisional Government and the Dáil that had received a broad democratic mandate and wide popular support (92 of 126 TDs elected in June 1922 – 72% of membership). Ironically, rather than pay a price for an attempt to overthrow the democratic government, republicans were rewarded by the voters.

In a Dáil with increased representation (153 instead of 128 members) the anti-Treaty grouping increased from thirty-six to forty-four (a gain of eight seats, almost 25 per cent – for a party that would not involve itself in parliamentary business for ideological reasons) as against a Cumann na nGaedheal advance from fifty-eight to sixty-three, just a 10 per cent gain in seats. The 1923 election result was far more representative than any election since 1918, with all the country's thirty constituencies being contested by all parties in what was the first general election since 1910 to take place in Ireland in 'normal' circumstances and free of both social turmoil and violent political upheaval. Éamon de Valera, the republicans' principal political leader, had been arrested in Ennis, County Clare as he arrived in the town in August to address an election meeting. He would spend the next year in jail.

Cumann na nGaedheal politicians vilified de Valera during the election campaign, holding him solely responsible for the Civil War. Éamon de Valera was certainly the anti-Treaty side's most articulate political voice during the Dáil debate on the Treaty and vociferously opposed the deal that Michael Collins and Arthur Griffith proposed as an acceptable settlement of the struggle for independence. The Civil War occurred primarily because of a military split in the IRA. The launch of de Valera's political party – Cumann na Poblachta – in mid-March 1922 saw de Valera embark on a week-long tour of Munster which acted as a *de facto* rally and recruiting drive to gain political influence over republicans in the province. De Valera also endorsed the seizure of the Four Courts carried out over Easter 1922, giving the rebel group political credibility and prestige without receiving any reciprocal influence over their actions. At this juncture de Valera's approval certainly represented a huge boost for the 'executive'. Once the Civil War began, the leadership on the republican side did not intend to compromise its objectives and so de Valera had no meaningful political role. Even when the 'republican government' was announced in late October 1922, its role – and his position – was largely to approve and articulate decisions the IRA had already made.

Ultimately Éamon de Valera was a crucial figure in bringing hostilities to an end in May 1923 and – even more importantly

– steering the defeated anti-Treaty wing of Sinn Féin – as the Fianna Fáil party – into a meaningful political role in the newly independent democracy. In the wake of the assassination of Kevin O'Higgins, TD, Minister for Home Affairs, in 1927, W. T. Cosgrave adroitly introduced legislation forcing all candidates to take a pledge that they would take their seats in the Dáil once elected. He then called a 'snap' election in September 1927 in the hope of securing a sympathy vote for the Cumann na nGaedheal party based on public revulsion at the death of a leading member of the government. Thus, Éamon de Valera led the Fianna Fáil TDs into the Dáil, where they took the oath of allegiance that had caused so much bloodshed and grief a mere five years previously. Explaining it away as 'mere formula', de Valera engaged in an act of legerdemain not unlike the circus rope conjurer, who on his first attempt could not remove the knot from the rope but found once he uttered the magic words the knot unravelled before his eyes.

Conclusion

The War of Independence, which began in January 1919 and ended on 11 July 1921, did not really gain momentum in Kerry until the summer of 1920. The Civil War, by contrast – even though it only lasted one third of that time – is remembered in Kerry as a far more bloody, bitterly waged and protracted conflict in terms of lives lost, damage to property, disruption of people's daily lives and its impact on the local economy than the war waged against the British.

In many ways the IRA in Kerry saw the Civil War as a continuation of the War of Independence and, in confronting the Provisional Government, saw themselves as defending the republic they had fought for between 1920 and 1921. During that conflict general headquarters staff, IRA in Dublin regarded Kerry's performance as disappointing. If comparing Kerry's profile in that war with the campaign in Cork or Tipperary, GHQ's assessment might have some validity, but once Kerry geared up for the conflict, the casualties the IRA inflicted on the RIC and the British army increased in terms of scale, level of success and volume of attacks across the county in the closing year of the war. Thus, when GHQ imposed a national organiser – in the summer of 1921 – to overhaul Kerry No. 1 and Kerry No. 2 brigades IRA there was considerable anger and resentment within the IRA leadership in the county. At a political level Austin Stack's opposition to the Treaty reinforced the IRA's military disenchantment and opposition to

a national body – closely aligned with Michael Collins' view
– on the 'settlement' with the British, which most of Kerry's
republican leadership regarded as surrendering the 'republic'.
At a most basic level local pride was hurt. The IRA in Kerry
had a grievance and a score to settle. If there was a conflict on
the Treaty issue, Kerry would have an opportunity to challenge
both GHQ's assessment of its War of Independence record
and the Provisional Government it would impose on Ireland
on behalf of the British.

The decision by the Provisional Government to establish a
garrison – 250 men recruited locally – in Listowel in late spring
1922 was followed about a month later – early May – by the arrival of 150 republican troops who took up positions around the
Free State outposts in the town. For the next two months there
was a military stand-off in Listowel, which only ended on 30
June (in the wake of the shelling of the Four Courts in Dublin
on 28 June that started the Civil War) when the republicans
deemed it necessary to bring the Free State military enclave
in Kerry to an end. Even then, both sides – all Kerrymen, with
officers from the War of Independence IRA – were reluctant
to fight and brokered a ceasefire, in a 'national conflict' that was
probably perceived in Kerry as a 'Dublin quarrel' at that point.
Sea-borne landings of Provisional Government troops at Tralee
and Tarbert on 2–3 August 1922 took the IRA in Kerry totally
by surprise. Seven hundred troops principally from Dublin
and the Clare/Galway area were well entrenched in Tralee and
across north Kerry by the time Kerry IRA contingents returned
from the Limerick 'front' to defend their own county.

During August and September thirty-five Free State soldiers were killed in Kerry – the equivalent of the RIC's entire

death toll during the War of Independence in the county – and casualties would have been much higher had the government forces had not the advantage of armoured cars and artillery which forced the republicans to abandon and abort several large-scale ambushes. The fact that the Free State army units in Kerry were from outside the county meant they had little or no empathy with their republican adversaries, who were regarded – especially by Collins' elite Dublin Guard regiment – as having done little to achieve national independence in the war against the British but were now doing their utmost to put the gains won in that victory at risk. In a campaign mostly of ambushes and sniping, the IRA in Kerry carried out two large-scale assaults – by Civil War standards – taking on the entire garrisons in Kenmare and Killorglin in September, the high-water mark of their campaign in the county.

The passing of the Emergency Powers Bill on 27 September 1922 gave the government draconian powers to execute republicans found in possession of arms and ammunition, a policy supported by the Irish bishops in their October pastoral. The legislation was an admission of sorts that the national army had not succeeded in defeating the republicans in a conventional conflict. Few republicans, either in Kerry or elsewhere, did anything to comply with the two-week amnesty – to surrender weapons – that accompanied the bill. The government, though disappointed with the republican response to the amnesty, were reluctant to use the powers the act gave them, and the first execution only occurred on 17 November, nearly two months after the act's introduction in the Dáil. Even then justice minister Kevin O'Higgins felt that unless the powers were exercised the republicans would not take their deterrent value seriously.

On the ground in Kerry the first 'legal' execution occurred in Ballymullen barracks, Tralee on 20 January 1923. In reality summary executions and reprisal killings of republicans had been the norm in the county as early as August 1922 – where the Squad cohort within the Dublin Guard returned and resorted to tried and tested methods in their war against republicans. During the autumn and winter of 1922–23 republican activity decreased considerably – with a corresponding fall in the Free State army death toll – while the army 'sweeps' carried out in those months captured sizeable numbers of prisoners and large quantities of arms and ammunition, radically limiting the republicans' ability to wage a coherent campaign.

The Irish Free State administration formally succeeded the Provisional Government on 6 December 1922, an occasion that ought to have been a signal to republicans that their campaign to destroy the Free State had failed. In a highly symbolic operation carried out on 6 December, the leading military commanders in Kerry, Brigadier Paddy O'Daly, O/C Dublin Guard and Colonel Michael Hogan, O/C 1st Westerns, recaptured Kenmare in a manoeuvre that they expected would usher in the ending of the war in Kerry by Christmas. This expectation proved premature, both at local and national level. The assassination of Seán Hales, a government TD, in Dublin on 7 December 1922 was followed the next day by the execution of the four principal republican prisoners in state custody since the fall of the Four Courts. Early January 1923 saw republicans launch what was in effect a 'blitz' on the Kerry rail network, culminating in the deaths of two rail workers at Liscahane, near Ardfert on 17 January 1923.

Events in early March 1923 that would come to epitomise the Civil War experience in Kerry represented the nadir of both the Kerry IRA's experience of the bitterness of the conflict and the government forces' campaign of retribution for what they saw as an unending conflict against an enemy that refused to admit defeat. Ballyseedy and related atrocities would cast a long shadow over Kerry, both in the way large segments of the population viewed the new state and the wider folk memory of the way the central government waged war against Kerrymen. Within the republican ranks in Kerry a strong tradition of opposition to the Free State would persist even generations after the Free State ceased to have any legal meaning (around the introduction of de Valera's constitution, 1937) and a republic – albeit a twenty-six county version – would be a political reality. For many republicans the outbreak of political unrest in Northern Ireland in the summer of 1969 and the eventual emergence of the Provisional IRA was seen both as a continuation of the War of Independence and an opportunity to reclaim the entire 'national territory' and redress the flawed settlement the south – as personified by Michael Collins – had accepted from the British in December 1921 that led to the Civil War.

In spite of the glib assessment of Irish politics and its political party system since the 1920s as 'Civil War politics', the Civil War represented the failure of politics and an inability within the Sinn Féin movement to deal with political compromise, where for many IRA activists – not just in Kerry – compromise represented surrender. Within Kerry over seventy republicans and – if one includes deaths due to accidents – over eighty-five Free State soldiers, as well as about a dozen civilians, lost their lives. Once in power in the 1930s de Valera found there was much wisdom in Michael Collins' argument that the Treaty offered a stepping-stone to achieve a wider and more comprehensive expression of national independence than was apparent at first sight. Though Irish democracy may have fallen at the first hurdle, both sides in the Civil War successfully established a working democracy within a decade of a bitter and bloody conflict.

APPENDIX 1

NATIONAL ARMY (KERRY)

KILLED – OR DIED OF WOUNDS: 1922/23

NAME	REG	KILLED	WHERE	HOME
BEHAN MICHAEL LIEUT			CURROW, CASTLEISLAND	DUBLIN
BROWN JOHN; CORP (28)	1ST W	25/04/23	DUAGH	EFFIN, COUNTY LIMERICK
BURKE JAMES; CPTN	1ST W	20/10/22	CASTLEMAINE	DUNMANWAY, COUNTY CORK
BYRNE EDWARD; PTE	DG	28/08/22	SPA, TRALEE	PIMLICO, DUBLIN
CADDIGAN JOHN; PTE		02/08/22	NA	NA
CARSON WILLIAM D.; CORP (19)	DG	02/11/22	PEMBROKE ST, TRALEE	UNIVERSITY ST, BELFAST
CASEY MICHAEL;		02/08/22	RATHMORE	NA
CONNOLLY; PTE	DG	26/11/22	MOORE ST, DUBLIN	KERRY
CONNORS; PTE	1 W	04/07/22	BALLYSEEDY	ENNISTYMON, COUNTY CLARE
CON ROY PATRICK	1W	28/08/22	BLENNERVILLE	LIMERICK
COOPER CLEMENT; LIEUT		04/11/22	CAHIRCIVEEN	COUNTY KERRY
COPELAND GEORGE		04/09/22	SNEEM/ KENMARE	NA
CORCORAN JOHN; CORP (33)	DG	28/03/23	ROCKFIELD, KILLARNEY	KENMARE PLACE, NCR, DUBLIN
COYLE PATRICK; CPTN	1W	22/10/22	KILMAINHAM, BROSNA	COUNTY CLARE
DALY MICHAEL; SERGT	DG	28/01/23	D. O. W CASTLEISLAND	DUBLIN
DUNNE MICHAEL; CAPTN	DG	23/08/22	KNOCKNAGOSHEL	DUBLIN
FARRELL MICHAEL; CORP (27)	DG	06/03/23	PEMBROKE ST, TRALEE	JAMES' ST, DUBLIN
FERCUSON MATTHEW; PTE	DG	02/08/22	BOWER, RATHMORE	VIRGINIA, COUNTY CAVAN
FITZGERALD CECIL; AMS (16)	DG	17/12/22	INNISFALLEN, KILLARNEY	GORT, COUNTY GALWAY
GALLAGHER THOMAS; PTE		04/11/22	BALLINEEN	NA
GALVIN MICHAEL; PTE	KYB	06/03/23	KNOCKNAGOSHEL	KILLARNEY
GALWORTHY JOHN; PTE	1W	24/08/22	D. O. W BALLYMULLEN BKS	INNISBOFFIN, GALWAY
GILCHRIST JOSEPH; CORP		25/10/22	BALLY ROBERT, ARDFERT	LONGFORD

APPENDIX 1 (CONTD.)

NATIONAL ARMY (KERRY)

KILLED – OR DIED OF WOUNDS: 1922/23

Name		Date	Place	Location
GILLESPIE FRED; SERGT (23)	DG	02/08/22	ROCK./PEMBROKE ST; TRALEE	KENMARE PLACE, NCR, DUBLIN
GILLIGAN	1W	14/10/22	Mc COWENS LANE, TRALEE	LIMERICK
GOGGIN TIMOTHY; PTE (22)	KYB	13/10/22	FENIT	TRALEE
GREENE CHRISTOPHER; PTE (19)	DG	07/03/23	BARRADUFF	INCHCORE, DUBLIN
HANNON DANIEL; PTE	DG	29/09/22	BRENNANS GLEN, FFORE	BELFAST
HARDING PATRICK; AMS (19)	DG	02/08/22	PEMBROKE ST; TRALEE	JAMES' ST; DUBLIN
HEALY WILLIAM; PTE	KYB	05/03/23	CAHIRCIVEEN	VALENTIA ISLAND, County KERRY
HOULIHAN BRIAN; CPTN	DG	05/08/22	DYSERT; FARRANFORE	KENMARE, KERRY
KAVANAGH THOMAS; PTE	DG	24/08/22	KILCUMMIN	SHERRARD AVE, NCR, DUBLIN
KENNY JOHN; PTE (19)	DG	02/08/22	ROCK/PEMBROKE ST; TRALEE	COOMBE ST; DUBLIN
LARKIN THOMAS; PTE (27)	DG	02/08/22	CASTLE ST; TRALEE	THE BAILEY, HOWTH
LEHANE DANIEL; CPTN (24)	1W	27/09/22	KILLORGLIN	LAHINCH, COUNTY CLARE
LYDEN JOHN; PTE AMS	1W	11/09/22	BLENNERVILLE	COUNTY GALWAY
LYDON JOHN; SERGT (28)	DG	18/08/22	LYONS PUB. SPA, TRALEE	JAMES' ST; TRALEE
McGOVERN		23/01/23	CASTLEMAINE	NA
McLOUGHLIN HENRY; PTE		29/12/22	CASTLEGREGORY	LISDEEN, COUNTY CLARE
MAGEE MICHAEL; DRIVER		11/09/22	D. O. W, CASTLEISLAND	DUBLIN
MARTIN MICHAEL; PTE	DG	27/09/22	BRENNANS GLEN, FFORE	DUNDALK, COUNTY LOUTH
MARTIN J		01/12/22	NA	NA
MARUM JAMES; SERGT (29)	DG	23/10/22	NA	BLACKROCK, COUNTY DUBLIN
MORAN THOMAS; PTE	DG	01/02/23	NA	KIMMAGE, DUBLIN
MULLEN F; PTE	DG	27/11/22	LIXNAW	DUBLIN

Name	Unit	Date	Place	Location
MULLHALL, PTE	DG	17/12/22	DINGLE	DUBLIN
MURPHY JOHN; PTE		20/09/22	NA	NA
MURPHY WILLIAM, SERGT		16/09/22	NA	NA
NAGLE; PTE	KYB	27/10/22	TONAVANE, CASTLEGREGORY	KILLARNEY, COUNTY KERRY
NOONAN EDWARD, SERGT	DG	28/09/22	RATHMORE	DUBLIN
O'CONNOR DENIS; PTE	KYB	29/09/22	D.O.W, KILLORGLIN	KERRY
O'CONNOR JAMES	DG	02/08/22	ROCK/PEMBROKE ST; TRALEE	SUMMERHILL, DUBLIN
O'CONNOR JOHN; CPTN (24)	KYB	09/09/22	KENMARE	KENMARE, COUNTY KERRY
O'CONNOR LAURENCE; PTE	KYB	06/03/23	KNOCKNAGOSHEL	CAUSEWAY
O'CONNOR PATRICK; LIEUT	KYB	06/03/23	KNOCKNAGOSHEL	CASTLEISLAND
O'CONNOR THOMAS; BRIG (20)	KYB	09/09/22	KENMARE	KENMARE, COUNTY KERRY
O'DONOGHUE J; SERGT		04/09/22	CAHIRCIVEEN	County KERRY
O'MEARA JOHN; AMS (20)	DG	17/08/22	INNISFALLEN, KILLARNEY	GALWAY CITY
O'NEILL; PTE	DG	16/04/23	CLASHMEALCON CAVE	NILE ST; DUBLIN
O'REILLY PATRICK;	DG	02/08/22	PEMBROKE ST; TRALEE	LR GARDINER ST; DUBLIN
PURCELL MICHAEL; PTE	KYB	5/08/22	TRALEE	ABBEY ST; TRALEE
PIERSON LIEUT H.D	1W	18/4/23	CLASHMEALCON CAVE	SCR, LIMERICK CITY
QUANE JOHN; PTE	1W	12/8/22	BEDFORD, LISTOWEL	MELEEK, COUNTY CLARE
QUANE JEREMIAH; SERGT	KYB	5/3/23	CAHIRCIVEEN	ARDFERT, COUNTY KERRY
QUINN PATRICK; PTE (23)	DG	2/8/22	KILFENORA	POOLBEG ST; DUBLIN
ROCHE PATRICK; PTE	KYB	25/1/23	WATERVILLE	WATERVILLE
SHEA TIMOTHY; LIEUT	KYB	5/3/23	CAHIRCIVEEN	CAHERCIVEEN, COUNTY KERRY
SHEEHY EDWARD; PTE (20)	KYB	30/6/22	LISTOWEL	LISTOWEL, COUNTY KERRY
SLATTERY THOMAS; LIEUT	KYB	20/2/23	NA	BALLYMACELLIGOTT
STAPELTON EDWARD; CAPTN	DG	6/3/23	KNOCKNAGOSHEL	DUBLIN
TALTY JOHN; PTE		29/12/22	CASTLEGREGORY	BUNCRANA, COUNTY DONEGAL
YOUNG JOHN; CPTN	DG	16/10/22	D.O.W, RATHMORE	DUBLIN

Killed or died of wounds

City/County of origin	Month 1922								1923					TOTAL
	J	J	A	S	O	N	D		J	F	M	A		
BELFAST			1	1				**2**						**2**
CAVAN						1		**1**						**1**
CLARE			2	1		1		**4**	1				**1**	**5**
CORK		1						**1**						**1**
DONEGAL							1	**1**						**1**
DUBLIN			11	2	3	2	2	**20**		1	2	3	**6**	**26**
GALWAY			3	1				**4**						**4**
KERRY	1	1	3	4	2			**11**	1	1	6		**8**	**19**
LONGFORD				1				**1**						**1**
LOUTH			1					**1**						**1**
LIMERICK					2	1		**3**				1	**1**	**4**
MONAGHAN									1				**1**	**1**
OTHER			1	3			2	**6**			1		**1**	**7**
	1	**1**	**22**	**13**	**8**	**5**	**5**	**55**	**3**	**2**	**10**	**3**	**18**	**73**

MILITARY RANKS
CPTN: CAPTAIN
LIEUT: LIEUTENANT
SERGT: SERGEANT
CORP: CORPORAL
PTE: PRIVATE
VOL: VOLUNTEER
AMS: ARMY MEDICAL SERVICE

MILITARY UNIT
DG: DUBLIN GUARD
1W: 1ST WESTERN
KYB: KERRY BRIGADE

Killed in accidents involving weapons, ordnance or other causes

	NAME OF SOLDIER	REGT	DATE KILLED	WHERE KILLED	HOME'ADDRESS
1	BEATTY JOHN; PTE.	1W	24/8/22	BASIN, TRALEE	LETTERMORE, COUNTY GALWAY
1	CLEARY MICHAEL; CAPT.	1W	14/3/23	LISTOWEL	WHITEGATE, COUNTY CLARE
4	FITZGERALD THOMAS; PTE		8/5/23	HEADFORD	
1	GLYNN ALFRED; LIEUT.	1W	14/3/23	LISTOWEL.	GORT, COUNTY GALWAY
3	HAYES	KYB	25/3/23	NEWTOWN SANDES	KILLARNEY, COUNTY KERRY
2	LOONEY J	KYB	24/9/22	KILLORGLIN BKS	DUBLIN
2	M°CABE STEPHEN; VOL	SAL PS	7/6/23	KILLORGLIN BKS	DUBLIN
3	M°CARTHY PATRICK; PTE (23)	KYB	14/1/23	LISTOWEL	LIXNAW, COUNTY KERRY
3	M°GRATH MATTHEW; CAPTN	1W	23/9/22	LISTOWEL	FEAKLE, COUNTY CLARE.
1	M°MAHON TIMOTHY; LIEUT (25)	1W	25/8/22	MOYDERWELL/BALLYMULLEN	MILTOWN MALBAY, CO CLARE
3	O'CALLAGHAN JOHN; SERGT.	CORK B	9/11/22	CAHIRCIVEEN	COUNTY CORK
2	RYAN JOHN; LIEUT	1W	27/2/23	BROSNA	LOUGHREA, COUNTY GALWAY
1	ROCHE MICHAEL; SERGT (28)	1W	25/8/22	MOYDERWELL/BALLYMULLEN	CONNOLLY, COUNTY CLARE
1	WOODS DENIS; PTE	1W	25/8/22	BASIN, TRALEE	MOUNTSHANNON, CO CLARE

1 KILLED IN GRENADE EXPLOSION
2 KILLED WHILE UNLOADING / CLEANING WEAPONS
3 SHOT DURING NIGHT PATROL, MISTAKEN FOR ENEMY
4 CRUSHED BY A TRAIN

328

APPENDIX 2

Republican Army – killed or died of wounds

NAME	LOCATION	DIED ON	HOME ADDRESS
AHERN MICHAEL	PALLAS, FOSSA	25/10/22	KILLORGLIN
BROSNAN MICHAEL	BALLYMULLEN BKS(FSQ)	20/01/23	RATHENNY, TRALEE
BUCKLEY, PATRICK	BALLYSEEDY	07/03/23	SCARTAGLIN
BUCKLEY STEPHEN	COUNTESS BRIDGE	07/03/23	TIERNABOUL, KILLARNEY
CASEY JEREMIAH	BEAUFORT	20/03/23	DUNLOE
CLIFFORD DANIEL	CAHERCIVEEN	05/03/23	
CLIFFORD JOHN	BALLYMULLEN BKS (FSQ)	20/01/23	CAHERCIVEEN
CONWAY-O'CONNOR LIAM	DERRYNA FENA, GLENCAR	06/04/23	KILLORGLIN
COURTNEY MICHAEL	CAHERCIVEEN	12/03/23	
CURRAN MICHAEL	CAHERCIVEEN	12/03/23	WATERVILLE
DALY CHARLES (26)	DROMBOE BKS, DONEGAL (FSQ)	14/03/23	KNOCKANE, FIRIES, KILLARNEY
DALY DANIEL (25)	TRALEE, RAILWAY STATION	23/01/23	KILLORGLIN
DALY JAMES	BALLYMULLEN BKS (FSQ)	20/01/23	KILLARNEY
DALY JOHN	BALLYSEEDY	07/03/23	WOODVIEW, CASTLEISLAND
DRUMMOND THOMAS (25)	BALLYMULLEN BKS 'D. O.W	24/08/22	32 RAE ST, TRALEE
ENRIGHT DANIEL	DROMBOE BKS, DONEGAL (FSQ)	14/03/23	LISTOWEL
FITZGERALD EUGENE	CURRANE	16/01/23	TRALEE
FLEMING JACK	TRALEE	29/03/23	TRALEE
FLYNN MICHAEL	DERRYMORE, CASTLEGREGORY	20/11/22	TRALEE
FLYNN THOMAS	BEACH, SPA, TRALEE	02/08/22	FENIT
FOLEY PATRICK	CAHERCIVEEN	25/01/23	WATERVILLE
FORAN PATRICK	D. O. W, LIMERICK CITY	26/07/22	LISSELTON
GALVIN JOHN	BALLYSEEDY WOOD	30/09/22	KILLORGLIN
GREANEY EDWARD	BALLYMULLEN BKS (FSQ)	25/04/23	BALLYDUFF
GRADY FRANK	MOUNTAIN STAGE, GLENBEIGH	11/03/23	GLENBEIGH
HANLON CHARLES	D. O. W, BRUREE, LIMERICK	04/08/22	LISTOWEL
HANLON JAMES	BALLYMULLEN BKS (FSQ)	20/01/23	CAUSEWAY

Name	Date	Location	Residence
HARRINGTON WILLIAM (23)	08/12/22	SKATING RINK, TRALEE	TRALEE
HARTNETT PATRICK	07/03/23	BALLYSEEDY	LISTOWEL
HATHAWAY REGINALD	25/04/23	BALLYMULLEN BKS (FSQ)	SLOUGH, UK
KEATING JEREMIAH	3/10/22	D. O. W, KILLORGLIN 27/9/22	CAHIRCIVEEN
KEATING TIMOTHY	11/3/23	D. O W CAHIRCIVEEN 5/3/23	BALLINASKELLIGS
KEVINS JOHN	15/3/23	CARRANAHONE, B'FORT	BEAUFORT
LAWLOR JOHN	30/10/22	BALLYHEIGUE	BALLYHEIGUE
LINNANE JOHN	13/4/23	TRINERAGH, LISTOWEL	LISTOWEL
LOONEY CON	27/9/22	KILLORGLIN	KENMARE
LYNCH PATRICK	30/11/22	MOYREISK, CAHIRCIVEEN	CAHIRCIVEEN
LYONS TIMOTHY	18/4/23	CLASHMEALCON CAVE	KILFLYNN
McCARTHY BOB	24/3/23	BALLYFERRITER	DINGLE
McENERY JAMES	25/4/23	BALLYMULLEN BKS (FSQ)	LIXNAW
McGRATH THOMAS	16/4/23	CLASHMEALCON CAVE	
McSWEENEY MICHAEL	6/2/23	SHRONE, RATHMORE	BOWER, RATHMORE
MORIARTY SEÁN (28)	27/8/22	BALLONAGH, TRALEE	WALPOLE LANE, TRALEE
MURPHY BERTIE (17)	27/9/22	G.S. HOTEL (ARMY POST), KILLARNEY	FARRANFORE
MURPHY DANIEL	24/3/23	KNOCKNAGOSHEL	KNOCKNAGOSHEL
MURPHY PATRICK	27/9/22	KILLORGLIN	DOOKS, GLENBEIGH
MURPHY TIMOTHY	7/3/23	COUNTESS BRIDGE	KILCUMMIN
MYLES WILLIAM	27/10/22	TONEVANE, CASTLEGREGORY	TRALEE
NAGLE GEORGE	6/4/23	DERRYNAFEANA, GLENCAR	BALLYGAMBOON, CMAINE
O'CONNELL JOHN	7/3/23	BALLYSEEDY	
O'CONNOR DENIS	28/1/23	KILMAINHAM	BROSNA
O'CONNOR JAMES	13/2/23	CURRAHANE	TRALEE
O'CONNOR T	7/3/23	BALLYSEEDY	WEST TERRACE, LIVERPOOL
O'DONOGHUE DANIEL	7/3/23	COUNTESS BRIDGE	LACKS, KILCUMMIN
O'DONOHUE JEREMIAH	7/3/23	COUNTESS BRIDGE	NEW STREET, KILLARNEY
O'DONOVAN JAMES	17/3/23	MAC GILLYCUDDY REEkS	KILLORGLIN
O'DWYER JOHN	12/3/23	CAHERCIVEEN	

Name	Date	Place	Place
ORIORDAN WILLIAM	25/10/22	DONGEEL, KILLORGLIN	GLENBEIGH
O'SHEA DANIEL	12/3/23	CAHIRCIVEEN	VELLOW ISTE
O'SHEA GEORGE	7/3/23	BALLYSEEDY	LIXNAW
O'SHEA TIMOTHY	18/4/23	CLASHMEALCON CAVE	CASTLEGREGORY
O'SULLIVAN JOHN	2/8/22	SAMMYSROCK, SPA	KILCUMMIN
O'SULLIVAN MICHAEL	2/11/22	CLOGHANE, HEADFORD	CAHIRCIVEEN
O'SULLIVAN SEAN T.	6/3/23	GLEESK	BALLYFERRITER
O'SULLIVAN THOMAS	18/2/23	BALLINEANIG	WILLIAM ST, LISTOWEL
O'SULLIVAN TIMOTHY	14/3/23	DROMBOE, BKS., DONEGAL (FSQ)	BALLYMACELLIGOTT
RYLE MICHAEL	5/8/22	BALLYSEEDY	TRALEE
SINNOTT MICHAEL	13/2/23	CURRAHANE	WATERVILLE
SUGRUE JOHN	12/3/23	CAHIRCIVEEN	GLENCAR
TAYLOR JAMES	8/3/23	BALLYSEEDY	LIXNAW
TWOMEY TIMOTHY	7/3/23	BALLYSEEDY	LOSDOIGUE, TRALEE
WALSH JAMES	7/3/23	BALLYSEEDY	KNOCKNAGOSHEL
WALSH JAMES	27/3/23	KNOCKNAGOSHEL	

FSQ = Killed by Firing Squad

MONTHLY DEATH TOLL – REPUBLICANS – KERRY 1922-23

MONTH	J	A	S	O	N	D	TOT	J	F	M	A	TOT	TOTAL
1922	2	5	4	5	3	1	20	8	4	32	9	53	73

APPENDIX 3

CIVILIANS KILLED / DIED OF GUNSHOT WOUNDS

1922	7	1923	5	FSA = FREE STATE ARMY	REP = REPUBLICANS

NAME	HOME' ADDRESS	DIED	BELLIGERENT (POSSIBLY) RESPONSIBLE FOR DEATH	
BROSNAN WILLIAM	CASTLEISLAND	07/12/1922		FSA
CONWAY JOHN	TRALEE	24/02/1923	WORKHOUSE, BARRACKS	FSA
CROWLEY DANIEL	CORK (50)	17/01/1923	G.S.+W.R, LISCAHANE	REP
LYONS THOMAS	KILLARNEY	17/09/1922	BALLYCARTY	*UNKNOWN
MANGAN JAMES	KILLARNEY (19)	26/12/1922	KILLBREAN	REP
McKENNA JEREMIAH	MILLTOWN (30)	13/11/1922	AMBUSH NEAR	CROSS
McKENNA MRS.	MILLTOWN (60)	13/11/1922	HOME: MOTHER+SON	FIRE
O'DRISCOLL MICHAEL	BARROW, CAMP	16/08/1922		*UNKNOWN
O'RIORDAN PADDY	TRALEE (36)	17/01/1923	G.S.+W.R, LISCAHANE	REP
O'SHEA MICHAEL	KEEL	02/04/1923		REP
POWER PATRICK	TRALEE	17/09/1922		*UNKNOWN
PRENDEVILLE THOMAS	CASTLEISLAND	17/01/1923	CASTLEISLAND, ARMY BK	FSA

APPENDIX 4

COMPENSATION CLAIMS: KERRY - CIVIL WAR

(TO 14 OCTOBER 1922)

PERSONAL INJURIES

EDMUND BURKE	TRALEE	£8,000.00
JOHN DAY	DINGLE	£8,000.00
MARY DRUMMOND	32 RAE STREET, TRALEE	£8,000.00
JOHN MORIARTY	WALPOLE LANE, TRALEE	£8,000.00
MICHAEL O'DRISCOLL	BARROW CAMP	£7,000.00
MRS COFFEY	DINGLE	£6,000.00
MRS LYDON	TRALEE	£5,000.00
MICHAEL PURCELL	2 LOWER ABBEY ST, TRALEE	£4,000.00
JAMES HEALY	11 COWENS LANE, TRALEE	£4,000.00
MICHAEL FOLEY	BASIN VIEW, TRALEE	£3,000.00
THOMAS HORAN	BALLYMULLEN, TRALEE	£3,000.00
DANIEL SULLIVAN	13 DOMINIC ST, TRALEE	£2,000.00
J MURPHY	MOYDERWELL, TRALEE	£1,000.00
JOHN CLIFFORD	11 CAHERINA, TRALEE	£500.00
MARIA DALY	COURT HOUSE, LISTOWEL	£500.00
SAMUEL DEVLIN	DOMINIC STREET, TRALEE	£500.00
ELLEN HANNON	WILLIAM STREET, LISTOWEL	£500.00
PATRICK HARMON	WILLIAM STREET, LISTOWEL	£500.00
T. McNALLY	CASTLEGREGORY	£500.00
		£70,000.00

DESTRUCTION / LOSS OF PROPERTY

TALBOT-CROSBIE	£100,000.00
DERRYQUINN CASTLE	£100,000.00

GREAT SOUTHERN & WESTERN RAILWAY: COMPANY

DESTRUCTION OF NEW (GREAT SOUTHERN) HOTEL, KILLARNEY	£30,000.00
DESTRUCTION OF STEAM LOCOMOTIVE, RAILWAY STATION, TRALEE	£15,000.00
DEMOLITION OF RAILWAY BRIDGE, CURRANS	£10,000.00
DESTRUCTION OF SIGNAL CABIN, GLENBANE, TRALEE	£2,000.00
DESTRUCTION OF RAILWAY BRIDGE, BALLYSEEDY	£1,500.00
DAMAGE OF PROPERTY ON THE LINE	£350.00
DAMAGE OF TELEPHONE EQUIPMENT, MONTANAGAY	£200.00
DAMAGE OF SWITCHBLADE, TUBRID MORE	£200.00
DAMAGE OF SWITCHBLADE, DROMCURRIG	£200.00
G.S+W.R SUB TOTAL	**£59,450.00**

MARQUISE OF LANDSDOWNE: DESTRUCTION, DIREEN HOUSE	£25,000.00
LORD HEADLEY DESTRUCTION: AGHADOE HOUSE	£20,000.00
TRALEE - DINGLE RAILWAY	£20,000.00
JULIA O'DONOVAN, KILLORGLIN	£10,000.00
EARL OF KENMARE: DESTRUCTION OF PROPERTY	£9,500.00
ANGLO- AMERICAN OIL COMPANY	£9,180.00
WHOLESALE CO-OPERATIVE SOCIETY (MANCHESTER) DESTRUCTION OF CREAMERY PREMISES-BALLYMAQUIN/CHAPELTOWN	£9,000.00

KERRY COUNTRY COUNCIL	£8,000.00
E. HAWNEY, BALLYBUNION: DAMAGE TO PREMISES	£4,000.00
MRS HANNAH DODD, KILLORGLIN	£2,000.00
M. SHEEHAN, SNEEM: GOODS STOLEN	£2,000.00
WILLIAM BROSNAN, RATHGANNY: DAMAGE TO PROPERTY	£1,500.00
JEOFFREY MORRIS, KILLORGLIN:	£1,500.00
MAURICE RYLE (KERRY PEOPLE): DAMAGE TO PROPERTY	£1,150.00
MUSGRAVE BROTHERS, TRALEE	£1,050.00
CONDENSED MILK COMPANY	£1,000.00
COLONEL W. WALKER	£1,000.00
POULSON - WARDEN	£1,000.00
	£387,310.00

WILLIAM MURPHY, KILLARNEY	£920.00
TYLERS: GOODS STOLEN	£900.00
CORNELIUS O'LEARY: LOSS OF LORRY	£800.00
GEORGE HEWSON: LOSS OF CAR	£800.00
O'DONOVANS/Mc KEUIHER/R. McCOWEN: DAMAGE TO PROPERTY	£771.00
J. J FOLEY/MRS. EGAN: DAMAGE TO PROPERTY	£700.00
R. LAHERN; 40 BRIDGE STREET, TRALEE	£650.00
J. J McKENNA, MARKET STREET, LISTOWEL: CON OF GOODS	£564.00
MAJOR McGILLYCUDDY: DAMAGE TO PROPERTY	£550.00
R. S BENNER: TRALEE	£530.00
DOWLINGS CHEMIST, TRALEE: DESTRUCTION OF PROPERTY	£500.00
HOWARD HARRINGTON, DUNLOE CASTLE: DEST. OF MOTORCAR	£500.00
SARAH KENNEDY, DINGLE	£500.00
R. LAVIN, TRALEE: DAMAGE TO PROPERTY	£500.00
DENIS O'SULLIVAN: KILLORGLIN	£500.00
TRALEE - RURAL DISTRICT COUNCIL.	£500.00
J. WALSH: DAMAGE TO PROPERTY	£500.00
E. LATCHFORD; TRALEE	£447.00
E. B WATSON; TRALEE	£439.00
MRS CATHERINE HOULIHAN, UPPER BRIDGE STREET, KILLORGLIN	£400.00
WILLIAM O'CONNOR, TARBERT: PROPERTY DAMAGED	£400.00
HARRIS O'DONNELL; TARBERT	£400.00
M. SHEEHAN; SNEEM	£400.00
CO-OP WHOLESALE SOCIETY, TRALEE	£360.00
ARTHUR R. /GEORGE V. ; BALLYORGAN, LISTOWEL.	£350.00
LORD VENTRY, DINGLE: LOSS OF STOCK	£322.00
BALLYMACELLIGOTT CO-OP: LORRY STOLEN.	£315.00
BACON FACTORY, TRALEE	£305.00
A. A HARDGRAVE, TRALEE: DAMAGE TO PROPERTY	£300.00
J. J STEPHENS, KILLORGLIN	£300.00
EDMUND PRICE: CAR STOLEN	£300.00
MARIA DALY, COURTHOUSE, LISTOWE: DAMAGE TO PROPERTY	£200.00
KATE GRIFFIN, MARKET STREET, LISTOWEL: LOSS OF PROPERTY	£200.00
JOHN O'CONNOR, TARBERT	£200.00
J. GALVIN, WILLIAM STREET, LISTOWEL.	£195.00
MAJOR C. R LESWE, TARBERT: GOODS STOLEN	£171.00
MUSGRAVE BROTHERS, TRALEE	£150.00
ROGER MORAN: DAMAGE TO HOUSE	£70.00
SPILLER AND BAKER: LOSS OF GOODS	£57.00
	£16,716.00

APPENDIX 5

Kerry constituency 1927–1932

C Na G – CUMANN nGAEDHEAL; FF – FIANNA FÁIL; SF – SINN FÉIN

1927 – 9 JUNE

ELECTORATE		SEATS
78,540		7
PARTY	*1 ST PREFER*	*SEATS*
C Na G	18,110	3
FF	17,893	3
SF	5,140	1
LABOUR	3,195	
FARMERS	3,842	
INDEP	3,243	
OTHER	1,362	
TOTAL POLL:	*52,785*	*67%*

C Na G	34.20%	1 ST PREF
FF	33.80%	"
SF	9.70%	"
FARMERS	4.90%	"
LABOUR	4%	"

1927 – 15 SEPT

ELECTORATE		SEATS
78,540		7
PARTY	*1 ST PREFER*	*SEATS*
C Na G	22,286	3
FF	29,011	4
FARMERS	4,594	
TOTAL POLL	*55,891*	*TURN OUT 71%*

FF	52.00%	1 ST PREF
C Na G	39.75%	"
FARMERS	8.25%	"

1932 – 16 FEB

ELECTORATE		SEATS
79,465		7
PARTY	*1 ST PREFER*	*SEATS*
C Na G	20,005	2
FF	35,757	5
FARMERS	4,548	
TOTAL POLL	*60,310*	*TURN OUT 75.9%*

FF 59.30% 1 ST PREF	59.30%	1ST PREF
C Na G 33.15%	33.15%	"
FARMERS 7.55%	7.55%	"

NOTES

1 – Ireland 1912–1918: A Revolution?

1 Walker, Brian M., *Parliamentary Election Results in Ireland, 1801–1922* (RIA, Dublin, 1978) 19, pp. 353–4. In the December 1910 election (Kerry South) J. P. Boland (Nat), 2,390 defeated T. P. Cronin (Ind Nat), 452, while (Kerry East) Timothy O'Sullivan (Nat), 2,561 defeated Patrick Guiney (Ind Nat), 1,308. Contested elections were the exception rather than the rule in Kerry prior to the First World War. In the 1900, 1906 and 1910 (two elections) elections the MPs for Kerry North, South and West constituencies only faced the electorate once, being returned without opposition on three occasions.

2 Census of Population, 1911

3 Dwyer, T. Ryle, *Tans, Terror and Troubles: Kerry's Real Fighting Story, 1913–1923* (Mercier Press, Cork, 2001) p. 34

4 Gaughan, J. Anthony, *Austin Stack: Portrait of a Separatist* (Kingdom Books, Dublin, 1976) pp. 10–13

5 Dwyer, *Tans, Terror and Troubles*, pp. 45–50

6 Strachan, Hew, *The First World War* (Simon & Schuster, London, 2003) p. 53

7 Stokesbury, James L., *A Short History of World War One* (Hale, London, 1981) p. 237

8 O'Mahony, Seán, *Frongoch, University of Revolution* (FRD Teo, Dublin, 1987) pp. 204–205

9 Dwyer, *Tans, Terror and Troubles*, pp. 126–30

2 – The War of Independence 1919–1921

1 Holt, Edgar, *Protest in Arms* (Putnam Press, London, 1960) p. 172

2 Abbott, Richard, *Police Casualties in Ireland, 1919–1922* (Mercier Press, Cork, 2000) pp. 30–33

3 Coogan, T. P., *Michael Collins* (Hutchinson, London, 1990) p. 117

4 Dwyer, *Tans, Terror and Troubles*, pp. 157–8

5 *Cork Examiner*, 18 January 1920

6 Dwyer, *Tans, Terror and Troubles*, p. 208

7 *Ibid.*, pp. 179–81

8 Townshend, Charles, *The British Campaign in Ireland, 1919–1921* (Oxford University Press, Oxford, 1975) p. 214

9 O'Farrell, Pádraig, *Who's Who in the Irish War of Independence and Civil War* (Lilliput Press, Dublin, 1996). Abstracts of information contained in pp. 102–20

3 – From the Truce to the Treaty

1 Coogan, *Michael Collins*, p. 217

2 Murphy, Jeremiah, *When Youth was Mine: A Memoir of Kerry, 1902–1925* (Mentor Press, Dublin, 1998) p. 171

3 Laffan, Michael, *The Resurrection of Ireland: the Sinn Féin Party 1916–1923* (Cambridge University Press, Cambridge, 1999) p. 299

4 Dwyer, T. Ryle, *Michael Collins and the Treaty* (Mercier Press, Cork, 1981)

5 Murphy, *When Youth was Mine*, p. 172

4 – A House Divided

1 Coogan, *Michael Collins*, p. 296
2 *Ibid.*, p. 296
3 Quote from Townshend, Charles, *Ireland: the Twentieth Century* (Arnold, London, 1999) p. 82
4 Coogan, *Michael Collins*, p. 301
5 *Cork Examiner*, 5 January, 1922
6 *Ibid.*, 2 January, 1922
7 *Ibid.*, 3 January, 1922
8 *Ibid.*, 6 January, 1922
9 Dwyer, *Tans, Terror and Troubles*, p. 333

5 – Things Fall Apart

1 Garvin, Tom, *1922: The Birth of Irish Democracy* (Gill & Macmillan, Dublin, 1996) p. 94
2 Dwyer, *Tans, Terror and Troubles*, p. 33
3 Blythe, Ernest, quoted in the *Cork Examiner*, 21 February 1923
4 Gaughan, J. Anthony, *Listowel and its Vicinity* (Mercier Press, Cork, 1973) pp. 433–5
5 *Cork Examiner*, 27 January 1922
6 Harrington, Niall C., *Kerry Landing, August 1922* (Anvil Press, Dublin, 1992) p. 89
7 *Cork Examiner*, 21 January 1922
8 *Ibid.*, 19 December 1921
9 Garvin, *1922: The Birth of Irish Democracy*, p. 83
10 Dwyer, *Tans, Terror and Troubles*, p. 343
11 *Cork Examiner*, 23 January & 4 February, 1922
12 *Kerry People*, 18 February, 1922
13 *Cork Examiner*, 29 December 1921
14 Harrington, Niall C., *Kerry Landing*, p. 10
15 Gaughan, *Listowel and its Vicinity*, pp. 404–5
16 Hopkinson, Michael, *Green against Green* (Gill & Macmillan, Dublin, 1988) pp. 89–90
17 *Cork Examiner*, 25 March 1922
18 *Ibid.*, 6 April 1922
19 *Ibid.*, 20 April 1922
20 *Ibid.*, 21 April 1922
21 *Ibid.*, 22 April 1922
22 *Ibid.*, 20 April 1922
23 Dwyer, *Tans, Terror and Troubles*, pp. 350–1
24 *Cork Examiner*, 2 May 1922
25 *Ibid.*, 17 May 1922
26 *Ibid.*, 18 May 1922
27 *Ibid.*, 24 May 1922

6 – From the Ballot to the Bullet

1 Bardon, Jonathan, *A History of Ulster* (Blackstaff Press, Belfast, 1989) p. 491
2 *Ibid.*, p. 491
3 *Cork Examiner*, 5 June 1922

4 *Ibid.*, 8 June 1922
5 *Ibid.*, late June 1922. Abstracts: first preference votes, seats gained by parties, etc., based on data in various editions.
6 *Ibid.*, 17 June 1922
7 *Ibid.*, 20 June 1922
8 *Ibid.*, 8 July 1922
9 Harrington, *Kerry Landing*, p. 167
10 *Cork Examiner*, 3 July 1922
11 *Ibid.*, 5 July 1922
12 *Kerry People*, 8 July 1922
13 Murray, Patrick, *Oracles of God: The Catholic Church and Irish Politics, 1922–1937* (UCD Press, Dublin, 2000) pp. 151-152
14 *Cork Examiner*, 3 July 1922
15 *Ibid.*, 5 July 1922
16 *Ibid.*, 14 July 1922
17 *Ibid.*, 14 July 1922
18 *Kerry People*, 29 July 1922
19 Gaughan, *Listowel and its Vicinity*, p. 415
20 *Cork Examiner*, 26 July 1922

7 – The Free State Archipelago

1 Younger, Calton, *Ireland's Civil War* (Fredrick Muller, London, 1968) p. 314
2 Harrington, *Kerry Landing*, pp. 74–5
3 *Ibid.*, pp. 93–4
4 *Cork Examiner*, 5 August 1922
5 Dwyer, *Tans, Terror and Troubles*, p. 355
6 *Cork Examiner*, 7 August 1922
7 Younger, *Ireland's Civil War*, p. 398
8 *Cork Examiner*, 9 September 1922
9 Ó Broin, Leon, *In Great Haste* (Gill & Macmillan, Dublin 1988) p. 216
10 *Cork Examiner*, 15 August 1922
11 Fitzgerald, Bobby (editor): *History of Ballymacelligott and its People* (Ballymacelligott Active Retirement Association, Ballymacelligott, 1997) p.12
12 *Irish Times*, 9 August 1922
13 Hopkinson, *Green against Green*, p. 43
14 *Cork Examiner*, 15 August 1922
15 *Ibid.*, 17 August 1922
16 *Irish Times*, 14 August 1922
17 *Freeman's Journal*, 30 August 1922
18 *Ibid.*, 16 August 1922
19 *Cork Examiner*, 16 August 1922
20 *Ibid.*, 18 August 1922
21 *Ibid.*, 4 February 1922
22 Valiulis, Maryann G., *Almost a Rebellion: The Irish Army Mutiny, 1924* (Tower Books, Cork, 1985) p. 37. Liam Tobin gives the composition of the Civil War Free State army as 50 per cent ex-British army, 40 per cent 'old' IRA, 10 per cent civilian.
23 *Cork Examiner*, 21 August 1922
24 *Ibid.*, 23 August 1922

338

25 Murphy, *When Youth was Mine*, pp. 201–2

26 *Freeman's Journal*, 21 August 1922

27 Harrington, *Kerry Landing*, p. 132

28 *Cork Examiner*, 23 August 1922

29 *Freeman's Journal*, 26 August 1922

30 *Cork Examiner*, 23 & 25 August 1922

31 *Freeman's Journal*, 25 August 1922

32 *Cork Examiner*, 28 August 1922

33 *Irish Times*, 24 August 1922

34 *Freeman's Journal*, 23 August 1922

35 *Cork Examiner*, 30 August 1922

36 Stoakley, T.E., *Sneem: The Knot in the Ring*, Second Edition (Sneem Tourism Association, Sneem, 1986) p.19-20

37 Harrington, *Kerry Landing*, p. 138

38 *Cork Examiner*, 28 August 1922

39 *Ibid.*, 16 December 1922

40 Valiulis, Maryann G., *Portrait of a Revolutionary: General Richard Mulcahy and the Foundation of the Irish Free State* (Irish Academic Press, Dublin, 1992) p. 188

41 *Irish Times*, 30 August 1922

42 *Cork Examiner*, 31 August 1922

43 *Freeman's Journal*, 3 September 1922

44 *Ibid.*, 8 September 1922

45 *Ibid.*

46 Regan, John M., *The Irish Counter Revolution, 1921–1936* (Gill & Macmillan, Dublin, 1991) p. 107

47 *Cork Examiner*, 4 September 1922

48 MacEoin, Uinseann, *Survivors* (Argenta Publications, Dublin, 1980) p. 359

49 *Freeman's Journal*, 8 September 1922

50 *Cork Examiner*, 21 September 1922

51 Murphy, *When Youth was Mine*, pp. 205–8

52 Younger, *Ireland's Civil War*, p. 450

53 MacEoin, Uinseann, *The IRA in the Twilight Years* (Argenta Publications, Dublin, 1997) p. 619

54 Younger, *Ireland's Civil War*, p. 451

55 Murphy, *When Youth was Mine*, pp. 205–8

56 Reminiscences of my mother, Anne Doyle [Houlihan], family folklore. An account of her uncle, Barth Houlihan, a butcher from Killorglin, who visited Kenmare shortly after the fall of the town (9 September 1922) to republicans.

57 Hopkinson, *Green against Green*, pp. 206–7

58 Younger, *Ireland's Civil War*, p. 451

59 Murphy, *When Youth was Mine*, pp. 210–11

60 *Cork Examiner*, 23 September 1922

61 *Freeman's Journal*, 12 & 16 September 1922

62 *Cork Examiner*, 26 September 1922

63 *Ibid.*, 13 September 1922

64 *Ibid.*, 26 September 1922

65 *Irish Times*, 23 September 1922

66 *Cork Examiner,* 22 September 1922
67 *Ibid.,* 30 September 1922
68 *Freeman's Journal,* 23 September 1922
69 *Irish Times,* 23 September 1922
70 *Freeman's Journal,* 27 September 1922
71 *Irish Times,* 29 September 1922
72 *Freeman's Journal,* 27 September 1922
73 The summary of the republican assault on Killorglin is based on accounts reported in the *Freeman's Journal* of 3 October 1922; the *Cork Examiner* of 30 September and 5 & 6 October 1922; Kieran Foley, *History of Killorglin* (Killorglin History and Folklore Society, Killorglin, 1988); and local knowledge collected by the author.
74 Regan, *The Irish Counter Revolution,* p. 108. Letter from David Robinson to Gavan Duffy
75 *Freeman's Journal,* 2 & 3 October 1922
76 *Irish Times,* 4 October 1922
77 Duggan, John P., *A History of the Irish Army* (Gill & Macmillan, Dublin, 1991) p. 95

8 – What We Have, We Hold

1 Harrington, *Kerry Landing,* p. 167
2 Ryan, Meda, *The Real Chief: Liam Lynch* (Mercier Press, Cork, 1986) p. 136
3 O'Farrell, *Who's Who,* Abstracts of details, pp. 102–20
4 *Ibid.*
5 *Irish Times,* 11 October 1922
6 *Cork Examiner,* 29/30 September 1922
7 Valiulis, *Portrait of a Revolutionary,* p. 188
8 *Cork Examiner,* 9 October 1922
9 *Ibid.*
10 *Ibid.,* 26 October 1922
11 *Freeman's Journal,* 21 October 1922
12 *Cork Examiner,* 21 October 1922
13 MacEoin, *Survivors,* p. 359. Interview, John Joe Sheehy
14 *Cork Examiner,* 12 October 1922
15 *Ibid.*
16 Cox, Pádraig, 'Memories of Rathmore in 1922–23', *Sliabh Luachra Journal,* Vol. 1, No. 6 November 1991, pp. 17–22
17 Murphy, *When Youth was Mine,* p. 208
18 *Cork Examiner,* 12 October 1922
19 *Ibid.,* 21 October 1922
20 *Ibid.,* 12 October 1922
21 *Ibid.,* 12 October 1922
22 *Ibid.*
23 *Ibid.,* 26 October 1922
24 *Ibid.,* 16 October 1922
25 *Freeman's Journal,* 16 October 1922
26 McCoole, Sinéad, *No Ordinary Women: Irish Female Activists, 1900–1923* (O'Brien Press, Dublin, 2003) p. 107
27 See Appendix 4, sample of personal injury claims, August–October 1922.

340

28 *Freeman's Journal*, 21 February 1923
29 *Cork Examiner*, 21 October 1922
30 *Ibid.*, 20 October 1922
31 *Freeman's Journal*, 24 November 1922
32 *Cork Examiner*, 23 November 1922
33 *Freeman's Journal*, 25 October 1922
34 *Ibid.*, 27 October 1922
35 *Cork Examiner*, 1 November 1922
36 *Ibid*
37 Account given to author by Seán Myers, Barleymount, Killarney, County Kerry
38 *Cork Examiner*, 1 November 1922
39 McMahon, Bryan, *The Story of Ballyheige* (Oidhreacht Press, Ballyheige, 1994) p. 153
40 Murphy, *When Youth was Mine*, pp. 217–18
41 *Ibid.*, pp. 225–6
42 O'Farrell, *Who's Who*, pp. 199–212
43 *Cork Examiner*, 9 November 1922
44 O'Farrell, *Who's Who*, pp. 199–212
45 *Cork Examiner*, 9 November 1922
46 *Ibid.*, 21 November 1922
47 *Ibid.*, 15 November 1922
48 Murray, *Oracles of God*, pp. 225–6
49 *Cork Examiner*, 13 November 1922
50 *Ibid.*, 15 November 1922
51 *Ibid.*, 17 November 1922
52 *Ibid.*, 12 November 1922
53 *Ibid.*, 11 November 1922
54 *Ibid.*, 15 November 1922
55 *Ibid.*, 21 November 1922
56 *Ibid.*, 20–27 November 1922
57 *Freeman's Journal*, 4 November 1922
58 Author's own figures, based on research carried out for this book
59 *Cork Examiner*, 27 November 1922
60 *Ibid.*, 28 November 1922
61 Mullins, Billy, *Memoirs of Billy Mullins* (Kerry's Eye, Tralee, 1983) p. 46.
62 Cox, 'Memories of Rathmore', p. 21
63 O'Farrell, *Who's Who*, pp. 199–212
64 Macardle, Dorothy, *Tragedies of Kerry* (Irish Freedom Press, Dublin, 1988, re-issue of original, 1924) p. 27.

9 – A Light at the End of the Tunnel?

1 *Freeman's Journal*, 4 December 1922
2 *Cork Examiner*, 8 December 1922
3 *Ibid.*
4 *Freeman's Journal*, 9 December 1922
5 *Cork Examiner*, 8 December 1922
6 Macardle, *Tragedies of Kerry*, p. 36
7 *Freeman's Journal*, 4 December 1922

8 *Ibid.,* 9 December 1922
9 *Ibid.,* 13 December 1922
10 *Cork Examiner,* 29 January 1923
11 *Freeman's Journal,* 13 December 1922
12 Hopkinson, *Green against Green,* p. 208
13 *Cork Examiner,* 8 December 1922
14 *Ibid.,* 12 December 1922
15 *Ibid.,* 20 December 1922
16 Murphy, *When Youth Was Mine,* pp. 236–7
17 O'Farrell, *Who's Who,* pp. 199–212
18 Dolan, Anne, *Commemorating the Civil War, 1923–2000* (Cambridge University Press, Cambridge, 2003) p. 133
19 *Cork Examiner,* 6 January 1923
20 *Freeman's Journal,* 20 December 1922
21 MacEoin, *Survivors,* p. 378. Interview with Con Casey
22 *Cork Examiner,* 27 December 1922
23 *Ibid.,* 19 December 1922
24 *Ibid.,* 27 December 1922
25 *Ibid.*
26 *Ibid.,* 1 January 1923
27 *Ibid.*
28 *Freeman's Journal,* 1 January 1923
29 *Cork Examiner,* 1 January 1923
30 *Ibid.,* 5 January 1923
31 *Ibid.,* 12 January 1923
32 *Ibid.,* 19 January 1923
33 *Ibid.,* 18 January 1923
34 *Freeman's Journal,* 23 January 1923
35 Macardle, *Tragedies of Kerry,* pp. 14–15
36 *Freeman's Journal,* 19 January 1923
37 *Ibid.,* 17 January 1923
38 *Ibid.,* 18 January 1923
39 *Cork Examiner,* 30 January 1923
40 *Freeman's Journal,* 20 January 1923
41 *Cork Examiner,* 23 January 1923
42 Younger, *Ireland's Civil War,* p. 488
43 *Cork Examiner,* 21–29 January 1923
44 *Freeman's Journal,* 25 January 1923
45 Murphy, *When Youth was Mine,* p. 240
46 *Cork Examiner,* 25 January 1923
47 Murphy, *When Youth was Mine,* p. 242
48 *Cork Examiner,* 25 January 1923
49 *Freeman's Journal,* 27 January 1923
50 *Ibid.,* 29 January 1923
51 Macardle, *Tragedies of Kerry,* p. 38
52 *Freeman's Journal,* 29 January 1923
53 *Ibid.,* 31 January 1923
54 *Ibid.,* 1 February 1923
55 *Ibid.,* 6 February 1923

56 *Ibid.*, 5 February 1923
57 Murphy, *When Youth was Mine*, pp. 245–50
58 Cox, 'Memories of Rathmore', p. 21
59 *Freeman's Journal*, 6 February 1923
60 *Irish Times*, 6 February 1923
61 *Ibid.*, 23 February 1923
62 *Cork Examiner*, 24 February 1923
63 *Ibid.*, 22 February 1923
64 *Ibid.*
65 *Ibid.*, 1 March 1923
66 *Ibid.*, 27 February 1923

10 – The Bitter End

1 *Cork Examiner*, 3 March 1923
2 Summary reports in *Cork Examiner*, 6 & 7 March and *Freeman's Journal*, 6 & 8 March 1923
3 Macardle, *Tragedies of Kerry*, p. 28
4 Dwyer, *Tans, Terror and Troubles*, p. 367
5 *Freeman's Journal*, 9 March 1923
6 Dwyer, *Tans, Terror and Troubles*, p. 369
7 *Ibid.*, p. 371
8 Macardle, *Tragedies of Kerry*, p. 16
9 Murray, *Oracles of God*, p. 89
10 *Cork Examiner*, 9 March 1923
11 *Ibid.*, 13 March 1923
12 *Freeman's Journal*, 1 March 1923
13 *Cork Examiner*, 14 March 1923
14 *Ibid.*, 28 March 1923
15 *Ibid.*, 20 March 1923
16 Macardle, *Tragedies of Kerry*, pp. 33–5
17 *Cork Examiner*, 20 March 1923
18 Macardle, *Tragedies of Kerry*, pp. 39–44
19 *Ibid.*
20 Griffith, Kenneth, *Curious Journey* (Mercier Press, Cork, 1998) pp. 305–6. Interview with Joe Sweeney
21 Hickey, Donal, *Queen of Them All: Killarney Golf Club, 1893–1993*, (Killarney Golf and Fishing Club, Killarney, 1993) p. 21
22 *Cork Examiner*, 20 March 1923
23 *Ibid.*, 27 March 1923
24 *Freeman's Journal*, 27 March 1923
25 *Cork Examiner*, 30 March 1923
26 Macardle, *Tragedies of Kerry*, p. 36
27 *Freeman's Journal*, 31 March 1923
28 *Cork Examiner*, 23 March 1923
29 *Ibid.*, 2 April 1923
30 *Ibid.*, 9 April 1923
31 *Ibid.*
32 Harrington, *Kerry Landing*, p. 132
33 *Cork Examiner*, 9 April 1923

34 *Ibid.,* 4 April 1923
35 *Freeman's Journal,* 6 April 1923
36 Dwyer, *Tans, Terror and Troubles,* p. 372
37 Valiulis, *Portrait of a Revolutionary,* pp. 190–1
38 *Cork Examiner,* 9 April 1923
39 *Ibid.,* 14 April 1923
40 Macardle, *Tragedies of Kerry,* pp. 54–63 gives her full account of the siege.
41 *Cork Examiner,* 18 April 1923
42 Macardle, *Tragedies of Kerry,* pp. 54–63
43 *Cork Examiner,* 21 April 1923
44 *Ibid.,* 26 April 1923
45 *Ibid.,* 28 April 1923
46 *Ibid.,* 3 May 1923
47 *Ibid.,* 30 April 1923

11 – Reconstruction

1 Murphy, *When Youth was Mine,* p. 266
2 *Cork Examiner,* 31 March 1923
3 *Ibid.,* 3 May 1923
4 *Ibid.,* 8 May 1923
5 *Freeman's Journal,* 24 May 1923
6 *Cork Examiner,* 12 May 1923
7   *Ibid.,* 23 May 1923
8 Kissane, Bill, *The Politics of the Irish Civil War* (Oxford University Press, Oxford, 2005) p. 93
9 *Cork Examiner,* 16 May 1923
10 *Ibid.,* 18 May 1923
11 *Ibid.,* 2 June 1923
12 *Ibid.,* 23 May 1923
13 *Ibid.,* 30 May 1923
14 *Ibid.,* 5 June 1923
15 Regan, *The Irish Counter Revolution,* pp. 173–5
16 *Cork Examiner,* 7 June 1923
17 *Freeman's Journal,* 27 June 1923
18 *Cork Examiner,* 16 July 1923
19 *Ibid.,* 23 July 1923
20 *Ibid.,* 3 August 1923
21 *Ibid.,* 14 August 1923
22 *Ibid.,* 15 August 1923
23 *Ibid.,* 28 August 1923
24 *Ibid.,* 29 & 30 August 1923

Bibliography

Abbott, Richard, *Police Casualities in Ireland, 1919–1922* (Mercier Press, Cork, 2000).

Bardon, Jonathan, *A History of Ulster* (Blackstaff Press, Belfast, 1992).

Caulfield, Max, *The Easter Rebellion* (Muller, London, 1964).

Coogan, T. P., *Michael Collins* (Hutchinson, London, 1990).

Dolan, Anne, *Commemorating The Civil War, 1923–2000* (Cambridge University Press, Cambridge, 2003).

Duggan, John P., *A History of the Irish Army* (Gill & Macmillan, Dublin, 1998).

Dwyer, T. Ryle, *Michael Collins and the Treaty* (Mercier Press, Cork, 1990).

—— *Tans, Terror and Troubles: Kerry's Real Fighting Story, 1913–1923* (Mercier Press, Cork, 1990).

Garvin, Tom, *1922: The Birth of Irish Democracy* (Gill & Macmillan, Dublin, 1996).

Gaughan, J. Anthony, *Austin Stack: Portrait of a Separatist* (Kingdom Books, Dublin, 1977).

—— *Listowel and its Vicinity* (Mercier Press, Cork, 1973).

Griffith, Kenneth, *Curious Journey* (Mercier Press, Cork, 1973).

Harrington, Niall C., *Kerry Landing, August 1922* (Anvil Books, Dublin, 1992).

Hopkinson, Michael, *Green against Green* (Gill & Macmillan, Dublin, 1998).

Joy, Sinéad, *The IRA in Kerry, 1916–1921* (Collins Press, Cork, 2005).

Kissane, Bill, *The Politics of the Irish Civil War* (Oxford University Press, Oxford, 2005).

Laffan, Michael, *The Resurrection of Ireland: The Sinn Féin Party 1916–1923* (Cambridge University Press, Cambridge, 1999).

Macardle, Dorothy, *Tragedies of Kerry* (Irish Freedom Press, Dublin, 1988).

McCoole, Sinéad, *No Ordinary Women: Irish Female Activists, 1900–1923* (O'Brien Press, Dublin, 2005).

MacEoin, Uinseann, *Survivors* (Argenta Publications, Dublin, 1980).

—— *The IRA in the Twilight Years* (Argenta Publications, Dublin, 1997).

Murphy, Jeremiah, *When Youth was Mine: A Memoir of Kerry, 1902–1925* (Mentor Press, Dublin, 1998).

Murray, Patrick, *Oracles of God: The Catholic Church and Irish Politics 1922–1937* (UCD Press, Dublin, 2000).

Neeson, Eoin, *The Civil War in Ireland* (Mercier Press, Cork, 1966).

O'Farrell, Pádraig, *Who's Who in the Irish War of Independence and Civil War* (Lilliput Press, Dublin, 1996).

O'Mahony, Seán, *Frongoch: University of Revolution* (FRD Teoranta, Dublin, 1987).

Regan, John M., *The Irish Counter Revolution, 1921–1936* (Gill & Macmillan, Dublin, 1991).

Ryan, Meda, *The Real Chief: The Story of Liam Lynch* (Mercier Press, Cork, 1986).

Townshend, Charles, *The British Campaign in Ireland, 1919–1921* (Oxford University Press, Oxford, 1975).

—— *Ireland: The Twentieth Century* (Arnold, London, 1999).

Valiulis, Maryann G., *Almost a Rebellion: The Irish Army Mutiny, 1924* (Tower Books, Cork, 1985).

—— *Portrait of a Revolutionary: General Richard Mulcahy and the Foundation of the Irish Free State* (Irish Academic Press, Dublin, 1992).

Younger, Calton, *Ireland's Civil War* (Fontana Books, London, 1968).

Walker, Brian M., *Irish Elections, 1801–1922* (Royal Irish Academy, Dublin, 1980).

Walker, Brian M., *Election Results, 1922 –1992* (Royal Irish Academy, Dublin, 1992).

Newspapers:
Cork Examiner
Freeman's Journal
Kerry People
Irish Times

INDEX